GROWING UP POOR

Growing Up Poor
A Literary Anthology

EDITED BY

ROBERT COLES

AND

RANDY TESTA

WITH

MICHAEL COLES

The New Press, New York

Published in the United States by The New Press, New York, 2001
Distributed by W. W. Norton & Company, Inc., New York.

Pages 277 through 279 constitute an extension of this copyright page.

LIBRARY OF CONGRESS CATALOGING-IN-PUBLICATION DATA

Growing up poor: a literary anthology / edited by Robert Coles and
Randy Testa, with Michael Coles.
p.   cm.
ISBN 1-56584-623-0 (hc.)
1. American literature—20th century.   2. Poor children—Literary collections.
3. Children of minorities—Literary collections.   4. Ethnic groups—Literary
collections.   I. Coles, Robert.   II. Testa, Randy.   III. Coles, Michael H.

PS509.P63 G76 2000
810.8'0355—dc21   00–055927

The New Press was established in 1990 as a not-for-profit alternative to
the large, commercial publishing houses currently dominating the book
publishing industry. The New Press operates in the public interest rather
than for private gain, and is committed to publishing, in innovative ways,
works of educational, cultural, and community value that are often
deemed insufficiently profitable.

The New Press, 450 West 41st Street, 6th Floor, New York, NY 10036
www.thenewpress.com

Printed in the United States of America
2   4   6   8   9   7   5   3   1

Contents

Acknowledgments

I'd like to thank my wife, Jane, and my sons Robert, Daniel, and Michael for all their love and support all these years.

—Robert Coles

I'd like to thank my mother and father, for struggling to make sure we were provided for.

—Randy Testa

Preface
Randy Testa

Early in his career as a child psychiatrist Robert Coles came to see "how complex, ironic, ambiguous and fateful life can be." He noticed that the categories he was learning about in psychiatry often left him stammering for deeper explanations of human fortitude in the face of trying circumstances.

When Coles began to write down the stories told to him, this simple truth was confirmed yet again by poor African American children living through the early days of southern school desegregation or the stories migrant workers' and sharecroppers' children recounted. The result of so much listening was a five-volume, Pulitzer Prize–winning series titled *Children of Crisis*. Two stories from that rich series appear in this anthology.

In 1978 Dr. Coles began teaching a course each fall at Harvard University titled "A Literature of Social Reflection." In it students read fiction and essays he hoped would engender the moral and social inquiry Coles himself was undertaking as he listened to the stories of those many vulnerable and often poor children.

Twenty-plus years later Coles and his course are still going strong, and excerpts from several works appearing in his course likewise appear here: works by William Carlos Williams, Ralph Ellison, Zora Neale Hurston, Raymond Carver and Richard Ford.

The pieces collected for this anthology can be thought of as inquiry in their own ways into the experience of growing up poor. Playwright George Bernard Shaw liked to say that the greatest crime against humanity was poverty. To underscore his point, Shaw did some social observation of his own, writing the play *Pygmalion*. The story of a destitute flower-seller named Eliza Doolittle transformed into a woman of society and position as a bet of sorts between two English gentlemen, *Pygmalion* revolves around Eliza Doolittle's comment that "the difference between a lady and a flower girl is not how she behaves but how she's treated."

This collection of writing spans twentieth-century America and concerns people of various ethnic backgrounds—Asian American, Hispanic American, African American, European American—who know or soon learn about their station in life and how others treat them, not for who they are, but for what they "lack."

One question posed by some stories is: how do lines between ethnicity and class blur, and what is the effect? Another question these stories collectively ask is "Just how poor is poor?" and we have tried to widen the scope of poverty's depiction in this anthology by including stories of the "working poor" as well.

Selections have been grouped using broad thematic links. "To Come Into a World Like This One" joins stories that navigate the circumstances of poverty—material and psychological—and the dawning implications of those circumstances. "They, Those People Over There" contains stories of denigration at the hands of others. "I Took My Place, Bent My Head and Went to Work" concerns working long hours at menial jobs in order to get by. "Take a Stand on High Ground" explores moments of resolve and resiliency.

What all the writers in this anthology share is their great desire to bring readers closer to understanding the lives and dreams and obstacles of a group so readily turned into a "they" in a world of shrill materialism. Perhaps the overall intention of this anthology lies in emphasizing what Dr.

Coles's father once explained when asked by his son why he was such an avid reader of literature.

Literature contains "reservoirs of wisdom," the elder Coles said. "Your mother and I feel rescued by these [stories]. We read them gratefully."

The stories included here about growing up poor in a land of restricted plenitude offer a certain richness. That same reservoir of wisdom and sense of gratitude Dr. Coles's parents passed on to him, we now pass on to you, the readers of this book.

Introduction
Robert Coles

To grow up poor is to begin to know, even in the first decade of life, what that adjectival word means, what its implications portend for the years ahead. Here is a young American, Jimmie, from Boston, who has figured out already at only ten, what *is*, what *will be*, in his life:

> You've got to be careful, my dad says, and my mom says "Amen," when he tells us that. He means you can't waste what you have, or else you'll be down to nothing—so you don't throw something out if you can eat it, and you don't leave soap in the water, or you'll have less and less to use. Sure, if you've got all you want, and if you want more, you can go to the store and buy all your heart tells you to buy, then you're "sitting pretty," dad says. But if "every penny counts," then you'd better remember [that], and when I'm all grown up, and out of school, I'll still remember, like my mom and dad—what can happen when there's no money to buy the food and pay the bills. "Find yourself a good job," dad tells us, my sister and my brothers, but don't be taking anything for granted, or you'll fall "flat on your face," that's his "philosophy," he says.

A pause, as a lad named Jimmie tries to become the man he hopes to be, named Jim:

> When I'm all grown up, I'll use my dad's name [Jim], and I'll try to get a job, and I'll try to save, so there'll be some "spare

cash." If you've got some "spare cash," my folks say, you're living on "easy street," but if you're strapped and no money is anywhere—then anything can come at you, around the corner, and boy, you're walking on thin ice, and you can just go under, fast, and that's it! "Plan in advance and hope for the best, but don't expect it," that's what "big Jim" says, and that's what I'll tell my kids when I'm older than I am now.

So it goes: parents teach children a felt jeopardy, vulnerability, and soon enough, those boys and girls are quite aware of their uncertain, if not grim prospects—to the point that they foresee clouds on the horizon, not only for themselves but for their own children. Not that those who grow up under modest circumstances, or indeed, amidst an obvious and unrelenting poverty, are necessarily without hope and ambition: many children born to parents struggling hard, against high odds, to make a go of it, nevertheless find their way to strong convictions about the desirable, and too, the possible. In the words of the youth just quoted:

> You can have a lot of trouble, and you're on the ropes, and you can be facing a knockout, but that doesn't mean you should give up. My uncle was on the boxing team [in high school] and he said, "If you're down that doesn't mean you're out," and my dad will say that a lot. He'll be sitting and trying to figure out "if we'll make it or we'll go to the poorhouse," but he always says: "Don't know where the poorhouse is, and no one I know has ever seen one, or been to one!" Maybe when I'm older I'll have enough money so I never think of a poorhouse, or talk about it to anyone.

Ironically, a family's poverty has enabled a son to think of the long run, to achieve a kind of distance on things—his dad's money problems, and his own ambitions as a boy who looks ahead, figures out what he wants from life. I came to know this boy, Jimmie, well enough, long enough, to understand from him (and his sister and one of his brothers, and his mom and dad) that a setback in life need not be regarded only as something that went wrong, badly awry—so the boy who spoke of his future life was able to point out clearly, in a forceful but polite reprimand for those who would gladly, even eagerly offer him compassion:

> Don't be ashamed, my folks tell us—it's no crime to be poor, so long as you keep working! Then [if someone does so] you should be proud of yourself. The worst thing is if you start feeling sorry for yourself—that means you've become a loser! I hear kids say, if you grow up and make a ton of dough, then you win, and if you grow up and you're poor, then you've lost. So, we argue, oh boy, *do* we! I'll say: "Hey you guys, you're *all* poor; everyone in this neighborhood, he's poor, she's poor, we're all poor." No one's walking around this street with wads of dough and a big bank book! But that doesn't mean you can count us out; and besides, some people with a lot of money are crooks—look at the news in the papers and the TV! If you feel sorry for yourself, you've lost; but if you can look yourself in the mirror, my dad says, you're on your way, because you can own your life, even if you have a lot of bills to pay, and you can't find the money to pay off what everyone wants from you (something for the food, something for the clothes, something for the rent). It's murder, all right, this life, but you shouldn't let yourself slip or fall!

In strongly vivid, compelling and colloquial language a child echoes a family's jeopardy, but also its willfulness, the latter (again, the irony) an occasional consequence of the former: his parents have told him candidly of their precarious financial situation, but they have also told him of their determination to persist, if not prevail—the fight they have in them no matter the strenuous odds they must daily face. To be sure, some parents have good reason to feel almost overwhelmed by poverty, to the point that they and their children have seemingly (and sadly) lost the kind of fighting spirit Jimmie has chosen to articulate with his friends, and in conversation with others, such as his teacher, and me, a doctor who sometimes worked at the school he attended. But some of us who want to know about the Jimmies of this world, want to understand the considerable hardships many poor families must endure, ought be mindful of the resourcefulness, the tenacity of mind and heart, that people who are hard-pressed, even down-and-out, socially and economically, can nevertheless muster—parents and children, both.

I start in this vein with Jimmie's help, because in the pages ahead his predicament keeps being conveyed in one story and statement after another—yes, poverty as, possibly, a hazard, a burden, a tough, demanding, exhausting ordeal, but poverty as also, now and then, a distinct challenge to those who experience it, and even a spur to those who feel hemmed in, or without much they wish they had, or know full well they need, yet who manage steadfastly to hold on tightly to their self-respect, their pride. The point, of course, is not to put on a pedestal those who often pay dearly in their minds for the tough life they have to endure—while at the same time, though, we can properly make allowance for the universal truth that suffering (illnesses, accidents, injuries, bad luck of various kinds) may also prompt those hurt, slapped down by fate and circumstance, to dig in, to summon all the strength and purpose they can find in their heads, in their bodies. In Ralph Ellison's novel, in Raymond Carver's stories and poems, or those of Richard Ford, even in Zora Neale Hurston's fictional account of harsh poverty as experienced by migrant farm families, one meets people of pluck and passion as well as travail—their eyes, after all, *are* "watching God." There is to such individuals, as the poet and physician William Carlos

Williams kept reminding us, based on his own firsthand acquaintance with working poor people of Paterson, New Jersey (where America's first factory was built), a *mulish* or stubbornly enduring side to their life, no matter the aches and worries that keep being experienced.

The challenge for *us* is to keep in mind what happens to the minds of *others* lest we be blind and deaf to how they must make do, and what they have to say, amidst the hard-fought lives that are theirs by dint of daily poverty. I have already referred to vulnerability and marginality as two aspects of poverty—both of them, not rarely, appreciated quite readily by children who have to live under such conditions. But let me move from social description to psychological experience. Here is Jimmie's sister, Sally, two years his senior, at thirteen on the edge of adolescence, speaking not of the future, as her brother was sometimes wont to do, but of the past—remembering, in fact, her own childhood as an elementary school girl who learned how to read and write and count, but who also learned how to read the world's values, take them in, realize their significance, and who learned how to write to herself, in a diary she kept, and not least, who learned how much she counted, in her parents' estimation, and how little she counted to others, or so it sometimes seemed to her:

I don't know how I became me, but I remember being in the second grade and the teacher was always upset with us, and she said we had to learn how to *behave*, and *dress right*, or we'd never get anywhere. Where is that "anywhere," I used to wonder to myself? Where she lives I suppose! Miss Carroll, she was totally full of herself, that's what my best friend Alice and I thought. I can remember a few kids, even back then, who were so stuck on themselves, and the teacher, that Miss Carroll, was stuck on them. Even so, Alice and me, we figured we'd rather live just where we do, right here in our own broken-down building [they lived in an apartment house that badly needed repairs] than be with those big-shot kids, so uppity their noses touch the clouds, and they're always sniffing at somebody, saying she's not so good, too bad!

Now [in junior high school], it's worse. The kids who have it made (their parents drive them to school in fancy cars) sit together when they can, especially in the cafeteria, and us, we come by bus and streetcar, and we hang together. My mom says, "That's life;" she says people stick with their own kind, that's how it goes, and you learn that when you grow up, and you leave your own because you go out in the world, to school where the kids are coming from all different places, and they have their different ideas, and some are "loaded," you just know.

I'll admit, it's hard; you see people, they've got fancy clothes—when you go downtown to the stores—and you think: some people have the luck and I'm not one of them. Mom says to forget that, but it's hard to stop your mind from "running all over the map"—you have these thoughts and you have to try and try to forget them. What thoughts? [I had asked.] Well, sometimes it's questions that I have, that I ask myself. I used to ask them when I was little, in the first grade, and now I'm still asking them, and I am in the seventh grade. I mean: why did it happen that some have everything that their heart wants and some don't know if there's the next meal around the corner, or a flat nothing will be there to eat, whether their stomach is growling or not? (I've heard my mom and dad talk like that, but they tell me to forget what they say and "get on with it.")

Another question I'll hear myself asking is—it's also one of the big ones: will good luck come and say hello to me, like it does to some people, or will I just be out of it all the time—you know, looking for a good deal, a good job, a good guy (who's nice, and *he* has a good deal, a good job) or will it be Mr. Nobody (who's going nowhere) who wants to take me with him?

I shouldn't have said that [she paused, then turned on herself with a scowl on her face]. I'm not being nice to all of us folks who live on this street when I get the idea in my head that nothing is green on this side of the fence, but on the other, you have heaven all over the place! Mom says, some people have their heaven, but we've got to make our own, right here, the best we can, and not be thinking, always, of what's out there, who's got it better than us—because that's not what the Lord wants heaven to be, a place where you're everyday thinking of others, "comparing, comparing, comparing," she says, my mom to us, when we say, "if only I could have this." "*If only*," mom will give it right back to us: "*if only* we could pay attention to who *we* are, and what *we* can do with the time the good Lord has given to us!"

I'll always remember when I asked if there's some way people having trouble can get out of it, and people looking for jobs that pay good can find them—and dad said: "Look" (he always starts that way!), "there are those who have a lot, and those who have a little, and we belong to the second, those kind of folks, but even so, bad can come to people who have a lot; they can get sick and die, like everyone else, or they can be mean to each other and selfish, just like bad can hit us (more than it hits them, who've got oodles of cash in their wallets and pocket books). One thing you should never lose sight of, *never ever*: that there's equality in this life. The sun shines on all of us, and the rain pours, the same way, down hard, and even if you've got a solid, expensive roof over your head, you have to go outside. Time belongs to no one—you can't buy it, you can only live during it (sure some people can spend their time buying, but that's *their* waste, you see!)." Dad tells us, when he says good night,

that you can be *down* but not *out*, and you can be way up
there, and take a big fall, and then you're really, really *out*,
because the longer, the steeper the fall, the harder it is. So,
we should stop comparing and comparing—just find our
dream, wherever it takes you, and try to build it, the best
you can.

So it went for Sally—a girl growing up poor, whose parents
had grown up poor, but a girl who owned her very own outlook on life, her very own notions of what is desirable, possible. Yes, at times those notions, part of a broader, overall
outlook, had their downside, even as she struggled long and
hard to be upbeat, to try earnestly (as her mom often put it,
drawing on the old and familiar lyrics of a song) to see the
"sunny side of the street." Indeed, to grow up poor (for Sally
and her brother Jimmie, for their parents, too, their kinfolk,
their neighbors near and far) could sometimes mean to scan
that other side of the street, to feel envy for it, to be rivalrous
or competitive with it, to long for what it has to offer, to hope
against hope that somehow, in some way, things would get
much better, money would be more available, good food and
shelter more reliable—and such being the case, life would be
more predictable and kindly, less harsh and precarious. Still,
as Sally knows in essence to remind not only herself but a
listener who converses with her, perspective matters, puts the
precarious in a larger framework of understanding, supplies a
certain "sense of things"—that phrase Sally has acquired from
her mom and dad, and she uses it as she tells how it is, living
in a given place:

> If you are upset, and if you feel it would be better if you
> had more (a beautiful dress and some really snazzy shoes),
> then what you need is to get a "sense of things"—that means
> you have to keep being yourself, and stop trying to be some-
> one else. Even rich people aren't satisfied with their eyes—

they want and they want and they want. So you can be greedy (with all you've got not enough for you) and you can live right here, where we do, and if you're "level-headed," dad says, and you have "a good sense of things"—why, that will keep you in harness, and you won't lose your head and go running in every which way, so you get confused and lost.

Such pointedly and poignantly expressed and averred words of awareness deserve to be in these pages, connected thereby to the words of various writers of fiction and nonfiction, of prose, and poetry, who like Sally and her brother Jimmie want all of us readers, students of literature and of life, both, to stop and consider what happens to us as we grow up poor, or not-so-very poor, but nevertheless, in families and on streets, where every penny counts, where enough dollars to fend off property owners and store owners can't be taken for granted, and where even the words "job" and "employment" are not every day's joyful vocabulary (but rather, signals, when used, of what is missing, and so, of distress and turmoil). The longer I have listened to poor children across this nation, and abroad, the more sharply I hear their self-consciousness conveyed—their intention, really, that I hear in no uncertain terms what they have come to figure out in their brains, feel strongly in their hearts. These are young people who know how close to the edge their parents, and they as boys and girls with them, live each day. These are children who sometimes long to live elsewhere, have a different kind of life, more secure and providing materially. These are children who now and then want what others may assume naturally to be theirs—want higher hopes and expectations not only felt but grounded in an observable, everyday existence. These are children already aware of what words like "loss" and "race" can come to mean—thus does a social and an economic background shape ideas, ideals, wishes and worries. These are children who have learned certain decisive social lessons, and don't forget them later, no matter the personal and professional breakthroughs they achieve.

Such children, of course, have their frailties and fears to confront—constant companions, alas, on a particular life's journey. Yet, such children can also be savvy in so many respects, alert in the face of any number of difficulties put in their way by events and individuals. To read the following stories (moments of lyrical affirmation or remembered incidents) is to be taught by those who have wanted to evoke and chronicle and render a kind of living—as writers or observers, they have aimed to document a kind of life, put on record its length and breadth (and depth).

That record of sorts, then, is what follows. Thereby, through words on pages, those who grow up poor can get close to the readers far away, and maybe distant by virtue of their lives— get to them through the magic of language, and too, amidst the magic of a classroom, wherein teachers search for direction, their own and that of their students. "I like it when we all get closer in school," Sally once told me as she contemplated the satisfactions of her life, gave frank acknowledgment of its not-rare hurdles, even vicissitudes. In a sense, one can dare say, this book will give her something else to welcome with eager excitement: she and so many others like her, like her brother, like some of the children who speak directly in the book, or are given expression through the narratives and reminiscences that fill the pages ahead, will now all "get closer in school," in school after school, to child after child whose reading eyes will stir a pondering mind to reflection, to interest, respect, concern, alarm—to those "motions of the heart" as they, in turn, have responded to the reading, learning mind's energetic activity.

PART ONE

To Come Into a World Like This One

Langston Hughes

Sometimes called the "poet laureate of African America," Langston Hughes was born in Joplin, Missouri, in 1902. Though Hughes's younger days were marked by relative privilege, he wrote not for a literary elite but for ordinary people. Always a man of his time, Hughes wrote over eight hundred poems about current issues and, in particular, life in black America: Harlem, prejudice, love, jazz—and poverty. Langston Hughes was part of an extraordinary period of artistic and political activity among African Americans, lasting from 1920 until about 1930, and later known as the Harlem Renaissance.

One of Langston Hughes's most famous poems, "Mother to Son," is from an early poetry collection titled *The Dream Keeper and Other Poems*, first published during the Depression. A mixture of dreams and reality is offered as advice for living in a world "with tacks in it" and "no boards on the floor."

Mother to Son

Well, son, I'll tell you:
Life for me ain't been no crystal stair.
It's had tacks in it,
And splinters,
And boards torn up,
And places with no carpet on the floor—
Bare.
But all the time
I'se been a-climbin' on,
And reachin' landin's,
And turnin' corners,
And sometimes goin' in the dark
Where there ain't been no light.
So, boy, don't you turn back.
Don't you set down on the steps
'Cause you finds it kinder hard.
Don't you fall now—
For I'se still goin', honey,
I'se still climbin',
And life for me ain't been no crystal stair.

William Carlos Williams

Distinguished American poet and novelist William Carlos Williams was also a physician who treated the im-
migrant poor in and around Paterson, New Jersey,
during the first half of the twentieth century. This excerpt is from the first of three novels Williams wrote
about Joe and Gurlie Strecher, poor European immigrants who come to New York at the turn of the twentieth century seeking a better life.

White Mule, the first novel in the Strecher family
saga (*In the Money* and *The Build-Up* are the sequels)
is the story of Joe and Gurlie's first baby, Flossie, and
her first year of life. Flossie had a kick like "White
Mule" whiskey, the reader learns, hence the novel's title. This scene of Flossie's birth opens the novel. The
nurse in attendance, Mrs. D., worries about what it
means for Flossie to "come into a world like this
one."

From *White Mule*

She entered, as Venus from the sea, dripping. The air enclosed her, she felt it all over her, touching, waking her. If Venus did not cry aloud after release from the pressures of that sea-womb, feeling the new and lighter flood springing in her chest, flinging out her arms—this one did. Screwing up her tiny smeared face, she let out three convulsive yells—and lay still.

Stop that crying, said Mrs. D, you should be glad to get outa that hole.

It's a girl. What? A girl. But I wanted a boy. Look again. It's a girl, Mam. No! Take it away. I don't want it. All this trouble for another girl.

What is it? said Joe, at the door. A little girl. That's too bad. Is it all right? Yes, a bit small though. That's all right then. Don't you think you'd better cover it up so it won't catch cold? Ah, you go on out of here now and let me manage, said Mrs. D. This appealed to him as proper so he went. Are you all right, Mama? Oh, leave me alone, what kind of a man are you? As he didn't exactly know what she meant he thought it better to close the door. So he did.

In prehistoric ooze it lay while Mrs. D wound the white twine about its pale blue stem with kindly clumsy knuckles and blunt fingers with black nails and with the wiped-off scissors from the cord at her waist, cut it—while it was twisting and flinging up its toes and fingers into the way—free.

Alone it lay upon its back on the bed, sagging down in the middle, by the smeared triple mountain of its mother's disgusted thighs and toppled belly.

The clotted rags were gathered. Struggling blindly against the squeezing touches of the puffing Mrs. D, it was lifted into a nice woolen blanket and covered. It sucked its under lip and then let out two more yells.

Ah, the little love. Hear it, Mam, it's trying to talk.

La, la, la, la, la, la, la! it said with its tongue—in the black softness of the new pressures—and jerking up its hand, shoved its right thumb into its eye, starting with surprise and pain and yelling and rolling in its new agony. But finding the thumb again at random it sobbingly subsided into stillness.

Mrs. D lifted the cover and looked at it. It lay still. Her heart stopped. It's dead! She shook the . . .

With a violent start the little arms and legs flew up into a tightened knot, the face convulsed again—then as the nurse sighed, slowly the tautened limbs relaxed. It did not seem to breathe.

And now if you're all right I'll wash the baby. All right, said the new mother drowsily.

In that two ridges lap with wind cut off at the bend of the neck it lay, half dropping, regrasped—it was rubbed with warm oil that rested in a saucer on the stove while Mrs. D with her feet on the step of the oven rubbed and looked it all over, from the top of its head to the shiny soles of its little feet.

About five pounds is my guess. You poor little mite, to come into a world like this one. Roll over here and stop wriggling or you'll be on the floor. Open your legs now till I rub some of this oil in there. You'll open them glad enough one of these days—if you're not sorry for it. So, in all of them creases. How it sticks. It's like lard. I wonder what they have that on them for. It's a hard thing to be born a girl. There you are now. Soon you'll be in your little bed and I wish I was the same this minute.

She rubbed the oil under the arm pits and carefully round the scrawny folds of its little neck pushing the wobbly head back and front. In behind the ears there was still that white grease of pre-birth. The matted hair, larded to the head, on the brow it lay buttered heavily while the whole back was caked with it, a yellow-white curd.

In the folds of the groin, the crotch where the genitals all bulging and angry red seemed presages of some future growth, she rubbed the warm oil, carefully—for she was a good woman—and thoroughly, cleaning her fingers on her apron. She parted the little parts looking and wondering at their smallness and perfection and shaking her head forebodingly.

The baby lay back at ease with closed eyes—lolling about as it was, lifted by a leg, an arm, and turned.

Mrs. D looked at the toes, counted them, admired the little perfect nails—and then taking each little hand, clenched tight at her approach, she smoothed it out and carefully anointed its small folds.

Into the little sleeping face she stared. The nose was flattened and askew, the mouth was still, the slits of the eyes were swollen closed—it seemed.

You're a homely little runt, God pardon you, she said—rubbing the spot in the top of the head. Better to leave that—I've heard you'd kill them if you pressed on that too hard. They say a bad nurse will stop a baby crying by pressing there—a cruel thing to do.

She looked again where further back upon the head a soft round lump was sticking up like a jockey cap askew. That'll all go down, she said to herself wisely because it was not the first baby Mrs. D had tended, nor the fifth nor the tenth nor the twentieth even.

She got out the wash boiler and put warm water in it. In that she carefully laid the new-born child. It half floated, half asleep—opening its eyes a moment then closing them and resting on Mrs. D's left hand, spread out behind its neck.

She soaped it thoroughly. The father came into the kitchen where they were and asked her if she thought he could have a cup of coffee before he left for work—or should he go and get it at the corner. He shouldn't have asked her—suddenly it flashed upon his mind. It's getting close to six o'clock, he said. How is it? Is it all right?

He leaned to look. The little thing opened its eyes, blinked and closed them in the flare of the kerosene oil lamp close by in the gilded bracket on the wall. Then it smiled a crooked little smile—or so it seemed to him.

It's the light that hurts its eyes, he thought, and taking a dish towel he hung it on the cord that ran across the kitchen so as to cast a shadow on the baby's face.

Hold it, said Mrs. D, getting up to fill the kettle.

He held it gingerly in his two hands, looking curiously, shyly at that ancient little face of a baby. He sat down, resting it on his knees, and covered its still wet body. That little female body. The baby rested. Squirming in the tender grip of his guarding hands, it sighed and opened its eyes wide.

He stared. The left eye was rolled deep in toward the nose; the other seemed to look straight at his own. There seemed to be a spot of blood upon it. He looked and a cold dread started through his arms. Cross eyed! Maybe blind. But as he looked—the eyes seemed straight. He was glad when Mrs. D relieved him—but he kept his peace. Somehow this bit of moving, unwelcome life had won him to itself forever. It was so ugly and so lost.

The pains he had seemed to feel in his own body while the child was being born, now relieved—it seemed almost as if it had been he that had been the mother. It was his baby girl. That's a funny feeling, he thought.

He merely shook his head.

Coffee was cooking on the back of the stove. The room was hot. He went into the front room. He looked through the crack of the door into their bedroom where she lay. Then he sat on the edge of the disheveled sofa where, in a blanket, he had slept that night—and waited. He was a good waiter. Almost time to go to work.

Mrs. D got the cornstarch from a box in the pantry. She

had to hunt for it among a disarray of pots and cooking things and made a mental note to put some order into the place before she left. Ah, these women with good husbands, they have no sense at all. They should thank God and get to work.

Now she took the baby once more on her lap, unwrapped it where it lay and powdered the shrivelling, gummy two inch stem of the gummy cord, fished a roll of Canton flannel from the basket at her feet and putting one end upon the little pad of cotton on the baby's middle wrapped the binder round it tightly, round and round, pinning the end in place across the back. The child was hard there as a board now—but did not wake.

She looked and saw a red spot grow upon the fabric. Tie it again. Once more she unwrapped the belly band. Out she took the stump of the cord and this time she wound it twenty times about with twine while the tiny creature heaved and vermiculated with joy at its relief from the too tight belly band.

Wrapping an end of cotton rag about her little finger, Mrs. D forced that in between the little lips and scrubbed those tender gums. The baby made a grimace and drew back from this assault, working its whole body to draw back.

Hold still, said Mrs. D, bruising the tiny mouth with sedulous care—until the mite began to cough and strain to vomit. She stopped at last.

Dried, diapered and dressed in elephantine clothes that hid it crinkily; stockinged, booted and capped, tied under the chin—now Mrs. D walked with her new creation from the sweaty kitchen into the double light of dawn and lamps, through the hallway to the front room where the father sat, to show him.

Where are you going? For a walk?, he said.

Look at it in its first clothes, she answered him.

Yes, he said, it looks fine. But he wondered why they put the cap and shoes on it.

Turning back again, Mrs. D held the baby in her left arm

and with her right hand turned the knob and came once more into the smells of the birth chamber. There it was dark and the lamp burned low. The mother was asleep.

She put out the lamp, opened the inner shutters. There was a dim light in the room.

Waking with a start—What is it? the mother said. Where am I? Is it over? Is the baby here?

It is, said Mrs. D, and dressed and ready to be sucked. Are you flooding any?

Is it a boy? said the mother.

It's a girl, I told you before. You're half asleep.

Another girl, Agh, I don't want girls. Take it away and let me rest. God pardon you for saying that. Where is it? Let me see it, said the mother, sitting up so that her great breasts hung outside her undershirt. Lay down, said Mrs. D. I'm all right. I could get up and do a washing. Where is it?

She took the little thing and turned it around to look at it. Where is its face? Take off that cap. What are these shoes on for? She took them off with a jerk. You miserable scrawny little brat, she thought, and disgust and anger fought inside her chest, she was not one to cry—except in a fury.

The baby lay still, its mouth stinging from its scrub, its belly half strangled, its legs forced apart by the great diaper—and slept, grunting now and then.

Take it away and let me sleep. Look at your breasts, said Mrs. D. And with that they began to put the baby to the breast. It wouldn't wake.

The poor miserable thing, repeated the mother. This will fix it. It's its own mother's milk it needs to make a fine baby of it, said Mrs. D. Maybe it does, said the mother, but I don't believe it. You'll see, said Mrs. D.

As they forced the great nipple into its little mouth, the baby yawned. They waited. It slept again. They tried again. It squirmed its head away. Hold your breast back from its nose. They did.

Mrs. D squeezed the baby's cheeks together between her thumb and index finger. It drew back, opened its jaws and in they shoved the dripping nipple. The baby drew back. Then for a moment it sucked.

There she goes, said Mrs. D, and straightened up with a sigh, pressing her two hands against her hips and leaning back to ease the pain in her loins.

The mother stroked the silky hair, looked at the gently pulsing fontanelle, and holding her breast with the left hand to bring it to a point, straightened back upon the pillows and frowned.

The baby ceased to suck, squirming and twisting. The nipple lay idle in its mouth. It slept. Looking down, the mother noticed what had happened. It won't nurse, Mrs. D. Take it away. Mrs. D come here at once and take this thing, I'm in a dripping perspiration.

Mrs. D came. She insisted it should nurse. They tried. The baby waked with a start, gagging on the huge nipple. It pushed with its tongue. Mrs. D had it by the back of the neck pushing. She flattened out the nipple and pushed it in the mouth. Milk ran down the little throat, a watery kind of milk. The baby gagged purple and vomited.

Take it. Take it away. What's the matter with it? You're too rough with it.

If you'd hold it up properly, facing you and not away off at an angle as if—Mrs. D's professional pride was hurt. They tried again, earnestly, tense, uncomfortable, one cramped over where she sat with knees spread out, the other half kneeling, half on her elbows—till anger against the little rebellious spitting imp, anger and fatigue, overcame them.

Take it away, that's all, said the mother finally.

Reluctantly, red in the face, Mrs. D had no choice but to do what she was told. I'd like to spank it, she said, flicking its fingers with her own.

What! said the mother in such menacing tones that Mrs. D

caught a fright and realized whom she was dealing with. She said no more.

But now, the baby began to rebel. First its face got red, its whole head suffused, it caught its breath and yelled in sobs and long shrill waves. It sobbed and forced its piercing little voice so small yet so disturbing in its penetrating puniness, mastering its whole surroundings till it seemed to madden them. It sobbed and squeezed its yell into their ears.

That's awful, said the mother, I can't have it in this room. I don't think it's any good. And she lay down upon her back exhausted.

Mrs. D with two red spots in her two cheeks and serious jaw and a headache took the yelling brat into the kitchen. Dose it up. What else?

She got the rancid castor oil and gave the baby some. It fought and spit. Letting it catch its breath, she fetched the fennel tea, already made upon the range, and sweetening it poured a portion into a bottle, sat down and rather roughly told the mite to take a drink. There, drat you. Sweet to un-sweeten that unhappy belly. The baby sucked the fermentative warm stuff and liked it—and wet its diaper after.

Feeling the wet through her skirt and petticoat and drawers right on her thighs, Mrs. D leaped up and holding the thing out at arm's length, got fresh clothes and changed it.

Feeling the nice fresh diaper, cool and enticing, now the baby grew red all over. Its face swelled, suffused with color. Gripping its tiny strength together, it tightened its belly band even more.

The little devil, said Mrs. D, to wait till it's a new dia-per on.

And with this final effort, the blessed little thing freed itself as best it could—and it did very well—of a quarter pound of tarrish, prenatal slime—some of which ran down one leg and got upon its stocking.

That's right, said Mrs. D.

Betty Smith

Elizabeth (Betty) Wehner grew up in the Williamsburg
slums of Brooklyn, New York, at the turn of the twentieth century. By 1943, she had married, changed her
name to Betty Smith, raised two daughters, divorced,
and was living on a playwriting fellowship at the University of North Carolina. On hearing that her memoir
was going to be published, Smith took her last hundred
dollars and traveled to New York City. *A Tree Grows
in Brooklyn* was an immediate success, selling 300,000
copies in just six weeks. Its tender but unflinching por-
trayal of urban poverty and its effects on one family
struck a deep chord in readers. Reviewers called the
book "profoundly moving," "authentic and poignant."
At the time of Smith's death in 1972 at the age of
seventy-five, the novel had gone through thirty-seven
printings, selling over 6 million copies.

A Tree Grows in Brooklyn is the story of the Nolan
family, from 1902 to 1919: Johnny, the father who
works—on and off—as a waiter; his proud, suffering
wife, Katie; and their two children, seven-year-old
Francie and her younger brother, Neeley. The tree
mentioned in the book's title is *Ailanthus altissima*, the
"tree of heaven," a Chinese sumac once common in
the yards of Brooklyn tenements, a tree thought inde-
structible, even if you cut it down. In this excerpt,
Francie learns a sobering lesson about school and how
others view students who are poor—even before school
has actually begun.

From *A Tree Grows in Brooklyn*

School days were eagerly anticipated by Francie. She wanted all of the things that she thought came with school. She was a lonely child and she longed for the companionship of other children. She wanted to drink from the school water fountains in the yard. The faucets were inverted and she thought that soda water came out instead of plain water. She had heard mama and papa speak of the school room. She wanted to see the map that pulled down like a shade. Most of all, she wanted "school supplies"; a notebook and tablet and a pencil box with a sliding top filled with new pencils, an eraser, a little tin pencil sharpener made in the shape of a cannon, a pen wiper, and a six-inch, soft wood, yellow ruler.

Before school, there had to be vaccination. That was the law. How it was dreaded! When the health authorities tried to explain to the poor and illiterate that vaccination was a giving of the harmless form of smallpox to work up immunity against the deadly form, the parents didn't believe it. All they got out of the explanation was that germs would be put into a healthy child's body. Some foreign-born parents refused to permit their children to be vaccinated. They were not allowed to enter school. Then the law got after them for keeping the children out of school. A free country? they asked. You should live so long. What's free about it, they reasoned when the law forces you to educate your children and then endangers their lives to get them into school? Weeping mothers brought bawling children to the health center for inoculation. They carried on as though bringing their innocents to the slaughter. The children screamed hysterically at the first sight of the needle and their mothers, waiting in the anteroom, threw their shawls over their heads and keened loudly as if wailing for the dead.

Francie was seven and Neeley six. Katie had held Francie back wishing both children to enter school together so that they could protect each other against the older children. On a dreadful Saturday in August, she stopped in the bedroom to speak to them before she went off to work. She awakened them and gave instructions.

"Now when you get up, wash yourselves good and when it gets to be eleven o'clock, go around the corner to the public health place, tell them to vaccinate you because you're going to school in September."

Francie began to tremble. Neeley burst into tears.

"You coming with us, Mama?" Francie pleaded.

"I've got to go to work. Who's going to do my work if I don't?" asked Katie covering up her conscience with indignation.

Francie said nothing more. Katie knew that she was letting them down. But she couldn't help it, she just couldn't help it. Yes, she should go with them to lend the comfort and authority of her presence but she knew she couldn't stand the ordeal. Yet, they had to be vaccinated. Her being with them or somewhere else couldn't take that fact away. So why shouldn't one of the three be spared? Besides, she said to her conscience, it's a hard and bitter world. They've got to live in it. Let them get hardened young to take care of themselves.

"Papa's going with us then," said Francie hopefully.

"Papa's at Headquarters waiting for a job. He won't be home all day. You're big enough to go alone. Besides, it won't hurt."

Neeley wailed on a higher key. Katie could hardly stand that. She loved the boy so much. Part of her reason for not going with them was that she couldn't bear to see the boy hurt ... not even by a pin prick. Almost she decided to go with them. But no. If she went she'd lose half a day's work and she'd have to make it up on Sunday morning. Besides, she'd be sick afterwards. They'd manage somehow without her. She hurried off to her work.

Francie tried to console the terrified Neeley. Some older boys had told him that they cut your arm off when they got you in the Health Center. To take his mind off the thing, Francie took him down into the yard and they made mud pies. They quite forgot to wash as mama had told them to.

They almost forgot about eleven o'clock, the mud pie making was so beguiling. Their hands and arms got very dirty playing in the mud. At ten to eleven, Mrs. Gaddis hung out the window and yelled down that their mother had told her to remind them when it was near eleven o'clock. Neeley finished off his last mud pie, watering it with his tears. Francie took his hand and with slow dragging steps the children walked around the corner.

They took their place on a bench. Next to them sat a Jewish mama who clutched a large six-year-old boy in her arms and wept and kissed his forehead passionately from time to time. Other mothers sat there with grim suffering furrowed on their faces. Behind the frosted glass door where the terrifying business was going on, there was a steady bawling punctuated by a shrill scream, resumption of the bawling and then a pale child would come out with a strip of pure white gauze about his left arm. His mother would rush and grab him and with a foreign curse and a shaken fist at the frosted door, hurry him out of the torture chamber.

Francie went in trembling. She had never seen a doctor or a nurse in all her small life. The whiteness of the uniforms, the shiny cruel instruments laid out on a napkin on a tray, the smell of antiseptics, and especially the cloudy sterilizer with its bloody red cross filled her with tongue-tied fright.

The nurse pulled up her sleeve and swabbed a spot clean on her left arm. Francie saw the white doctor coming towards her with the cruelly-poised needle. He loomed larger and larger until he seemed to blend into a great needle. She closed her eyes waiting to die. Nothing happened, she felt nothing. She opened her eyes slowly, hardly daring to hope that it was all over. She found to her agony, that the doctor was still there, poised needle and all. He was staring at her arm in distaste. Francie looked too. She saw a small white area on a dirty dark brown arm. She heard the doctor talking to the nurse.

"Filth, filth, filth, from morning to night. I know they're poor but they could wash. Water is free and soap is cheap. Just look at that arm, nurse."

The nurse looked and clucked in horror. Francie stood there with the hot flamepoints of shame burning her face. The doctor was a Harvard man, interning at the neighborhood hospital. Once a week, he was obligated to put in a few hours at one of the free clinics. He was going into a smart practice in Boston when his internship was over. Adopting the phraseology of the neighborhood, he referred to his Brooklyn internship as going through Purgatory when he wrote to his socially prominent fiancée in Boston.

The nurse was a Williamsburg girl. You could tell that by her accent. The child of poor Polish immigrants, she had been ambitious, worked days in a sweatshop and gone to school at night. Somehow she had gotten her training. She hoped some day to marry a doctor. She didn't want anyone to know she had come from the slums.

After the doctor's outburst, Francie stood hanging her head. She was a dirty girl. That's what the doctor meant. He was talking more quietly now asking the nurse how that kind of people could survive; that it would be a better world if they were all sterilized and couldn't breed anymore. Did that mean he wanted her to die? Would he do something to make her die because her hands and arms were dirty from the mud pies?

She looked at the nurse. To Francie, all women were mamas like her own mother and Aunt Sissy and Aunt Evy. She thought the nurse might say something like:

"Maybe this little girl's mother works, and didn't have time to wash her good this morning," or, "You know how it is, Doctor, children *will* play in dirt." But what the nurse actually said was, "I know. Isn't it terrible? I sympathize with you, Doctor. There is no excuse for these people living in filth."

A person who pulls himself up from a low environment via the boot-strap route has two choices. Having risen above his environment, he can forget it; or, he can rise above it and never forget it and keep compassion and understanding in his heart for those he has left behind him in the cruel up climb. The nurse had chosen the forgetting way. Yet, as she stood there, she knew that years later she would be haunted by the sorrow in the face of that starveling child and that she would wish bitterly that she had said a comforting word then and done *something* towards the saving of her immortal soul. She had the knowledge that she was small but she lacked the courage to be otherwise.

When the needle jabbed, Francie never felt it. The waves of hurt started by the doctor's words were racking her body and drove out all other feeling. While the nurse was expertly tying a strip of gauze around her arm and the doctor was putting his instrument in the sterilizer and taking out a fresh needle, Francie spoke up.

"My brother is next. His arm is just as dirty as mine so don't be surprised. And you don't have to tell him. You told me." They stared at this bit of humanity who had become so strangely articulate. Francie's voice went ragged with a sob. "You don't have to tell him. Besides it won't do no good. He's a boy and he don't care if he is dirty." She turned, stumbled a little and walked out of the room. As the door closed, she heard the doctor's surprised voice.

"I had no idea she'd understand what I was saying." She heard the nurse say, "Oh, well," on a sighing note.

—

Katie was home for lunch when the children got back. She looked at their bandaged arms with misery in her eyes. Francie spoke out passionately.

"Why, Mama, why? Why do they have to . . . to . . . say things and then stick a needle in your arm?"

"Vaccination," said mama firmly, now that it was all over, "is a very good thing. It makes you tell your left hand from your right. You have to write with your right hand when you go to school and that sore will be there to say, uh-uh, not this hand. Use the other hand."

This explanation satisfied Francie because she had never been able to tell her left hand from her right. She ate, and drew pictures with her left hand. Katie was always correcting her and transferring the chalk or the needle from her left hand to her right. After mama explained about vaccination, Francie began to think that maybe it was a wonderful thing. It was a small price to pay if it simplified such a great problem and let you know which hand was which. Francie began using her right hand instead of the left after the vaccination and never had trouble afterwards.

—

Francie worked up a fever that night and the site of the injection itched painfully. She told mama who became greatly alarmed. She gave intense instructions.

"You're not to scratch it, no matter how it bites you."

"Why can't I scratch it?"

"Because if you do, your whole arm will swell up and turn black and drop right off. So don't scratch it."

Katie did not mean to terrify the child. She, herself, was badly frightened. She believed that blood-poisoning would set in if the arm were touched. She wanted to frighten the child into not scratching it.

Francie had to concentrate on not scratching the painfully itching area. The next day, shots of pain were shooting up the arm. While preparing for bed, she peered under the bandage. To her horror, the place where the needle had entered was swollen, dark-green and festering yellowly. And Francie had not scratched it! *She knew she had not scratched it.* But wait! Maybe she had scratched it in her sleep the night before. Yes, she must have done it then. She was afraid to tell mama. Mama would say, "I told you and I told you and still you wouldn't listen. Now look."

It was Sunday night. Papa was out working. She couldn't sleep. She got up from her cot and went into the front room and sat at the window. She leaned her head on her arms and waited to die.

At three in the morning she heard a Graham Avenue trolley grind to a stop on the corner. That meant someone was getting off. She leaned out the window. Yes, it was papa. He sauntered down the street with his light dancer's step whistling "My Sweetheart's the Man in the Moon." The figure in its tuxedo and derby hat, with a rolled-up waiter's apron in a neat packet under its arm, seemed like life itself to Francie. She called to him when he got to the door. He looked up and tipped his hat gallantly. She opened the kitchen door for him.

"What are you doing up so late, Prima Donna?" he asked. "It's not Saturday night, you know."

"I was sitting at the window," she whispered, "waiting for my arm to drop off."

He choked back a laugh. She explained about the arm. He closed the door leading into the bedrooms and turned up the gas. He removed the bandage and his stomach turned over at sight of the swollen festering arm. But he never let her know. He never let her know.

"Why, Baby, that's nothing at all. Just nothing at all. You should have seen my arm when I was vaccinated. It was twice as swollen and red, white and blue instead of green and yellow and now look how hard and strong it is." He lied gallantly for he had never been vaccinated.

He poured warm water into a basin and added a few drops of carbolic acid. He washed the ugly sore over and over again. She winced when it stung but Johnny said that stinging meant curing. He sang a foolish sentimental song in a whisper as he washed it.

He never cares to wander from his own fireside.
He never cares to ramble or to roam . . .

He looked around for a clean bit of cloth to serve as a bandage. Finding none, he took off his coat and shirt dicky, pulled his undershirt off over his head and dramatically ripped a strip of cloth from it.

"Your good undershirt," she protested.

"Aw, it was all full of holes anyhow."

He bandaged the arm. The cloth smelled of Johnny, warm and cigarish. But it was a comforting thing to the child. It smelled of protection and love.

"There! You're all fixed up, Prima Donna. Whatever gave you the idea your arm was going to drop off?"

"Mama said it would if I scratched it. I didn't mean to scratch it but I guess I did while I was sleeping."

"Maybe." He kissed her thin cheek. "Now go back to bed." She went and slept peacefully the rest of the night. In the morning, the throbbing had stopped and in a few days the arm was normal again.

After Francie had gone to bed, Johnny smoked another cigar. Then he undressed slowly and got into Katie's bed. She was sleepily aware of his presence and in one of her rare impulses of affection, she threw her arm across his chest. He removed it gently and edged as far away from her as he could. He lay close to the wall. He folded his hands under his head and lay staring into the darkness all the rest of that night.

Sandra Cisneros

Internationally acclaimed author Sandra Cisneros was born in Chicago in 1954. *The House on Mango Street,* Cisneros's first novel, gives voice to her Latina upbringing through forty-four short vignettes. Like the novel's heroine, twelve-year-old Esperanza Cordero who grows up on a poor Chicago street in a family of six, Cisneros says she too grew up "rat poor," the only sister of six brothers, in a predominantly Puerto Rican district of Chicago.

From *The House on Mango Street*

THE HOUSE ON MANGO STREET

We didn't always live on Mango Street. Before that we lived on Loomis on the third floor, and before that we lived on Keeler. Before Keeler it was Paulina, and before that I can't remember. But what I remember most is moving a lot. Each time it seemed there'd be one more of us. By the time we got to Mango Street we were six—Mama, Papa, Carlos, Kiki, my sister Nenny and me.

The house on Mango Street is ours, and we don't have to pay rent to anybody, or share the yard with the people downstairs, or be careful not to make too much noise, and there isn't a landlord banging on the ceiling with a broom. But even so, it's not the house we'd thought we'd get.

We had to leave the flat on Loomis quick. The water pipes broke and the landlord wouldn't fix them because the house was too old. We had to leave fast. We were using the washroom next door and carrying water over in empty milk gallons. That's why Mama and Papa looked for a house, and that's why we moved into the house on Mango Street, far away, on the other side of town.

They always told us that one day we would move into a house, a real house that would be ours for always so we wouldn't have to move each year. And our house would have running water and pipes that worked. And inside it would have real stairs, not hallway stairs, but stairs inside like the houses on T.V. And we'd have a basement and at least three washrooms so when we took a bath we wouldn't have to tell everybody. Our house would be white with trees around it, a great big yard and grass growing without a fence. This was the house Papa talked about when he held a lottery ticket and this was the house Mama dreamed up in the stories she told us before we went to bed.

But the house on Mango Street is not the way they told it at all. It's small and red with tight steps in front and windows so small you'd think they were holding their breath. Bricks are crumbling in places, and the front door is so swollen you have to push hard to get in. There is no front yard, only four little elms the city planted by the curb. Out back is a small garage for the car we don't own yet and a small yard that looks smaller between the two buildings on either side. There are stairs in our house, but they're ordinary hallway stairs, and the house has only one washroom. Everybody has to share a bedroom—Mama and Papa, Carlos and Kiki, me and Nenny.

Once when we were living on Loomis, a nun from my school passed by and saw me playing out front. The laundromat downstairs had been boarded up because it had been robbed two days before and the owner had painted on the wood YES WE'RE OPEN so as not to lose business.

Where do you live? she asked.

There, I said pointing up to the third floor.

You live *there*?

There. I had to look to where she pointed—the third floor, the paint peeling, wooden bars Papa had nailed on the windows so we wouldn't fall out. You live *there?* The way she said it made me feel like nothing. *There.* I lived *there.* I nodded.

I knew then I had to have a house. A real house. One I could point to. But this isn't it. The house on Mango Street isn't it. For the time being, Mama says. Temporary, says Papa. But I know how those things go.

OUR GOOD DAY

If you give me five dollars I will be your friend forever. That's what the little one tells me.

Five dollars is cheap since I don't have any friends except Cathy who is only my friend till Tuesday.

Five dollars, five dollars.

She is trying to get somebody to chip in so they can buy a bicycle from this kid named Tito. They already have ten dollars and all they need is five more.

Only five dollars, she says.

Don't talk to them, says Cathy. Can't you see they smell like a broom.

But I like them. Their clothes are crooked and old. They are wearing shiny Sunday shoes without socks. It makes their bald ankles all red, but I like them. Especially the big one who laughs with all her teeth. I like her even though she lets the little one do all the talking.

Five dollars, the little one says, only five.

Cathy is tugging my arm and I know whatever I do next will make her mad forever.

Wait a minute, I say, and run inside to get the five dollars. I have three dollars saved and I take two of Nenny's. She's not home, but I'm sure she'll be glad when she finds out we own a bike. When I get back, Cathy is gone like I knew she would be, but I don't care. I have two new friends and a bike too.

My name is Lucy, the big one says. This here is Rachel my sister.

I'm her sister, says Rachel. Who are you?

And I wish my name was Cassandra or Alexis or Maritza—anything but Esperanza—but when I tell them my name they don't laugh.

We come from Texas, Lucy says and grins. Her was born here, but me I'm Texas.

You mean *she,* I say.

No, I'm from Texas, and doesn't get it.

This bike is three ways ours, says Rachel who is thinking ahead already. Mine today, Lucy's tomorrow and yours day after.

But everybody wants to ride it today because the bike is new, so we decide to take turns *after* tomorrow. Today it belongs to all of us.

I don't tell them about Nenny just yet. It's too complicated. Especially since Rachel almost put out Lucy's eye about who was going to ride it first. But finally we agree to ride it together. Why not?

Because Lucy has long legs she pedals. I sit on the back seat and Rachel is skinny enough to get up on the handlebars which makes the bike all wobbly as if the wheels are spaghetti, but after a bit you get used to it.

We ride fast and faster. Past my house, sad and red and crumbly in places, past Mr. Benny's grocery on the corner, and down the avenue which is dangerous. Laundromat, junk store, drugstore, windows and cars and more cars, and around the block back to Mango.

People on the bus wave. A very fat lady crossing the street says, You sure got quite a load there.

Rachel shouts, You got quite a load there too. She is very sassy.

Down, down Mango Street we go. Rachel, Lucy, me. Our new bicycle. Laughing the crooked ride back.

THE FIRST JOB

It wasn't as if I didn't want to work. I did. I had even gone to the social security office the month before to get my social security number. I needed money. The Catholic high school cost a lot, and Papa said nobody went to public school unless you wanted to turn out bad.

I thought I'd find an easy job, the kind other kids had, working in the dime store or maybe a hotdog stand. And though I hadn't started looking yet, I thought I might the week after next. But when I came home that afternoon, all wet because Tito had pushed me into the open water hydrant—only I had sort of let him—Mama called me in the kitchen before I could even go and change, and Aunt Lala was sitting there drinking her coffee with a spoon. Aunt Lala said she had found a job for me at the Peter Pan Photo Finishers on North Broadway where she worked, and how old was I, and to show up tomorrow saying I was one year older, and that was that.

So the next morning I put on the navy blue dress that made me look older and borrowed money for lunch and bus fare because Aunt Lala said I wouldn't get paid till the next Friday, and I went in and saw the boss of the Peter Pan Photo Finishers on North Broadway where Aunt Lala worked and lied about my age like she told me to and sure enough, I started that same day.

In my job I had to wear white gloves. I was supposed to match negatives with their prints, just look at the picture and look for the same one on the negative strip, put it in the envelope, and do the next one. That's all. I didn't know where these envelopes were coming from or where they were going. I just did what I was told.

It was real easy, and I guess I wouldn't have minded it except that you got tired after a while and I didn't know if I could sit down or not, and then I started sitting down only when the two ladies next to me did. After a while they started to laugh and came up to me and said I could sit when I wanted to, and I said I knew.

When lunchtime came, I was scared to eat alone in the company lunchroom with all those men and ladies looking, so I ate real fast standing in one of the washroom stalls and had lots of time left over, so I went back to work early. But then break time came, and not knowing where else to go, I went into the coatroom because there was a bench there.

I guess it was the time for the night shift or middle shift to arrive because a few people came in and punched the time clock, and an older Oriental man said hello and we talked for a while about my just starting, and he said we could be friends and next time to go in the lunchroom and sit with him, and I felt better. He had nice eyes and I didn't feel so nervous anymore. Then he asked if I knew what day it was, and when I said I didn't, he said it was his birthday and would I please give him a birthday kiss. I thought I would because he was so old and just as I was about to put my lips on his cheek, he grabs my face with both hands and kisses me hard on the mouth and doesn't let go.

THE FAMILY OF LITTLE FEET

There was a family. All were little. Their arms were little, and their hands were little, and their height was not tall, and their feet very small.

The grandpa slept on the living room couch and snored through his teeth. His feet were fat and doughy like thick tamales, and these he powdered and stuffed into white socks and brown leather shoes.

The grandma's feet were lovely as pink pearls and dressed in velvety high heels that made her walk with a wobble, but she wore them anyway because they were pretty.

The baby's feet had ten tiny toes, pale and see-through like a salamander's, and these he popped into his mouth whenever he was hungry.

The mother's feet, plump and polite, descended like white pigeons from the sea of pillow, across the linoleum roses, down the wooden stairs, over the chalk hopscotch squares, 5, 6, 7, blue sky.

Do you want this? And gave us a paper bag with one pair of lemon shoes and one red and one pair of dancing shoes that used to be white but were now pale blue. Here, and we said thank you and waited until she went upstairs.

Hurray! Today we are Cinderella because our feet fit exactly, and we laugh at Rachel's one foot with a girl's grey sock and a lady's high heel. Do you like these shoes? But the truth is it is scary to look down at your foot that is no longer yours and see attached a long long leg.

Everybody wants to trade. The lemon shoes for the red shoes, the red for the pair that were once white but are now pale blue, the pale blue for the lemon, and take them off and put them back on and keep on like this a long time until we are tired.

Then Lucy screams to take our socks off and yes, it's true.

We have legs. Skinny and spotted with satin scars where scabs were picked, but legs, all our own, good to look at, and long.

It's Rachel who learns to walk the best all strutted in those magic high heels. She teaches us to cross and uncross our legs, and to run like a double-dutch rope, and how to walk down to the corner so that the shoes talk back to you with every step. Lucy, Rachel, me tee-tottering like so. Down to the corner where the men can't take their eyes off us. We must be Christmas.

Mr. Benny at the corner grocery puts down his important cigar: Your mother know you got shoes like that? Who give you those?

Nobody.

Them are dangerous, he says. You girls too young to be wearing shoes like that. Take them shoes off before I call the cops, but we just run.

On the avenue a boy on a homemade bicycle calls out: Ladies, lead me to heaven.

But there is nobody around but us.

Do you like these shoes? Rachel says yes, and Lucy says yes, and yes I say, these are the best shoes. We will never go back to wearing the other kind again. Do you like these shoes?

In front of the laundromat six girls with the same fat face pretend we are invisible. They are the cousins, Lucy says, and always jealous. We just keep strutting.

Across the street in front of the tavern a bum man on the stoop.

Do you like these shoes?

Bum man says, Yes, little girl. Your little lemon shoes are so beautiful. But come closer. I can't see very well. Come closer. Please.

You are a pretty girl, bum man continues. What's your name, pretty girl?

And Rachel says Rachel, just like that.

Now you know to talk to drunks is crazy and to tell them

your name is worse, but who can blame her. She is young and dizzy to hear so many sweet things in one day, even if it is a bum man's whiskey words saying them.

Rachel, you are prettier than a yellow taxicab. You know that?

But we don't like it. We got to go, Lucy says.

If I give you a dollar will you kiss me? How about a dollar. I give you a dollar and he looks in his pocket for wrinkled money.

We have to go right now, Lucy says taking Rachel's hand because she looks like she's thinking about that dollar.

Bum man is yelling something to the air but by now we are running fast and far away, our high heel shoes taking us all the way down the avenue and around the block, past the ugly cousins, past Mr. Benny's up Mango Street, the back way, just in case.

We are tired of being beautiful. Lucy hides the lemon shoes and the red shoes and the shoes that used to be white but are now pale blue under a powerful bushel basket on the back porch, until one Tuesday her mother, who is very clean, throws them away. But no one complains.

What Sally Said

He never hits me hard. She said her mama rubs lard on all the places where it hurts. Then at school she'd say she fell. That's where all the blue places come from. That's why her skin is always scarred.

But who believes her. A girl that big, a girl who comes in with her pretty face all beaten and black can't be falling off the stairs. He never hits me hard.

But Sally doesn't tell about that time he hit her with his hands just like a dog, she said, like if I was an animal. He thinks I'm going to run away like his sisters who made the family ashamed. Just because I'm a daughter, and then she doesn't say.

Sally was going to get permission to stay with us a little and one Thursday she came finally with a sack full of clothes and a paper bag of sweetbread her mama sent. And would've stayed too except when the dark came her father, whose eyes were little from crying, knocked on the door and said please come back, this is the last time. And she said Daddy and went home.

Then we didn't need to worry. Until one day Sally's father catches her talking to a boy and the next day she doesn't come to school. And the next. Until the way Sally tells it, he just went crazy, he just forgot he was her father between the buckle and the belt.

You're not my daughter, you're not my daughter. And then he broke into his hands.

Jesse Hill Ford

Born in 1930 in Troy, Alabama, Jesse Hill Ford grew up in Nashville and studied writing at Vanderbilt University and then at the University of Florida. He was the author of dozens of short stories and several screenplays, many of which examined life in the South and the tensions between races and classes of people. Ford settled in the west Tennessee town of Humboldt. His most famous novel is *The Liberation of Lord Byron Jones*. When some of its citizens recognized themselves in Ford's novel, the town of Humboldt was scandalized. He died in 1996 at the age of 66.

In the short story "Big Boy," Ford looks at rural poverty and its effect on the future of one family. When lawyer Oman Hedgepath pulls into the farmyard where Hake Morris and his family are sharecropping, offering Morris's son Big Boy a chance to improve his station in life, Hake Morris tells lawyer Hedgepath he can't afford for Big Boy to be off the farm. Then, wealthy lawyer and struggling farmer strike a deal to provide Big Boy the economic chance of a lifetime— but at considerable moral cost. "Big Boy" was originally published in the *Atlantic Monthly*.

Big Boy

Hake Morris married a big-boned woman. Hake was a low-built white man and the woman he married stood taller than Hake and she was part Cherokee Indian. Hake was in no shape or condition to do better.

He was a poor man. He cropped in Sligo County first on one place and then on another. He seemed always to be saving enough old plowline to tie what little he and his Indian woman had to a wagon—borrowed wagon, borrowed mules—for the next move to the next place.

Children came along. Hake paid them little nevermind. Then along came Big Boy. And he was the last.

By now Hake had landed east of Somerton on a sizable farm owned by Mr. Jefferson Purser. Seven families lived on the farm and each had its own parcel of acreage to tend and plant, till and harvest.

Big Boy grew up on that farm and because the authorities had got strict, Big Boy had to board the school bus of a morning and be gone all day sometimes until after dark nine months of the year. Thus he was little use to Hake except in the summers when he did good work until the corn was laid by.

It was during this time that tractors started coming on strong in West Tennessee and Mr. Purser took in mind to buy a cotton picker and a bean combine and a corn sheller—three expensive machines. It changed Hake's luck. When the other hands had been turned off the place Hake Morris remained. Mr. Jefferson Purser had kept Hake because Hake knew what a clutch was and could shift gears and never left any machinery out in the weather.

Thus Hake, who always was a bad hand with mules and

never could work them properly nor speak to them so they wouldn't kick him now and again and try to break his bones, Hake was just fine and could stay where he was, once the tractors and the machines came on, for Hake Morris was a wonder with machines.

And Big Boy came fifteen. He was big too. He was three of Hake and two of his mother. Big Boy seemed like he ate more than all the rest of the Morris family put together.

Big Boy was fifteen and it was cotton-picking time and Hake was running the picker night and day, getting the crop out while he had a chance during a dry spell. Experience had taught lessons to Hake and Mr. Jefferson Purser. They knew never to let wet weather close in and be depending on something that weighs several tons and has to go about on wheels. Come wet weather and you could leave your cotton in the field or take the chance of bogging down your picker. So when it came a dry spell during picking season it was night and day. . . .

Just in the midst of this here came Lawyer Hedgepath from Somerton wanting to see Hake. Lawyer Hedgepath drove the biggest car made and was not somebody anybody ever told the word "no."

When Hake came in for dinner it was already after dark. There sat Lawyer Hedgepath before the teevee in the one stuffed easy chair. Hake had seen the big gleaming automobile outside. He had guessed it might be trouble.

Lawyer Hedgepath stood up. He was a good bit taller than Hake and didn't offer to shake hands. He wanted to know how the cotton was.

"Yessir. OK if the weather holds," says Hake.

"For some years, as you may know, I've had more than a passing interest in our Somerton High School," says Lawyer Hedgepath. "I try to help the football coach. I've been president of the Quarterback Club. Take a ball team, one that wins, and it's a source of pride, Hake. So like my daddy who was a lawyer before me I try to maintain an interest in our high school football."

"Yessir," says Hake.

"I want your boy to play for Somerton, Hake. The coach wants him. He's got the makings of a fine football player."

"I've disallowed for him to play ball," says Hake. And not knowing what else to do or say he sat down to his supper then. His woman brought his food. Hake commenced eating and was more at his ease for knowing it was not trouble but football the lawyer had in mind. Big Boy had mentioned to Hake about Lawyer Hedgepath and the coach talking to him about playing ball. Hake had merely told the boy: "That's disallowed, as you know."

Uninvited, Lawyer Hedgepath came to where Hake was and took a chair at the table. He was big and he was finely dressed. He had brown eyes and a level look about him and he started talking. He said what a chance it was if a boy got the right start with a big high school where football was liked. The coaches would train him. Scouts from the big colleges would come watch him play. Here was a way a boy could get himself a big expensive education and help Somerton at the same time. If he was the right boy.

"Yessir," says Hake. "But he is needed here. He has spoke to me once about it already but I have disallowed him, as I already said just now. Just like I have disallowed him to hunt. Can't afford license nor gun nor shotgun shells. Disallowed him a dog. Can't feed a dog. Hereabout this place in my condition everything mighty nigh has to be disallowed. Take a rich man, he would not understand it. That I know, a rich man. Could he understand it he would not be rich."

"My daddy farmed. My granddaddy farmed," says Oman Hedgepath. "My great-granddaddy farmed before them. Back as far as the history of my family goes, we have farmed. So be sure, Mr. Morris, that I appreciate the problems. I know the obstacles, the hardships, and all the disappointments of farming. I know them at first hand because I grew up on the farm myself, sir."

Hake was near about to believing. Even though he knew the truth. Big money wasn't made by farming. Farm money hadn't bought the lawyer's car standing outside in the early frost just falling. That car was the biggest thing made. Even if Oman Hedgepath lived on a farm, which he did, that didn't make him a farmer. Hake knew what he knew. And he knew that Oman Hedgepath had servants to wait on him and servants to drive him about when he didn't feel like driving himself. And more servants worked in Lawyer Hedgepath's flower beds and weeded his shrubs than lived on this whole place. And this place measured some fifteen hundred acres.

Still, just listening, Hake gradually came to feel he knew this man and he felt something close to pride at having Oman Hedgepath here visiting him, Hake Morris, in a personal way. All this did something for Hake that he was glad for, such that far from jumping up from the table when he was finished eating he accepted one of Lawyer Hedgepath's cigars. And they sat smoking as though they had all the time there was in the world, and didn't have several acres of cotton out there waiting to be picked while the ground was yet dry.

And while they sat thus smoking and visiting, Big Boy pulled into the company, right up to the table like a full-grown man. His cheeks were chapped by the cold. He wore a faded denim jacket that was too small for him and had on the big old Army GI shoes Hake had found for him in the surplus store at Pinoak. It's said those shoes come from battlefields, pulled from the feet of dead soldiers. Hake paid no attention to that. He found the shoes, they were big enough, and he had reached straight down into his overalls and bought them for Big Boy.

"We'd arrange things so Big Boy could work on the weekends and pick up a little money," Oman Hedgepath was saying. "Somerton Warriors need a linesman. Big Boy needs a good education."

"How much money?" says Hake. "On the weekends."

Oman Hedgepath named sixty dollars a month. Hake let his cigar lie so long in the coffee can lid ashtray that it went out and Oman—he insisted on being called Oman now—went on about the call of a man's patriotic duty, and the call of a man to football, and likened both to the call men get when it comes to them that God has chosen them to preach. "Tell you, Hake, I b'lieve this boy has a *call* to play football for the Warriors. Wouldn't surprise me next year to see him make twenty dollars a week during school and move up to twice that or more during the summer."

"I can't *hardly* stand in his way, on that," Hake heard himself saying. And he looked at Big Boy. "What about it, son? How you feel about going and moving to Somerton and playing for the—ah—"

"The Warriors," says Oman. "Need a light there, Hake?" The lawyer brought a kitchen match out of his pocket and struck it on his thumbnail with a swift, businesslike movement. He held the flame across the table and Hake puffed hard to relight his cigar.

"Strong, but it's good. Kind is it?"

"Cuban," says Oman Hedgepath. "Friends smuggle 'em in for me when they come from Europe. Can't get 'em anymore in this country."

"Can't?" says Hake, puffing the big, black, strong cigar. "Ever now and then I might buy me a King Edward. Give you a King Edward sometime, how about that—ah—Oman?" Hake didn't want to seem like a man who would remain beholden.

"You let Big Boy move to town and wouldn't surprise me if somebody didn't lay down a full box of King Edwards on this table," says Oman. "Plus maybe a *bottle* of something!"

The way Oman said it was so funny Hake had to laugh in spite of himself. Then he heard himself asking Big Boy again what about it and Big Boy just nodded *yes,* that he wanted to move into Somerton.

"About when would he go, then?" says Hake. "If I was to say *yes,* I mean."

"Take him in tonight," says Oman Hedgepath. "Let him ride in town with me."

"Tonight?"

"Wait here a minute. Something in the car I forgot—wait a minute." And the lawyer left the table and went outdoors.

Hake looked at the boy. "What about it? You willing? You want to go?"

Big Boy looked down at his hands.

"Looks like a fine chance to me, son," says Hake. "Go call your mama and tell her I said to come in here."

Big Boy went into the next room and came back with her. One thing about her she was shy about talking to strangers. It was easy to see how close the boy favored her. He had her same high cheekbones and her same proud black eyes. His teeth were good like hers and his skin was that same dark golden color. And he was big and he'd grow bigger still and he was part her and part Hake. And Hake, being the age he was, would never hope to have more children. Hake Morris would die without a purebred white child to his name and credit and all his descendants would henceforth and forever be off-brand sort of folks. But he'd had no choice. It had been her or nothing and besides all that he loved her. She could saw wood and swing an axe like a man, and she was tough so that if anything bothered her or hurt her she never let on and whined. She stood silent, waiting.

"Boy wants to go live in Somerton. Wants to play ball."

"Ball," she said.

"Football," says Hake. "Warriors need him real bad. Want to get his clothes together?"

The outside door opened. It was Oman Hedgepath. He had

a bottle in his hand. He shut the door. "Mrs. Morris? I thought so. I'd know in a minute you were Big Boy's mother. How are you?"

"Fine." Almost a whisper.

"How you feel about Big Boy coming to play football for Somerton?"

"Fine." The same near whisper.

"She needs to get his clothes together," says Hake. "Go on now and get him ready. Lawyer Hedgepath can't wait all night on him. This is busy times."

"Don't hurry on my account," says Oman. "Take your time, Mrs. Morris."

She and the boy have gone into the tacked-on shed room where he sleeps. The two of them move back and forth in the room, getting him ready.

"Wouldn't have a couple of glasses, would you, Hake?" says Oman. He opens the bottle.

"Some old jelly glasses here somewhere," says Hake, getting up and fetching two glasses from the shelf over the kitchen sink. "You like yours with R.C., Oman?"

"Straight, thanks," says Oman.

"I seen some of the highway patrol take theirs with R.C.," says Hake, bringing the glasses. "We keep R.C. for Big Boy. I take mine straight. Always did. But I don't but rarely take a drink."

"Now's a good time," Oman says. He pours a drink into each glass. "Big Boy's success."

"I'll go for that," says Hake. He empties his glass in a swallow. Oman pours him another. Hake takes a closer look at the bottle. "Good stuff," he says.

The liquor has started to stir Hake's blood when his woman walks out with Big Boy's things rolled in a bed blanket. She's tied up both ends with a piece of binder twine. Big Boy comes behind her with some things in a grocery sack.

"You could have took my suitcase," says Hake.

"This is fine," says Big Boy.

"Wouldn't of minded you taking my suitcase. You're welcome to it. Old suitcase ain't worth much. But—if you're satisfied with a bed blanket, Big Boy, then I guess that satisfies me."

"It's OK," says Big Boy.

Oman Hedgepath stands up. "Well," he says. "We ready— are we?"

"Set and stay a spell. You don't have to rush off," says Hake. "Don't forget your bottle, Oman."

"That stays here," says Oman. "Handy for cold weather like tonight."

Hake stands up then. He wants to hug Big Boy but he can't bring himself to do it. They've long since got beyond all that. "Y'all better get on the road, then, I guess," says Hake.

"You'll come watch him play, Hake," says Oman Hedgepath. "We'll take good care of him. You'll be proud of him."

"Sure will. That'll be just fine," says Hake. "Bye now and Big Boy you mind and do what they tell you and . . . " But he could not think what else. The woman stood in beside him. Big Boy and Oman went out the door into the cold. The car doors slammed. The big car's engine turned over and started. The lights flashed on bright and the car moved slowly away down between the fences dividing the fields.

Hake watched until the car reached the main road and swung left and went purring softly away on the gravel. When he finally shut the door the woman was already sitting down at the table in her usual chair. Hake got her a jelly glass from the shelf. Without saying anything she took the glass in her big, blunt hand and looked at it.

"Fine bourbon," says Hake. " 'Early Times' and they don't make no finer. I bet they don't make no whiskey in the world the equal of 'Early Times.' "

"Good spirits."

"Huh?" Hake poured her a little drink.

"My grandmother took about this much four or five times a day. Said it made good spirits."

"Injun?"

The woman nodded. "I never tasted it but I remember the smell. This has the same smell."

"Drink up," says Hake. "Try it."

"I don't want to waste it. How much does it cost?"

Hake sighed. "It's a gift. Lawyer Hedgepath is known for one of the richest men around here anywhere. You heard of him, ain't you? Well, that's who that was. Know where this cigar come from—I swear if it's not gone out again. The Cubans could take a page out of King Edward's book to make a cigar that will stay lit. Where's a match?"

She went to the cupboard and brought him the kitchen matches. When she sat down she pulled her blue cotton dress close and held it gathered at her throat.

Hake lit the cigar. For the third time he puffed to get it started. It had a dark taste and was too strong to be inhaled. Nor was it in any way sweet-tasting like cigars Hake now and then bought at the grocery in Pinoak where he traded. He sat then and smoked doggedly, determined to enjoy the cigar.

"You ain't gonna even try it?" says Hake. One hand still held her dress gathered at the throat as though she were cold. She held the jelly glass in the other hand. Hake felt thick about the mouth.

"Don't know what my grandmother saw in it," she says.

"Just forget about her."

"Why?"

"Well—she's been dead a long time, ain't she?"

"Whiskey reminds me of her, that's all."

"But you ain't all total Injun. You got a deal of white blood. Couldn't tell you from a white woman myself didn't I know what you really was. Take some horses, or even now and then you find a dog and you can't look at him to tell if he wasn't a registered animal. Same with cattle. I seen whiteface cows you'd never know had a wild drop of blood in 'em if you didn't just happen to have the inside dope on it what their breeding was."

He saw that her glass was empty and poured her another drink. Heck fire, he was thinking. He thought of the lawyer's big automobile and how it had moved off so comfortable like and the exhaust had fanned around real slow like a white peacock tail and the big machine had whirred. Big Boy riding in that automobile. Big Boy gone to live in town somewhere. Big Boy a grown-up, educated man. Big Boy, with buttonholes in his shirt collars like Oman Hedgepath's.

"She sang the rain song."

"Sang what? How's that?"

"The rain song." Her glass was empty again. The woman sure could pour it down, Hake was thinking.

"Who?" says Hake. His mind was on that big car, a Lincoln Continental at least, if not something larger. Could of been a Cadillac. It had got so lately a man couldn't tell one from another whereas in his youth he might have known them all by sight, by year and brand.

"My grandmother."

"Aw?" says Hake. "Had a singin' voice? Never knew Injuns sang. Never seen no Injun perform a song on teevee," he said thoughtfully. And as though to reward himself for this discovery he poured himself another nip—but a little one this time. Whiskey must be saved. Maybe just one nip on Christmas Day. A nip each for him and the woman.

"She sang to me. Took me on her lap and sang."

"Sang what? Hymns or regular songs?"

"Just the rain song." Her fingers began to move up and down on the table. She was singing something in a low voice and it made him nervous. She was showing a side of herself he hadn't glimpsed before, never in all the years of their life together. And something was dawning on him. He felt the start of a feeling he sometimes had the next day after a bad trade, a trade done in haste, whereas a little waiting, a little deliberation might have saved him fifty dollars. He was glad when she hushed and couldn't seem to remember any more of whatever it was she had been singing. "Good spirits," she said, and looked at her glass.

"Listen," he said. "You know that Big Boy is the last—?"

"Yes."

"We got no more kids. It never come to me Big Boy was the last. Yet I knew he was the youngest. This leaves me alone. Nothing but me. No kin of mine in the house or on the place. They are all gone. The baby's gone."

She was not listening, though. She was singing again. She reminded him of a gosh damned tomtom. Almost in spite of himself he poured some more whiskey in her glass.

She stopped singing and took a drink. "Big Boy will be famous," she said. "The night before the day he was born I dreamed it. Big Boy Morris. Wait and watch and see if he won't be famous." It wasn't like her. She was talking so much her tongue was loose as a wiggling snake.

Hake gave her a look. She had picked up Oman Hedgepath's abandoned cigar. She struck a match and lit it, putting her mouth where another's mouth had been. She drew the smoke down into her lungs and breathed it out again like a creature of steel.

"Big Boy's gonna be on teevee," she said. "Cherokee Indian on teevee, Big Boy Morris. Um!"

"Doing what?" says Hake.

"Football. Um," she inhaled again.

The remembrance of that stuff she had been singing rose to the back of his mind. *Rain!* It hit him and made his scalp move. He sprang up. She didn't move. While he piled into his coat and readied himself to rush outside she sat very still. He went out and pulled the door shut and ran to the cotton picker. Frost was on the windshield. He scraped it away and started the big machine. He made a turn in close to the house and had a glimpse of her through the window sitting in the same place she had been sitting when he had jumped up. He was still frightened by that dreadful thought—*rain.* Seeing the woman was like looking at a dummy in a store window. He completed the turn and headed through the gate into the field past the picked-over rows. Shreds and scraps of cotton hung from the brown, aging bolls. With a sigh he swung into the white gleam of the fresh locks. He seemed to feel in his own hands the steel work of those chattering spindles.

He was cold. But by the time he had made his first pass to the rows' end the cab had begun to warm up and when he felt the warmth Hake wondered where C. B. his Negro helper, was, for C. B. was supposed to follow him. Was the man waiting here somewhere in the field? Had he been too shy to approach the house to see why Hake did not come back right away after supper? Hake wondered if the Negro had stayed in the cold all this time or if he had given up on Hake and gone home.

Then, beginning the second pass, he saw C. B. and pulled the picker to a halt, put it in neutral, and climbed down out of the cab.

C. B.'s head was wrapped in a thick, bulging scarf—an old sweater, perhaps.

"What kept me was Big Boy he left and went in town to live and play football," Hake said in a loud voice.

"Say he sick?"

"Naw, got him a job in Somerton. Left home. Now mind and follow me."

C. B. nodded. Hake climbed back into the warm cab and engaged the gears. Big Boy—gone. And well, Hake didn't even know where the boy was staying. Gone, all that quick. It was like death and Hake was still pondering it when they finally shut down for the night. Big Boy was still on his mind when he crawled into bed beside the woman. She lay snoring, dead asleep. Hake pondered what it could mean and he wondered where his own life had gone. And while he lay awake, knowing that Big Boy's bed was empty, another part of him was listening and fearful lest something hit the windows or strike the roof. A part of him was listening to make sure rain didn't come up and catch him. It was the way of rain to sneak up on a man unawares. Hake lay thus, for what seemed a long time, staring into darkness and feeling the abandoned shed room, feeling the emptiness where Big Boy had been.

Ralph Ellison

Ralph Waldo Ellison was an African American scholarship music student from Oklahoma who served in the merchant marine during the Second World War, won a writing fellowship, and went on to become one of the most important American writers of the twentieth century. First published in 1952 when Ellison was thirty-eight (two years before segregation in the United States would be declared illegal), *Invisible Man* became an instant American classic. The book takes the reader through the post-Depression South, through Harlem and into the mind of a black man driven to the brink of madness by the twin horrors of poverty and racism.

The idea for the book first came to Ellison at the end of World War II. During his time in the merchant marine, Ellison says he heard "vivid accounts of the less-than-democratic conditions under which [Negro soldiers] fought and labored" arising from what Ellison called "an archetypal American dilemma: How could you treat a Negro as equal in war and then deny him equality during time of peace?" Ellison gradually revised the novel's central theme, "the human universals hidden within the plight of one who was both black and American."

The nameless black protagonist of *Invisible Man*, a bright high school student unable to afford college, has been asked to give a speech "at a gathering of the town's leading white citizens" held "in the main ballroom of the leading hotel." Thinking that after he gives his speech he will be given his scholarship, the narrator is instead awarded a rich lesson in exploitation at the hands of well-to-do whites.

From *Invisible Man*

He was an odd old guy, my grandfather, and I am told I take
after him. It was he who caused the trouble. On his deathbed
he called my father to him and said, "Son, after I'm gone I
want you to keep up the good fight. I never told you, but our
life is a war and I have been a traitor all my born days, a spy
in the enemy's country ever since I give up my gun back in the
Reconstruction. Live with your head in the lion's mouth. I
want you to overcome 'em with yeses, undermine 'em with
grins, agree 'em to death and destruction, let 'em swoller you
till they vomit or bust wide open." They thought the old man
had gone out of his mind. He had been the meekest of men.
The younger children were rushed from the room, the shades
drawn and the flame of the lamp turned so low that it sputtered on the wick like the old man's breathing. "Learn it to
the younguns," he whispered fiercely; then he died. . . .
 Grandfather had been a quiet old man who never made any
trouble, yet on his deathbed he had called himself a traitor and
a spy, and he had spoken of his meekness as a dangerous activity. It became a constant puzzle which lay unanswered in
the back of my mind. And whenever things went well for me
I remembered my grandfather and felt guilty and uncomfortable. It was as though I was carrying out his advice in spite of
myself. And to make it worse, everyone loved me for it. I was
praised by the most lily-white men of the town. I was considered an example of desirable conduct—just as my grandfather
had been. And what puzzled me was that the old man had
defined it as *treachery*. When I was praised for my conduct I
felt guilty that in some way I was doing something that was
really against the wishes of the white folks, that if they had

understood they would have desired me to act just the opposite, that I should have been sulky and mean, and that that
really would have been what they wanted, even though they
were fooled and though they wanted me to act as I did. It
made me afraid that some day they would look upon me as a
traitor and I would be lost. Still I was more afraid to act any
other way because they didn't like that at all. The old man's
words were like a curse. On my graduation day I delivered an
oration in which I showed that humanity was the secret, indeed, the very essence of progress. (Not that I believed this—
how could I remembering my grandfather?—I only believed
that it worked.) It was a great success. Everyone praised me
and I was invited to give the speech at a gathering of the
town's leading white citizens. It was a triumph for our whole
community.

It was in the main ballroom of the leading hotel. When I
got there I discovered that it was on the occasion of a smoker,
and I was told that since I was to be there anyway I might as
well take part in the battle royal to be fought by some of my
schoolmates as part of the entertainment. The battle royal
came first.

All of the town's big shots were there in their tuxedoes,
wolfing down the buffet foods, drinking beer and whiskey and
smoking black cigars. It was a large room with a high ceiling.
Chairs were arranged in neat rows around three sides of a
portable boxing ring. The fourth side was clear, revealing a
gleaming space of polished floor. I had some misgivings over
the battle royal, by the way. Not from a distaste for fighting,
but because I didn't care too much for the other fellows who
were to take part. They were tough guys who seemed to have
no grandfather's curse worrying their minds. No one could
mistake their toughness. And besides, I suspected that fighting
a battle royal might detract from the dignity of my speech. In
those pre-invisible days I visualized myself as a potential
Booker T. Washington. But the other fellows didn't care too

much for me either, and there were nine of them. I felt superior to them in my way, and I didn't like the manner in which we were all crowded together into the servants' elevator. Nor did they like my being there. In fact, as the warmly lighted floors flashed past the elevator we had words over the fact that I, by taking part in the fight, had knocked one of their friends out of a night's work.

We were led out of the elevator through a rococo hall into an anteroom and told to get into our fighting togs. Each of us was issued a pair of boxing gloves and ushered out into the big mirrored hall, which we entered looking cautiously about us and whispering, lest we might accidentally be heard above the noise of the room. It was foggy with cigar smoke. And already the whiskey was taking effect. I was shocked to see some of the most important men of the town quite tipsy. They were all there—bankers, lawyers, judges, doctors, fire chiefs, teachers, merchants. Even one of the more fashionable pastors. We were a small tight group, clustered together, our bare upper bodies touching and shining with anticipatory sweat; while up front the big shots were becoming increasingly excited over something we still could not see. Suddenly I heard the school superintendent, who had told me to come, yell, "Bring up the shines, gentlemen! Bring up the little shines!"

We were rushed up to the front of the ballroom, where it smelled even more strongly of tobacco and whiskey. Then we were pushed into place. I almost wet my pants. A sea of faces, some hostile, some amused, ringed around us . . .

But as we tried to leave we were stopped and ordered to get into the ring. There was nothing to do but what we were told. All ten of us climbed under the ropes and allowed ourselves to be blindfolded with broad bands of white cloth. One of the men seemed to feel a bit sympathetic and tried to cheer us up as we stood with our backs against the ropes. Some of us tried to grin. "See that boy over there?" one of the men said. "I want you to run across at the bell and give it to him right in the belly. If you don't get him, I'm going to get you. I don't like his looks." Each of us was told the same. The blindfolds were put on. Yet even then I had been going over my speech. In my mind each word was as bright as flame. I felt the cloth pressed into place, and frowned so that it would be loosened when I relaxed.

But now I felt a sudden fit of blind terror. I was unused to darkness. It was as though I had suddenly found myself in a dark room filled with poisonous cottonmouths. I could hear the bleary voices yelling insistently for the battle royal to begin.

"Get going in there!"

"Let me at that big nigger!"

I strained to pick up the school superintendent's voice, as though to squeeze some security out of that slightly more familiar sound.

"Let me at those black sonsabitches!" someone yelled.

"No, Jackson, no!" another voice yelled. "Here, somebody, help me hold Jack."

"I want to get at that ginger-colored nigger. Tear him limb from limb," the first voice yelled.

I stood against the ropes trembling. For in those days I was what they called ginger-colored, and he sounded as though he might crunch me between his teeth like a crisp ginger cookie.

Quite a struggle was going on. Chairs were being kicked about and I could hear voices grunting as with a terrific effort. I wanted to see, to see more desperately than ever before. But the blindfold was tight as a thick skin-puckering scab and when I raised my gloved hands to push the layers of white aside a voice yelled, "Oh, no you don't, black bastard! Leave that alone!"

"Ring the bell before Jackson kills him a coon!" someone boomed in the sudden silence. And I heard the bell clang and the sound of the feet scuffling forward.

A glove smacked against my head. I pivoted, striking out stiffly as someone went past, and felt the jar ripple along the length of my arm to my shoulder. Then it seemed as though all nine of the boys had turned upon me at once. Blows pounded me from all sides while I struck out as best I could. So many blows landed upon me that I wondered if I were not the only blindfolded fighter in the ring, or if the man called Jackson hadn't succeeded in getting me after all.

Blindfolded, I could no longer control my motions. I had no dignity. I stumbled about like a baby or a drunken man. The smoke had become thicker and with each new blow it seemed to sear and further restrict my lungs. My saliva became like hot bitter glue. A glove connected with my head, filling my mouth with warm blood. It was everywhere. I could not tell if the moisture I felt upon my body was sweat or blood. A blow landed hard against the nape of my neck. I felt myself going over, my head hitting the floor. Streaks of blue light filled the black world behind the blindfold. I lay prone, pretending that I was knocked out, but felt myself seized by hands and yanked to my feet. "Get going, black boy! Mix it up!" My arms were like lead, my head smarting from blows. I managed to feel my way to the ropes and held on, trying to catch my breath. A glove landed in my mid-section and I went over again, feeling as though the smoke had become a knife jabbed into my guts. Pushed this way and that by the legs milling around me, I finally pulled erect and discovered that I could see the black, sweat-washed forms weaving in the smoky-blue atmosphere like drunken dancers weaving to the rapid drum-like thuds of blows.

Everyone fought hysterically. It was complete anarchy. Everybody fought everybody else. No group fought together for long. Two, three, four, fought one, then turned to fight each other, were themselves attacked. Blows landed below the belt and in the kidney, with the gloves open as well as closed, and with my eye partly opened now there was not so much terror. I moved carefully, avoiding blows, although not too many to attract attention, fighting from group to group. The

boys groped about like blind, cautious crabs crouching to protect their mid-sections, their heads pulled in short against their
shoulders, their arms stretched nervously before them, with
their fists testing the smoke-filled air like the knobbed feelers
of hypersensitive snails. In one corner I glimpsed a boy violently punching the air and heard him scream in pain as he
smashed his hand against a ring post. For a second I saw him
bent over holding his hand, then going down as a blow caught
his unprotected head. I played one group against the other,
slipping in and throwing a punch then stepping out of range
while pushing the others into the melee to take the blows
blindly aimed at me. The smoke was agonizing and there were
no rounds, no bells at three minute intervals to relieve our
exhaustion. The room spun around me, a swirl of lights,
smoke, sweating bodies surrounded by tense white faces. I bled
from both nose and mouth, the blood spattering upon my
chest.

The men kept yelling, "Slug him, black boy! Knock his guts
out!"

"Uppercut him! Kill him! Kill that big boy!"

Taking a fake fall, I saw a boy going down heavily beside
me as though we were felled by a single blow, saw a sneaker-
clad foot shoot into his groin as the two who had knocked
him down stumbled upon him. I rolled out of range, feeling a
twinge of nausea.

The harder we fought the more threatening the men became.
And yet, I had begun to worry about my speech again. How
would it go? Would they recognize my ability? What would
they give me?

I was fighting automatically when suddenly I noticed that
one after another of the boys was leaving the ring. I was surprised, filled with panic, as though I had been left alone with
an unknown danger. Then I understood. The boys had arranged it among themselves. It was the custom for the two
men left in the ring to slug it out for the winner's prize. I

discovered this too late. When the bell sounded two men in tuxedoes leaped into the ring and removed the blindfold. I found myself facing Tatlock, the biggest of the gang. I felt sick at my stomach. Hardly had the bell stopped ringing in my ears than it clanged again and I saw him moving swiftly toward me. Thinking of nothing else to do I hit him smash on the nose. He kept coming, bringing the rank sharp violence of stale sweat. His face was a black blank of a face, only his eyes alive—with hate of me and aglow with a feverish terror from what had happened to us all. I became anxious. I wanted to deliver my speech and he came at me as though he meant to beat it out of me. I smashed him again and again, taking his blows as they came. Then on a sudden impulse I struck him lightly and as we clinched, I whispered, "Fake like I knocked you out, you can have the prize."

"I'll break your behind," he whispered hoarsely.

"For *them?*"

"For *me,* sonofabitch!"

They were yelling for us to break it up and Tatlock spun me half around with a blow, and as a joggled camera sweeps in a reeling scene, I saw the howling red faces crouching tense beneath the cloud of blue-gray smoke. For a moment the world wavered, unraveled, flowed, then my head cleared and Tatlock bounced before me. That fluttering shadow before my eyes was his jabbing left hand. Then falling forward, my head against his damp shoulder, I whispered,

"I'll make it five dollars more."

"Go to hell!"

But his muscles relaxed a trifle beneath my pressure and I breathed, "Seven?"

"Give it to your ma," he said, ripping me beneath the heart.

And while I still held him I butted him and moved away. I felt myself bombarded with punches. I fought back with hopeless desperation. I wanted to deliver my speech more than anything else in the world, because I felt that only these men could judge truly my ability, and now this stupid clown was ruining my chances. I began fighting carefully now, moving in to punch him and out again with my greater speed. A lucky blow to his chin and I had him going too—until I heard a loud voice yell, "I got my money on the big boy."

Hearing this, I almost dropped my guard. I was confused: Should I try to win against the voice out there? Would not this go against my speech, and was not this a moment for humility, for nonresistance? A blow to my head as I danced about sent my right eye popping like a jack-in-the-box and settled my dilemma. The room went red as I fell. It was a dream fall, my body languid and fastidious as to where to land, until the floor became impatient and smashed up to meet me. A moment later I came to. An hypnotic voice said FIVE emphatically. And I lay there, hazily watching a dark red spot of my own blood shaping itself into a butterfly, glistening and soaking into the soiled gray world of the canvas.

When the voice drawled TEN I was lifted up and dragged to a chair. I sat dazed. My eye pained and swelled with each throb of my pounding heart and I wondered if now I would be allowed to speak. I was wringing wet, my mouth still bleeding. We were grouped along the wall now. The other boys ignored me as they congratulated Tatlock and speculated as to how much they would be paid. One boy whimpered over his smashed hand. Looking up front, I saw attendants in white jackets rolling the portable ring away and placing a small square rug in the vacant space surrounded by chairs. Perhaps, I thought, I will stand on the rug to deliver my speech.

Then the M.C. called to us, "Come on up here boys and get your money."

We ran forward to where the men laughed and talked in their chairs, waiting. Everyone seemed friendly now.

"There it is on the rug," the man said. I saw the rug covered with coins of all dimensions and a few crumpled bills. But what excited me, scattered here and there, were the gold pieces.

"Boys, it's all yours," the man said. "You get all you grab."

"That's right, Sambo," a blond man said, winking at me confidentially.

I trembled with excitement, forgetting my pain. I would get the gold and the bills, I thought. I would use both hands. I would throw my body against the boys nearest me to block them from the gold.

"Get down around the rug now," the man commanded, "and don't anyone touch it until I give the signal."

"This ought to be good," I heard.

As told, we got around the square rug on our knees. Slowly the man raised his freckled hand as we followed it upward with our eyes.

I heard, "These niggers look like they're about to pray!"

Then, "Ready," the man said. "Go!"

I lunged for a yellow coin lying on the blue design of the carpet, touching it and sending a surprised shriek to join those rising around me. I tried frantically to remove my hand but could not let go. A hot, violent force tore through my body, shaking me like a wet rat. The rug was electrified. The hair bristled up on my head as I shook myself free. My muscles jumped, my nerves jangled, writhed. But I saw that this was not stopping the other boys. Laughing in fear and embarrassment, some were holding back and scooping up the coins knocked off by the painful contortions of the others. The men roared above us as we struggled.

"Pick it up, goddamnit, pick it up!" someone called like a bass-voiced parrot. "Go on, get it!"

I crawled rapidly around the floor, picking up the coins, trying to avoid the coppers and to get greenbacks and the gold. Ignoring the shock by laughing, as I brushed the coins off quickly, I discovered that I could contain the electricity—a contradiction, but it works. Then the men began to push us onto the rug. Laughing embarrassedly, we struggled out of their hands and kept after the coins. We were all wet and slippery and hard to hold. Suddenly I saw a boy lifted into the air, glistening with a sweat like a circus seal, and dropped, his wet back landing flush upon the charged rug, heard him yell and saw him literally dance upon his back, his elbows beating a frenzied tattoo upon the floor, his muscles twitching like the flesh of a horse stung by many flies. When he finally rolled off, his face was gray and no one stopped him when he ran from the floor amid booming laughter.

"Get the money," the M.C. called. "That's good hard American cash!"

And we snatched and grabbed, snatched and grabbed. I was careful not to come too close to the rug now, and when I felt the hot whiskey breath descend upon me like a cloud of foul air I reached out and grabbed the leg of a chair. It was occupied and I held on desperately.

"Leggo, nigger! Leggo!"

The huge face wavered down to mine as he tried to push me free. But my body was slippery and he was too drunk. It was Mr. Colcord, who owned a chain of movie houses and "entertainment palaces." Each time he grabbed me I slipped out of his hands. It became a real struggle. I feared the rug more than I did the drunk, so I held on, surprising myself for a moment by trying to topple *him* upon the rug. It was such an enormous idea that I found myself actually carrying it out. I tried not to be obvious, yet when I grabbed his leg, trying to tumble him out of the chair, he raised up roaring with laughter, and, looking at me with soberness dead in the eye, kicked me viciously in the chest. The chair leg flew out of my hand and I felt myself going and rolled. It was as though I had rolled through a bed of hot coals. It seemed a whole century would pass before I would roll free, a century in which I was seared through the deepest levels of my body to the fearful breath within me and the breath seared and heated to the point of explosion. It'll all be over in a flash, I thought as I rolled clear. It'll all be over in a flash.

But not yet, the men on the other side were waiting, red faces swollen as though from apoplexy as they bent forward in their chairs. Seeing their fingers coming toward me I rolled away as a fumbled football rolls off the receiver's fingertips, back into the coals. That time I luckily sent the rug sliding out of place and heard the coins ringing against the floor and the boys scuffling to pick them up and the M.C. calling, "All right, boys, that's all. Go get dressed and get your money."

I was limp as a dish rag. My back felt as though it had been beaten with wires.

When we had dressed the M.C. came in and gave us each five dollars, except Tatlock, who got ten for being last in the ring. Then he told us to leave. I was not to get a chance to deliver my speech, I thought. I was going out into the dim alley in despair when I was stopped and told to go back. I returned to the ballroom, where the men were pushing back their chairs and gathering in groups to talk.

The M.C. knocked on a table for quiet. "Gentlemen," he said, "we almost forgot an important part of the program. A most serious part, gentlemen. This boy was brought here to deliver a speech which he made at his graduation yesterday . . ."

"Bravo!"

"I'm told that he is the smartest boy we've got out there in Greenwood. I'm told that he knows more big words than a pocket-sized dictionary."

Much applause and laughter.

"So now, gentlemen, I want you to give him your attention."

There was still laughter as I faced them, my mouth dry, my eye throbbing. I began slowly, but evidently my throat was tense, because they began shouting, "Louder! Louder!"

"We of the younger generation extol the wisdom of that

great leader and educator," I shouted, "who first spoke these flaming words of wisdom: 'A ship lost at sea for many days suddenly sighted a friendly vessel. From the mast of the unfortunate vessel was seen a signal: "Water, water; we die of thirst!" The answer from the friendly vessel came back: "Cast down your bucket where you are." The captain of the distressed vessel, at last heeding the injunction, cast down his bucket, and it came up full of fresh sparkling water from the mouth of the Amazon River.' And like him I say, and in his words, 'To those of my race who depend upon bettering their condition in a foreign land, or who underestimate the importance of cultivating friendly relations with the Southern white man, who is his next-door neighbor, I would say: "Cast down your bucket where you are"—cast it down in making friends in every manly way of the people of all races by whom we are surrounded . . .' "

I spoke automatically and with such fervor that I did not realize that the men were still talking and laughing until my dry mouth, filling up with blood from the cut, almost strangled me. I coughed, wanting to stop and go to one of the tall brass, sand-filled spittoons to relieve myself, but a few of the men, especially the superintendent, were listening and I was afraid. So I gulped it down, blood, saliva and all, and continued. (What powers of endurance I had during those days! What enthusiasm! What a belief in the rightness of things!) I spoke even louder in spite of the pain. But still they talked and still they laughed, as though deaf with cotton in dirty ears. So I spoke with greater emotional emphasis. I closed my ears and swallowed blood until I was nauseated. The speech seemed a hundred times as long as before, but I could not leave out a single word. All had to be said, each memorized nuance considered, rendered. Nor was that all. Whenever I uttered a word of three or more syllables a group of voices would yell for me to repeat it. I used the phrase "social responsibility" and they yelled:

"What's that word you say, boy?"

"Social responsibility," I said.

"What?"

"Social . . ."

"Louder."

". . . responsibility."

"More!"

"Respon____"

"Repeat!"

"____sibility."

The room filled with the uproar of laughter until, no doubt, distracted by having to gulp down my blood, I made a mistake and yelled a phrase I had often seen denounced in newspaper editorials, heard debated in private.

"Social . . ."

"What?" they yelled.

". . . equality—"

The laughter hung smokelike in the sudden stillness. I opened my eyes, puzzled. Sounds of displeasure filled the room. The M.C. rushed forward. They shouted hostile phrases at me. But I did not understand.

A small dry mustached man in the front row blared out, "Say that slowly, son!"

"What, sir?"

"What you just said!"

"Social responsibility, sir," I said.

"You weren't being smart, were you, boy?" he said, not unkindly.

"No, sir!"

"You sure that about 'equality' was a mistake?"

"Oh, yes, sir," I said. "I was swallowing blood."

"Well, you had better speak more slowly so we can understand. We mean to do right by you, but you've got to know your place at all times. All right, now, go on with your speech."

I was afraid. I wanted to leave but I wanted also to speak and I was afraid they'd snatch me down.

"Thank you, sir," I said, beginning where I had left off, and having them ignore me as before.

Yet when I finished there was a thunderous applause. I was surprised to see the superintendent come forth with a package wrapped in white tissue paper, and, gesturing for quiet, address the men.

"Gentlemen, you see that I did not overpraise this boy. He makes a good speech and some day he'll lead his people in the proper paths. And I don't have to tell you that that is important in these days and times. This is a good, smart boy, and so to encourage him in the right direction, in the name of the Board of Education I wish to present him a prize in the form of this . . ."

He paused, removing the tissue paper and revealing a gleaming calfskin brief case.

". . . in the form of this fist-class article from Shad Whitmore's shop."

"Boy," he said, addressing me, "take this prize and keep it well. Consider it a badge of office. Prize it. Keep developing as you are and some day it will be filled with important papers that will help shape the destiny of your people."

I was so moved that I could hardly express my thanks. A rope of bloody saliva forming a shape like an undiscovered continent drooled upon the leather and I wiped it quickly away. I felt an importance that I had never dreamed.

"Open it and see what's inside," I was told.

My fingers a-tremble, I complied, smelling the fresh leather and finding an official-looking document inside. It was a scholarship to the state college for Negroes. My eyes filled with tears and I ran awkwardly off the floor.

I was overjoyed; I did not even mind when I discovered that the gold pieces I had scrambled for were brass pocket tokens advertising a certain make of automobile.

When I reached home everyone was excited. Next day the neighbors came to congratulate me. I even felt safe from grandfather, whose deathbed curse usually spoiled my triumphs. I stood beneath his photograph with my brief case in hand and smiled triumphantly into his stolid black peasant's face. It was a face that fascinated me. The eyes seemed to follow everywhere I went.

That night I dreamed I was at a circus with him and that he refused to laugh at the clowns no matter what they did. Then later he told me to open my brief case and read what was inside and I did, finding an official envelope stamped with the state seal; and inside the envelope I found another and another, endlessly, and I thought I would fall of weariness. "Them's years," he said. "Now open that one." And I did and in it I found an engraved document containing a short message in letters of gold. "Read it," my grandfather said. "Out loud!"

"To Whom It May Concern," I intoned. "Keep This Nigger-Boy Running."

I awoke with the old man's laughter ringing in my ears.

Max Moran

Describing himself as an "intelligent young Hispanic male who will never commit a crime," high school senior Max Moran writes about the realities of urban poverty and his temporary escape from them by riding the New York subway all night long. There he dreams of "travel to a . . . place where life is worth living."

No Way Out

Here I am chilling on the last car of a Brooklyn-bound train. Don't ask me how, but I always end up all the way back here. I'm dressed as if I'm ready for war. This is what I do when I want to get away from reality. I ride the trains all night long.

Now I close my eyes and travel to a good place, a place where life is worth living. No crime, no rapes, no sound of gunshots, and no discrimination. A place so far away from here that it is hard to imagine.

People I know be saying there's no way out from the streets, but I will find a way. I'm not ashamed of where I'm from, but I'm tired of this ghetto world. Even where I live in Staten Island there are so many clowns acting wild.

A couple of years ago a kid was shot and killed on my block. Why? Because he was staring at the murderer. Staring is a fool's game, yet sometimes I can be the biggest fool when I'm stressed out, which is basically every day.

My new roommate has a gun in our room and yesterday we got into a big argument. Then he gave me that speech: "You better chill, you don't know where I'm from." I laughed at him and told him that real men don't need guns.

When I lived in the Bronx, I grew up with kids who always carried guns. One of my friends is dead and the other is doing time for a stick-up. I don't want to end up like that. I know better.

This is my senior year in high school and I'm feeling the pressure. I got two choices: a dead-end job or college. I can't picture myself in school in the future, but I don't want to keep on making $5 an hour from nine to five and feeling like a slave.

I'm worth more than $5 and I'm too proud to beg for quarters. I'm an intelligent young Hispanic male who will never commit a crime because my mind is too precious to be trapped in a dark cell.

I got so many things on my mind that I can't even get in the Christmas spirit. I really don't have to, because I celebrate Christmas every day by showing love to those who care and respect me. My love is worth much more than some stupid presents.

Wow! There's a cutie sitting across from me, let me smile at her. Oh! She smiled back. Should I talk to her? No, let's just continue with my journey.

At times like this I wish I wasn't so shy, but the past has taught me how easy it is to fall in love with a pretty face. Then again, she could look much prettier if she wasn't dressed like me.

Today's world got me bugging, I don't understand why we guys call girls b-tches. When I become a father, I surely won't want anybody calling my little girl a b-tch. Even when a girl disses me, I refuse to call her that.

Just last week this girl played me out lovely. We knew each other for three months and it was all good. Then things started to get serious and she wanted to know more about me.

She told me that she liked me, but her parents wouldn't approve of me because I live in a group home. I told her my living situation doesn't matter if she likes me, forget her parents. I mean, I was interested in her, not her parents.

But I realized I was in a no-win situation. I simply smiled at her and wished her a good life. It's her loss because I got mad love to give.

Well, by the next stop I'll be in Coney Island. I'm going to sit under the boardwalk and listen to the ocean, feeling the cold air that sends chills up my spine.

I'm thinking about a couple of friends who are getting caught up in the drug game. Sometimes it brings tears to my eyes.

It is so quiet here, no phone ringing, no beepers beeping, nobody screaming out my name. People be saying that I be acting like I'm all that, just because I don't say much and keep things to myself. Just because I'm shy, that doesn't mean I like being alone. I always have been misunderstood.

I'm going to sit here for a while and hopefully I will not fall asleep like I did the last time. This time I will try to reach a star and also look at the moon, imagining that bright powder falling off. I guess I'm going crazy and things I be thinking about make me scared. At times like this I could do anything for a kiss or a hug, yet I only like giving a pound to those whose hearts are in their hands.

Great! This girl beeped me again. If I didn't call her the first time, what makes her think I will do it now? Back in the days I used to have a beeper for all the wrong reasons.

I'm simply tired of this world, where a typical criminal description fits me almost perfectly. Christmas and birthdays have missed me for the last eight years, no family to talk about, so don't ask me why I'm depressed all the time. As I sit here, I can put everything in perspective.

Today I will watch the sunrise. But I never want the sun to set on me. I'm too young, I need the warmth of the sun. Only eighteen but I'm running out of time. I will leave the streets behind me. Come and follow me if you want, but if you don't, I won't think any less of you. In this life only the strong survive and I've survived long enough. I will find a way out, some day.

PART TWO

They, Those People Over There

Dorothy Allison

Dorothy Allison is known for her best-selling first novel, *Bastard Out of Carolina,* published in 1992. Drawn from Allison's childhood in South Carolina, it chronicles her impoverished rural childhood and repeated sexual abuse at the hands of her stepfather. In the years since her book's publication, Allison has become one of the country's best-known openly lesbian authors, whose sexuality figures prominently in her fiction and nonfiction.

The following excerpt is taken from a collection titled *Skin: Talking About Sex, Class and Literature.* In it, Allison lays out what it means "to be queer in a world that hates queers" and "poor in a world that despises the poor."

A Question of Class

The first time I heard, "They're different than us, don't value human life the way we do," I was in high school in Central Florida. The man speaking was an army recruiter talking to a bunch of boys, telling them what the army was really like, what they could expect overseas. A cold angry feeling swept over me. I had heard the word *they* pronounced in that same callous tone before. *They,* those people over there, those people who are not us, they die so easily, kill each other so casually. They are different. *We,* I thought. *Me.*

When I was six or eight back in Greenville, South Carolina, I had heard that same matter-of-fact tone of dismissal applied to me. "Don't you play with her. I don't want you talking to them." Me and my family, we had always been *they.* Who am I? I wondered, listening to that recruiter. Who are my people? We die so easily, disappear so completely—we/they, the poor and the queer. I pressed my bony white trash fists to my stubborn lesbian mouth. The rage was a good feeling, stronger and purer than the shame that followed it, the fear and the sudden urge to run and hide, to deny, to pretend I did not know who I was and what the world would do to me.

My people were not remarkable. We were ordinary, but even so we were mythical. We were the *they* everyone talks about—the ungrateful poor. I grew up trying to run away from the fate that destroyed so many of the people I loved, and having learned the habit of hiding, I found I had also learned to hide from myself. I did not know who I was, only that I did not want to be *they,* the ones who are destroyed or dismissed to make the "real" people, the important people, feel safer. By the time I understood that I was queer, that habit of hiding was deeply set in me, so deeply that it was not a choice but an instinct. Hide, hide to survive, I thought, knowing that if I told the truth about my life, my family, my sexual desire, my history, I would move over into that unknown territory, the land of they, would never have the chance to name my own life, to understand it or claim it.

Why are you so afraid? my lovers and friends have asked me the many times I have suddenly seemed a stranger, someone who would not speak to them, would not do the things they believed I should do, simple things like applying for a job, or a grant, or some award they were sure I could acquire easily. Entitlement, I have told them, is a matter of feeling like we rather than they. You think you have a right to things, a place in the world, and it is so intrinsically a part of you that you cannot imagine people like me, people who seem to live in your world, who don't have it. I have explained what I know over and over, in every way I can, but I have never been able to make clear the degree of my fear, the extent to which I feel myself denied: not only that I am queer in a world that hates queers, but that I was born poor into a world that despises the poor. The need to make my world believable to people who have never experienced it is part of why I write fiction. I know that some things must be felt to be understood, that despair, for example, can never be adequately analyzed; it must be lived. But if I can write a story that so draws the reader in that she imagines herself like my characters, feels their sense of fear and uncertainty, their hopes and terrors, then I have come closer to knowing myself as real, important as the very people I have always watched with awe.

—

I have known I was a lesbian since I was a teenager, and I have spent a good twenty years making peace with the effects of incest and physical abuse. But what may be the central fact of my life is that I was born in 1949 in Greenville, South Carolina, the bastard daughter of a white woman from a desperately poor family, a girl who had left the seventh grade the year before, worked as a waitress, and was just a month past fifteen when she had me. That fact, the inescapable impact of being born in a condition of poverty that this society finds shameful, contemptible, and somehow deserved, has had dominion over me to such an extent that I have spent my life trying to overcome or deny it. I have learned with great difficulty that the vast majority of people believe that poverty is a voluntary condition. . . .

My family's lives were not on television, not in books, not even comic books. There was a myth of the poor in this country, but it did not include us, no matter how hard I tried to squeeze us in. There was an idea of the good poor—hardworking, ragged but clean, and intrinsically honorable. I understood that we were the bad poor: men who drank and couldn't keep a job; women, invariably pregnant before marriage, who quickly became worn, fat, and old from working too many hours and bearing too many children; and children with runny noses, watery eyes, and the wrong attitudes. My cousins quit school, stole cars, used drugs, and took dead-end jobs pumping gas or waiting tables. We were not noble, not grateful, not even hopeful. We knew ourselves despised. My family was ashamed of being poor, of feeling hopeless. What was there to work for, to save money for, to fight for or struggle against? We had generations before us to teach us that nothing ever changed, and that those who did try to escape failed.

—

My mama had eleven brothers and sisters, of whom I can name only six. No one is left alive to tell me the names of the others. It was my grandmother who told me about my real daddy, a shiftless pretty man who was supposed to have married, had six children, and sold cut-rate life insurance to poor

Black people. My mama married when I was a year old, but her husband died just after my little sister was born a year later.

When I was five, Mama married the man she lived with until she died. Within the first year of their marriage Mama miscarried, and while we waited out in the hospital parking lot, my stepfather molested me for the first time, something he continued to do until I was past thirteen. When I was eight or so, Mama took us away to a motel after my stepfather beat me so badly it caused a family scandal, but we returned after two weeks. Mama told me that she really had no choice: she could not support us alone. When I was eleven I told one of my cousins that my stepfather was molesting me. Mama packed up my sisters and me and took us away for a few days, but again, my stepfather swore he would stop, and again we went back after a few weeks. I stopped talking for a while, and I have only vague memories of the next two years.

My stepfather worked as a route salesman, my mama as a waitress, laundry worker, cook, or fruit packer. I could never understand, since they both worked so hard and such long hours, how we never had enough money, but it was also true of my mama's brothers and sisters who worked hard in the mills or the furnace industry. In fact, my parents did better than anyone else in the family. But eventually my stepfather was fired and we hit bottom—nightmarish months of marshals at the door, repossessed furniture, and rubber checks. My parents worked out a scheme so that it appeared my stepfather had abandoned us, but instead he went down to Florida, got a new job, and rented us a house. He returned with a U-Haul trailer in the dead of night, packed us up, and moved us south.

The night we left South Carolina for Florida, my mama leaned over the backseat of her old Pontiac and promised us girls, "It'll be better there." I don't know if we believed her, but I remember crossing Georgia in the early morning, watching the red clay hills and swaying grey blankets of moss recede through the back window. I kept looking at the trailer behind us, ridiculously small to contain everything we owned. Mama had packed nothing that wasn't fully paid off, which meant she had only two things of worth: her washing and sewing machines, both of them tied securely to the trailer walls. Throughout the trip I fantasized an accident that would burst that trailer, scattering old clothes and cracked dishes on the tarmac.

I was only thirteen. I wanted us to start over completely, to begin again as new people with nothing of the past left over. I wanted to run away from who we had been seen to be, who we had been. That desire is one I have seen in other members of my family. It is the first thing I think of when trouble comes—the geographic solution. Change your name, leave town, disappear, make yourself over. What hides behind that impulse is the conviction that the life you have lived, the person you are, is valueless, better off abandoned, that running away is easier than trying to change things, that change itself is not possible. Sometimes I think it is this conviction—more seductive than alcohol or violence, more subtle than sexual hatred or gender injustice—that has dominated my life and made real change so painful and difficult.

Moving to Central Florida did not fix our lives. It did not stop my stepfather's violence, heal my shame, or make my mother happy. Once there, our lives became controlled by my mother's illness and medical bills. She had a hysterectomy when I was about eight and endured a series of hospitalizations for ulcers and a chronic back problem. Through most of my adolescence she superstitiously refused to allow anyone to mention the word *cancer*. When she was not sick, Mama and my stepfather went on working, struggling to pay off what seemed an insurmountable load of debts.

By the time I was fourteen, my sisters and I had found ways to discourage most of our stepfather's sexual advances. We were not close, but we united against him. Our efforts were helped along when he was referred to a psychotherapist after he lost his temper at work, and was prescribed drugs that made him sullen but less violent. We were growing up quickly, my sisters moving toward dropping out of school while I got good grades and took every scholarship exam I could find. I was the first person in my family to graduate from high school, and the fact that I went on to college was nothing short of astonishing.

We all imagine our lives are normal, and I did not know my life was not everyone's. It was in Central Florida that I began to realize just how different we were. The people we met there had not been shaped by the rigid class structure that dominated the South Carolina Piedmont. The first time I looked around my junior high classroom and realized I did not know who those people were—not only as individuals but as categories, who their people were and how they saw themselves—I also realized that they did not know me. In Greenville, everyone knew my family, knew we were trash, and that meant we were supposed to be poor, supposed to have grim low-paid jobs, have babies in our teens, and never finish school. But Central Florida in the 1960s was full of runaways and immigrants, and our mostly white working-class suburban school sorted us out not by income and family background but by intelligence and aptitude tests. Suddenly I was boosted into the college-bound track, and while there was plenty of contempt for my inept social skills, pitiful wardrobe, and slow drawling accent, there was also something I had never experienced before: a protective anonymity, and a kind of grudging respect and curiosity about who I might become. Because they did not see poverty and hopelessness as a foregone conclusion for my life, I could begin to imagine other futures for myself.

In that new country, we were unknown. The myth of the poor settled over us and glamorized us. I saw it in the eyes of my teachers, the Lion's Club representative who paid for my new glasses, and the lady from the Junior League who told me about the scholarship I had won. Better, far better, to be one of the mythical poor than to be part of the *they* I had known before. I also experienced a new level of fear, a fear of losing what had never before been imaginable. Don't let me lose this chance, I prayed, and lived in terror that I might suddenly be seen again as what I knew myself to be.

—

As an adolescent I thought that my family's escape from South Carolina played like a bad movie. We fled the way runaway serfs might have done, with the sheriff who would have arrested my stepfather the imagined border guard. I am certain that if we had remained in South Carolina, I would have been trapped by my family's heritage of poverty, jail, and illegitimate children—that even being smart, stubborn, and a lesbian would have made no difference.

My grandmother died when I was twenty, and after Mama went home for the funeral, I had a series of dreams in which we still lived up in Greenville, just down the road from where Granny died. In the dreams I had two children and only one eye, lived in a trailer, and worked at the textile mill. Most of my time was taken up with deciding when I would finally kill my children and myself. The dreams were so vivid, I became convinced they were about the life I was meant to have had, and I began to work even harder to put as much distance as I could between my family and me. I copied the dress, mannerisms, attitudes, and ambitions of the girls I met in college, changing or hiding my own tastes, interests, and desires. I kept my lesbianism a secret, forming a relationship with an effeminate male friend that served to shelter and disguise us both. I explained to friends that I went home so rarely because my stepfather and I fought too much for me to be comfortable in his house. But that was only part of the reason I avoided home, the easiest reason. The truth was that I feared the person I might become in my mama's house, the woman of my dreams—hateful, violent, and hopeless.

It is hard to explain how deliberately and thoroughly I ran away from my own life. I did not forget where I came from, but I gritted my teeth and hid it. When I could not get enough scholarship money to pay for graduate school, I spent a year of rage working as a salad girl, substitute teacher, and maid. I finally managed to find a job by agreeing to take any city assignment where the Social Security Administration needed a clerk. Once I had a job and my own place far away from anyone in my family, I became sexually and politically active, joining the Women's Center support staff and falling in love with a series of middle-class women who thought my accent and stories thoroughly charming. The stories I told about my family, about South Carolina, about being poor itself, were all lies, carefully edited to seem droll or funny. I knew damn well that no one would want to hear the truth about poverty, the hopelessness and fear, the feeling that nothing I did would ever make any difference and the raging resentment that burned beneath my jokes. Even when my lovers and I formed an alternative lesbian family, sharing what we could of our resources, I kept the truth about my background and who I knew myself to be a carefully obscured mystery. I worked as hard as I could to make myself a new person, an emotionally healthy radical lesbian activist, and I believed completely that by remaking myself I was helping to remake the world. . . .

My aunt Dot used to joke, "There are two or three things I know for sure, but never the same things and I'm never as sure as I'd like." What I know for sure is that class, gender, sexual preference, and prejudice—racial, ethnic, and religious— form an intricate lattice that restricts and shapes our lives, and that resistance to hatred is not a simple act. Claiming your identity in the cauldron of hatred and resistance to hatred is infinitely complicated, and worse, almost unexplainable. . . .

One of my favorite cousins went to jail when I was eight

years old, for breaking into pay phones with another boy. The other boy was returned to the custody of his parents. My cousin was sent to the boys' facility at the county farm. After three months, my mama took us down there to visit, carrying a big basket of fried chicken, cold cornbread, and potato salad. Along with a hundred others we sat out on the lawn with my cousin and watched him eat like he hadn't had a full meal in the whole three months. I stared at his near-bald head and his ears marked with fine blue scars from the carelessly handled razor. People were laughing, music was playing, and a tall, lazy, uniformed man walked past us chewing on toothpicks and watching us all closely. My cousin kept his head down, his face hard with hatred, only looking back at the guard when he turned away.

"Sons-a-bitches," he whispered, and my mama shushed him. We all sat still when the guard turned back to us. There was a long moment of quiet, and then that man let his face relax into a big wide grin.

"Uh-huh," he said. That was all he said. Then he turned and walked away. None of us spoke. None of us ate. He went back inside soon after, and we left. When we got back to the car, my mama sat there for a while crying quietly. The next week my cousin was reported for fighting and had his stay extended by six months.

My cousin was fifteen. He never went back to school, and after jail he couldn't join the army. When he finally did come home we never talked, never had to. I knew without asking that the guard had had his little revenge, knew too that my cousin would break into another phone booth as soon as he could, but do it sober and not get caught. I knew without asking the source of his rage, the way he felt about clean, well-dressed, contemptuous people who looked at him like his life wasn't as important as a dog's. I knew because I felt it too. That guard had looked at me and Mama with the same expression he used on my cousin. We were trash. We were the ones they built the county farm to house and break. The boy who was sent home was the son of a deacon in the church, the man who managed the hardware store.

As much as I hated that man, and his boy, there was a way in which I also hated my cousin. He should have known better, I told myself, should have known the risk he ran. He should have been more careful. As I grew older and started living on my own, it was a litany I used against myself even more angrily than I used it against my cousin. I knew who I was, knew that the most important thing I had to do was protect myself and hide my despised identity, blend into the myth of both the good poor and the reasonable lesbian. When I became a feminist activist, that litany went on reverberating in my head, but by then it had become a groundnote, something so deep and omnipresent I no longer heard it, even when everything I did was set to its cadence. . . .

For me, the bottom line has simply become the need to resist that omnipresent fear, that urge to hide and disappear, to disguise my life, my desires, and the truth about how little any of us understand—even as we try to make the world a more just and human place. Most of all, I have tried to understand the politics of *they,* why human beings fear and stigmatize the different while secretly dreading that they might be one of the different themselves. Class, race, sexuality, gender—and all the other categories by which we categorize and dismiss each other—need to be excavated from the inside.

—

The horror of class stratification, racism, and prejudice is that some people begin to believe that the security of their families and communities depends on the oppression of others, that for some to have good lives there must be others whose lives are truncated and brutal. It is a belief that dominates this culture. It is what makes the poor whites of the South so determinedly racist and the middle class so contemptuous of the poor. It is a myth that allows some to imagine that they build their lives on the ruin of others, a secret core of shame for the middle class, a goad and a spur to the marginal working class, and cause enough for the homeless and poor to feel no constraints on hatred or violence. The power of the myth is made even more apparent when we examine how, within the lesbian and feminist communities where we have addressed considerable attention to the politics of marginalization, there is still so much exclusion and fear, so many of us who do not feel safe.

I grew up poor, hated, the victim of physical, emotional, and sexual violence, and I know that suffering does not ennoble. It destroys. To resist destruction, self-hatred, or lifelong hopelessness, we have to throw off the conditioning of being despised, the fear of becoming the *they* that is talked about so dismissively, to refuse lying myths and easy moralities, to see ourselves as human, flawed, and extraordinary. All of us—extraordinary.

Danielle Joseph

One of the fixtures of poverty is the breakup of families and placement of children in foster care. Meant to offer children relief from their previous circumstances, foster homes, as beginning New York City writer Danielle Joseph describes with smoldering outrage, can be a hell all their own.

Joseph offers a firsthand account of her experience of foster care, and makes an eloquent plea for reform on behalf of those who are "innocent, defenseless . . . and unable to take care of themselves."

The essay comes from New York City's Youth Communication Writing Program, a program dedicated to encouraging urban "teens writing for teens."

Who Will Speak for Lizzy?

"Close your stupid eyes and go to sleep, now!" My foster mother's voice echoed through the house as she shouted at four-year-old Lizzy, who at 7:00 P.M. was simply lying on her bed and staring at the top bunk, where I would later go to sleep.

With a gloomy expression on her face, poor Lizzy seemed distant, and every time she breathed she seemed like she was gasping for her last breath on earth. Perhaps she was wondering why she had been abruptly placed in a strange new environment, or maybe she was just missing her family (if she had one).

Little Lizzy shook and immediately snapped out of her world of bewilderment. She turned on her side and quickly closed her eyes in fear. You see, little Lizzy had a real bad case of the flu and Bernice, instead of taking Lizzy to the doctor (which would have cost her only two tokens), decided instead to put Lizzy in her own version of quarantine. (Bernice had the time to take Lizzy to the doctor. She did nothing all day.)

"Whatever you do, Lizzy, just keep your butt away from my baby!" Bernice shouted.

How dare Bernice talk to a four-year-old like that? Didn't she see what she was doing to poor Lizzy? (You may say, hey, people get upset sometimes and they say things that they don't mean. I agree, but this was an everyday occurrence.) I don't think it was necessary for Bernice to use words such as "hell" and "stupid" when addressing a four-year-old. It was like she was talking to a little nobody, someone unimportant, nonexistent almost.

I still remember that evening five months ago when I first

visits always gave Ms. Jones the opportunity to make her home appear spotless.

Is it too much trouble for agencies to at least make sure that foster parents have food in the home? Most of the foster homes I've known have had little food available to the children.

The agencies should also ask potential foster parents why they "honestly" want to become foster parents. (And they shouldn't accept the usual "because I love kids" crap. That is totally unacceptable. Any idiot or child-hater could say that and not mean a word of it.)

What should they say? How about, "I enjoy the company of children, I know they are our future, and I want to give those kids who feel unloved and uncared for a home to call their own. All hope is not lost, and I want to help them achieve success."

Educational achievement should be a key factor in selecting foster parents. Very few, if any, of my foster parents had gone to college. Three out of four did not even graduate high school. So it is not difficult to understand why they look to the foster care system to help them make ends meet, to collect a few extra dollars.

———

People in authority, particularly social workers, may not believe this, but we foster children are the ones who are too often deprived of food, proper clothing (coats in the winter), and proper heat.

I have one last thing to say to foster parents: "All of you who do not have a job, get one!" (Especially you, Ms. Jones.) Stop being parasites and preying on innocent, defenseless children who are unable to take care of themselves.

I refuse to believe that in the United States, one of the most developed countries in the world, children are being treated like criminals, being made to pay for what their parents did.

Society has to start taking responsibility for its children because we are the products of the society. If the abuse of children doesn't stop immediately, society will pay. And pay dearly.

I can identify with poor little Lizzy because had I been younger and unable to speak up about my living conditions, I would almost definitely be in her shoes.

I told my social worker about Lizzy's condition, but he coldly stated that it was not his case. I can speak up for myself, but the little ones, who will speak for them?

Poor neglected, unloved little Lizzy, what are you going to grow up to be? I do not know if you still live in that hellhole, but if you do, I hope you beat the odds and someday find the love, happiness, understanding, and food that you both need and deserve.

Deborah Stern, editor

Deborah Stern is a high school teacher, school reform activist in Chicago, and author of *Teaching English So It Matters*.

The intention of the inner-city students who designed this test is to prove to you through frank humor "that many tests are altogether biased," particularly against the poor and those of color.

From *City Kids, City Teachers:*
Reports from the Front Row

The Love Test
(LIFTING OUR VIBRATIONS HIGHER FOR EQUALITY)

Many tests are altogether biased—especially intelligence tests. Intelligence tests are often biased because they are based on certain information which is part of a certain specific culture. When people of other cultures take these tests, they might fail them, because they haven't been exposed to the same information. Then, these people are considered to be unintelligent.

We think this bias is unfair. To prove our point, we have created a test which you will pass only if you're from *our* culture.

Introduction by Nubia Manning. Test considered and created by Andre Adams, Erika Akins, Darrell Allen, Courtney Alston, Ronald Banks, Katrina Banner, Elliott Baskerville, Marie Battle, Aziel Bell, Cherita Broughton, Stephanie Brown, Mary Buckley, Rachel Byrd, Cozetta Castleberry, Lavanda Coats, James Coleman, Sagan Cowan, Jamie Davis, Adrian Densmore, Latossha Farrior, Joe Gaither, Ida Garner, Patricia Gibson, Darryl Glinsey, Ronnisa Griffin, Kenyatta Hardy, Raymond Jackson, Cecil James, Carl Jones, Phillip Jones, Lamont Kent, Twana Lewis, Zipporah Lewis, Shannon Lomax, Nubia Manning, Tyronza McCline, Donyale McCray, Eddie McGee, Laquita McGoogin, Lashandra McKenzie, Charles Mean, Larry Morris, Tykeith Nelson, Contrell Palmer, Claudia Ratliff, Rhonda Reed, Octavious Roberson, Arnika Scott, Rashawn Sigle, Lewis Strong, Latasha Thomas, Wallace Todd, Negal Trotter, Christopher Tucker, Monica Tucker, Brandi

Wallace, Tiffany Warr, Hosea West, Mario Wigfall, Linda Wilkins, Craig Williams, Dorothy Williams, Monique Wilson, Calvin Young, and Izelda. Students from DuSable High School, Chicago, Illinois.

1. "Tripping" means a) falling down b) talking nonsense c) taking a trip d) getting high

2. "Ends" is a) pants legs b) money c) shoes d) an overdose

3. "Chillin' " means a) killing b) relaxing with friends c) getting frostbite d) being rude to

4. A "crib" is a) a baby's bed b) someone's house c) both a and b) d) none of the above

5. "Fifty ones"/"Five-o's" means a) 51st Street b) old people c) police d) a gang

6. "Homie" means a) go home b) get out of town c) friend d) ugly

7. If you want someone to "show some love," you are asking for a) a hug or handshake b) a kiss c) sex d) a love letter

8. A "hype" is a) a drug addict b) someone who is happy c) a heterogeneous mixture d) a new dance

9. A "player" is a) a DJ b) a gambler c) a drug dealer d) a ladies' man

10. "To bone" is a) to make chicken b) to have sex c) to cheat d) to beat up

11. A "tootsie roll" is a type of a) gang initiation ceremony b) dance c) haircut d) marijuana cigarette

12. If you are "blown," you have been a) discovered committing a crime b) convicted of a crime c) drinking and/or smoking drugs d) none of the above

13. A "187" is a) a malt liquor b) a gun c) a good alibi d) a gang code

14. "Snoop" is a) a beer b) a nosy person c) an informant d) a new dance

15. "Fimp" is a) a junky car b) a fat wimp c) money d) food

16. A "boody call" is a) a marriage proposal b) a singles bar c) an invitation to have sex d) a phone call

17. "G" stands for a) great b) gangster c) gorgeous d) green (as in money)

18. "Dokin" is the same as a) getting busy b) using the bathroom c) fighting d) dancing

19. A "dove sac" is a) a bag used to catch pigeons b) $20 worth of marijuana c) people getting ready to fight d) Mexican beer

20. A "ride" is a) a gang b) a sex partner c) a car d) the person who supports you

21. A "forty" is a) a term meaning "rent money" b) a soft drink c) an old timer d) a beer

22. What is a "Nelson"? a) an action figure b) a prison sentence c) a type of candy d) a gun

23. A "hood rat" is a) a mouse b) a juvenile delinquent c) a promiscuous slut d) an excuse

24. A "blunt" is a) a heavy object used to hurt someone b) a marijuana cigarette c) a person of mixed race d) a fight that ends in a tie

25. If someone is "fresh," they a) look good b) are rude c) are young d) are right out of jail

26. "Wake up" is a) a talk show b) money c) a type of rap d) a drug

27. "Kay low" means a) a house b) "All right" c) "I'm unhappy" d) a hat

28. "Dank" is a) lunch b) breakfast c) a child's game d) marijuana

Answers

1. b 2. b 3. b 4. c 5. c 6. c 7. a 8. a 9. d 10. b
11. b 12. c 13. b 14. a 15. c 16. c 17. b 18. a 19. b
20. c 21. d 22. d 23. c 24. b 25. a 26. b 27. a
28. d

Love Shiloh,
Young Tay B2,
and Anonymous

These three selections are from *The Beat Within*, a weekly newsletter of writing and art by incarcerated youth in northern California detention facilities. In the first essay, a young man describes smoking crack and the high he feels "until the next score."

In the second piece, a young man who's been around low-income housing projects his "whole life" tells of the stigma of growing up so poor that you're eligible for "Section 8" housing assistance.

The third piece is a poem by a young woman who wonders aloud if God hears the prayers of people behind bars.

From *The Beat Within*

THE DAILY ROUTINE OF A DOPE FIEND

I walk to the bathroom with butterflies in my stomach. I get in a stall sit on the toilet I pull out my dollar bill and my foil and the piece I have in my back pocket. I take my lighter and burn both sides of the foil then take toilet paper and put the foil against the wall and wipe the ash off. Then I take my flat crisp foil and put it on the toilet paper dispenser. Next I take a piece of dark sticky chiva and break a piece off with my pocket knife I have hidden in my sock. It is too hard to stick on the foil, so I breathe hot air on it to melt it down, then I take the piece in my left hand and put the sweet smelling chiva on the foil that's in my right hand and pick up my already rolled up tutor (dollar bill) and put it in my mouth waiting to let my feelings become numb, then I get my lighter out and put it under the foil closing my eyes as the flame melts the chiva white. I taste the sweet brown sugar and vinegar go in my lungs, I hold it in as long as I can. I lean back against the toilet seat and let all my problems fade away as I blow the smoke out. Then I repeat the same act over and over until every last drip and crush is gone. I take my dollar put it in my pocket then flush the foil down the toilet. I slowly stand up feeling a light sensation run through my body. I walk out of the stall look in the mirror run my fingers through my hair then walk back out into my own sense of peace my own reality acting as if everything is normal, wondering when I can come up on my next score.

—Love Shiloh

PUBLIC HOUSIN' IS STRAIGHT HATIN' ON US MINORITIES

They trying to put us out on the streets. And the Section 8 population ain't right. See, I'm young but I'm up on G-A-M-E, 'cause every set of projects they tear down, all they gonna do is put a few Section 8 people back in, that's 10% of the people, and about 40% middle class people with money and the other 50% will be people with good jobs living wealthy who don't have to beg for anything. This type of stuff be kinda hectic 'cause you have to look at it like this, if they move all the Blacks out of the projects, and only put 10% back in where are the rest gonna go?

See, they play people these days if you don't have a lot of money or a good job then I guess you out on the streets slangin' crack cocaine or you're either smoking crack, weed, or snorting hop, 'cause if you don't have no place to go you're always on the streets and the police get to know you and they're always bothering you 'cause they see your face a lot then you end up in jail. That's a problem for your family because your family's poor. So, they can't help you too much with the predicament you put yourself in. All they can do is pray for you and help you when you come home. See now a days when you're out on the block slangin' rocks it's mandatory you have a strap. But then you got to look at it this way, if you get caught with a Glock, they giving 10 years off the top, but Glocks carry 17 bullets and now the sentence is 10 years off the top, plus (you get years for) the number of bullets loaded in the gun.

Back to the projects, but then again this is life in the projects 'cause I look at it like this, if there's 17 playboys on the block, I'm gonna guarantee 15 got straps and that's just the way we live, especially in neighborhoods like the Fillmore and Hunters Point.

I've been around the projects my whole life. When I was young about 9 years old, we use to play with kids from the projects in football. Everytime we played them in football, it was mandatory we fought after every game, and that was just the way it was being a youngsta growing up in my neighborhood in the Fillmore. When I used to go to the projects sometimes with my uncle, OG Joe, he's the one who put me up on game as a youngsta, 'cause my father wasn't there for me. He was in and out of jail when I was younger. So I look up to my uncle like if he was my father. After, my father was missing out of my life for a few years, then he got out of jail and moved to Hayes Valley Projects, where my uncle had a spot too. So, I had two spots to go to.

See my dad started snorting coke and I started doing whatever I wanted. I was 12. Then I started slangin' rocks (at 12), stealing cars, smoking weed, following my big cousin trying to do what he was doing. 'Cause like I got cousins from the Mac Block aka McAllister Street to Harbor Road in Hunters Point. Like, I seen all my cousins having money and I wanted to have money like them so I started hangin' on the block pulling all nighters, bringing guns into my mom's house. See, I was showing no respect to my mom. I was just ripping and running the streets all night long just trying to get paid. Ya know, that's just a part of life. Feel me like? 'Cause I know you want to get yours too when you see everybody else with paypa. You'll want your pockets to be on phat too. When I touchdown, I'm gonna have mine fo' sho, no matter if you haters trying to get me, or talk down, I'm gonna prevail on all y'all. That's just how I'm gonna do it. I'm gonna get mine, I got to have it, yeah, I must have it!!!

—Young Tay B2

JESUS WASN'T LISTENING

The needle is my perfect God
Smack is my soul,
say what you will,
but it's the only thing that saves me, from wanting
to hate and destroy.
Jesus wasn't listening,
when I said,
"Hey you up there?"
Jesus wasn't listening, when I asked Him for a
   prayer.
I'm addicted to pain,
'simply cause pleasure hurts.
I'm sick of falling in love with all these screwed up
   jerks.

—No Name

Sherman Alexie

Sherman Alexie is a Spokane/Coeur d'Alene Indian raised amid the poverty of the Spokane Indian Reservation in Washington State. As of this writing Alexie has published six books of poetry, two novels, and two short story collections. The recent film *Smoke Signals* is also based on Alexie's short stories.

With his family, the scrappy narrator of this partially autobiographical story lives close to the bone, eating canned beef "that even the dogs wouldn't eat." He realizes by first grade that he is a "they," and describes the cumulative effects of his "Indian education."

Indian Education

My hair was too short and my U.S. Government glasses were horn-rimmed, ugly, and all that first winter in school, the other Indian boys chased me from one corner of the playground to the other. They pushed me down, buried me in the snow until I couldn't breathe, thought I'd never breathe again.

They stole my glasses and threw them over my head, around my outstretched hands, just beyond my reach, until someone tripped me and sent me falling again, facedown in the snow.

I was always falling down; my Indian name was Junior Falls Down. Sometimes it was Bloody Nose or Steal-His-Lunch. Once, it was Cries-Like-a-White-Boy, even though none of us had seen a white boy cry.

Then it was a Friday morning recess and Frenchy SiJohn threw snowballs at me while the rest of the Indian boys tortured some other *top-yogh-yaught* kid, another weakling. But Frenchy was confident enough to torment me all by himself, and most days I would have let him.

But the little warrior in me roared to life that day and knocked Frenchy to the ground, held his head against the snow, and punched him so hard that my knuckles and the snow made symmetrical bruises on his face. He almost looked like he was wearing war paint.

But he wasn't the warrior. I was. And I chanted *It's a good day to die, it's a good day to die*, all the way down to the principal's office.

Second Grade

Betty Towle, missionary teacher, redheaded and so ugly that no one ever had a puppy crush on her, made me stay in for recess fourteen days straight.

"Tell me you're sorry," she said.

"Sorry for what?" I asked.

"Everything," she said and made me stand straight for fifteen minutes, eagle-armed with books in each hand. One was a match book; the other was English. But all I learned was that gravity can be painful.

For Halloween I drew a picture of her riding a broom with a scrawny cat on the back. She said that her God would never forgive me for that.

Once, she gave the class a spelling test but set me aside and gave me a test designed for junior high students. When I spelled all the words right, she crumpled up the paper and made me eat it.

"You'll learn respect," she said.

She sent a letter home with me that told my parents to either cut my braids or keep me home from class. My parents came in the next day and dragged their braids across Betty Towle's desk.

"Indians, indians, indians." She said it without capitalization. She called me "indian, indian, indian."

And I said, *Yes, I am. I am Indian. Indian, I am.*

Third Grade

My traditional Native American art career began and ended with my very first portrait: *Stick Indian Taking a Piss in My Backyard.*

As I circulated the original print around the classroom, Mrs. Schluter intercepted and confiscated my art.

Censorship, I might cry now. *Freedom of expression,* I would write in editorials to the tribal newspaper.

In third grade, though, I stood alone in the corner, faced the wall, and waited for the punishment to end.

I'm still waiting.

FOURTH GRADE

"You should be a doctor when you grow up," Mr. Schluter told me, even though his wife, the third grade teacher, thought I was crazy beyond my years. My eyes always looked like I had just hit-and-run someone.

"Guilty," she said. "You always look guilty."

"Why should I be a doctor?" I asked Mr. Schluter.

"So you can come back and help the tribe. So you can heal people."

That was the year my father drank a gallon of vodka a day and the same year that my mother started two hundred different quilts but never finished any. They sat in separate, dark places in our HUD house and wept savagely.

I ran home after school, heard their Indian tears, and looked in the mirror. *Doctor Victor,* I called myself, invented an education, talked to my reflection. *Doctor Victor to the emergency room.*

FIFTH GRADE

I picked up a basketball for the first time and made my first shot. No. I missed my first shot, missed the basket completely, and the ball landed in the dirt and sawdust, sat there just like I had sat there only minutes before.

But it felt good, that ball in my hands, all those possibilities and angles. It was mathematics, geometry. It was beautiful.

At that same moment, my cousin Steven Ford sniffed rubber cement from a paper bag and leaned back on the merry-go-round. His ears rang, his mouth was dry, and everyone seemed so far away.

But it felt good, that buzz in his head, all those colors and noises. It was chemistry, biology. It was beautiful.

Oh, do you remember those sweet, almost innocent choices that the Indian boys were forced to make?

SIXTH GRADE

Randy, the new Indian kid from the white town of Springdale, got into a fight an hour after he first walked into the reservation school.

Stevie Flett called him out, called him a squawman, called him a pussy, and called him a punk.

Randy and Stevie, and the rest of the Indian boys, walked out into the playground.

"Throw the first punch," Stevie said as they squared off.

"No," Randy said.

"Throw the first punch," Stevie said again.

"No," Randy said again.

"Throw the first punch!" Stevie said for the third time, and Randy reared back and pitched a knuckle fastball that broke Stevie's nose.

We all stood there in silence, in awe.

That was Randy, my soon-to-be first and best friend, who taught me the most valuable lesson about living in the white world: *Always throw the first punch.*

SEVENTH GRADE

I leaned through the basement window of the HUD house and kissed the white girl who would later be raped by her foster-parent father, who was also white. They both lived on the reservation, though, and when the headlines and stories filled the papers later, not one word was made of their color.

Just Indians being Indians, someone must have said somewhere and they were wrong.

But on the day I leaned through the basement window of the HUD house and kissed the white girl, I felt the good-byes I was saying to my entire tribe. I held my lips tight against her lips, a dry, clumsy, and ultimately stupid kiss.

But I was saying good-bye to my tribe, to all the Indian girls and women I might have loved, to all the Indian men who might have called me cousin, even brother.

I kissed that white girl and when I opened my eyes, she was gone from the reservation, and when I opened my eyes, I was gone from the reservation, living in a farm town where a beautiful white girl asked my name.

"Junior Polatkin," I said, and she laughed.

After that, no one spoke to me for another five hundred years.

EIGHTH GRADE

At the farm town junior high, in the boys' bathroom, I could hear voices from the girls' bathroom, nervous whispers of anorexia and bulimia. I could hear the white girls' forced vomiting, a sound so familiar and natural to me after years of listening to my father's hangovers.

"Give me your lunch if you're just going to throw it up," I said to one of those girls once.

I sat back and watched them grow skinny from self-pity.

Back on the reservation, my mother stood in line to get us commodities. We carried them home, happy to have food, and opened the canned beef that even the dogs wouldn't eat.

But we ate it day after day and grew skinny from self-pity.

There is more than one way to starve.

NINTH GRADE

At the farm town high school dance, after a basketball game in an overheated gym where I had scored twenty-seven points and pulled down thirteen rebounds, I passed out during a slow song.

As my white friends revived me and prepared to take me to the emergency room where doctors would later diagnose my diabetes, the Chicano teacher ran up to us.

"Hey," he said. "What's that boy been drinking? I know all about these Indian kids. They start drinking real young."

Sharing dark skin doesn't necessarily make two men brothers.

TENTH GRADE

I passed the written test easily and nearly flunked the driving, but still received my Washington State driver's license on the same day that Wally Jim killed himself by driving his car into a pine tree.

No traces of alcohol in his blood, good job, wife and two kids.

"Why'd he do it?" asked a white Washington State trooper.

All the Indians shrugged their shoulders, looked down at the ground.

"Don't know," we all said, but when we look in the mirror, see the history of our tribe in our eyes, taste failure in the tap water, and shake with old tears, we understand completely.

Believe me, everything looks like a noose if you stare at it long enough.

ELEVENTH GRADE

Last night I missed two free throws which would have won the game against the best team in the state. The farm town high school I play for is nicknamed the "Indians," and I'm probably the only actual Indian ever to play for a team with such a mascot.

This morning I pick up the sports page and read the headline: INDIANS LOSE AGAIN.

Go ahead and tell me none of this is supposed to hurt me very much.

TWELFTH GRADE

I walk down the aisle, valedictorian of this farm town high school, and my cap doesn't fit because I've grown my hair longer than it's ever been. Later, I stand as the school board chairman recites my awards, accomplishments, and scholarships.

I try to remain stoic for the photographers as I look toward the future.

Back home on the reservation, my former classmates graduate: a few can't read, one or two are just given attendance diplomas, most look forward to the parties. The bright students are shaken, frightened, because they don't know what comes next.

They smile for the photographer as they look back toward tradition.

The tribal newspaper runs my photograph and the photograph of my former classmates side by side.

POSTSCRIPT: CLASS REUNION

Victor said, "Why should we organize a reservation high school reunion? My graduating class has a reunion every weekend at the Powwow Tavern."

Gary Soto

Nominated for a National Book Award in 1995 for his work, writer Gary Soto was born in Fresno, California, in 1952. Taken from a collection of stories called *Baseball in April,* based on Soto's childhood in Fresno, "Mother and Daughter" is a bittersweet story about the fragility of dignity. One of Soto's poems, entitled "Field Poem," also appears in this anthology.

Mother and Daughter

Yollie's mother, Mrs. Moreno, was a large woman who wore a muumuu and butterfly-shaped glasses. She liked to water her lawn in the evening and wave at low-riders, who would stare at her behind their smoky sunglasses and laugh. Now and then a low-rider from Belmont Avenue would make his car jump and shout "*Mamacita!*" But most of the time they just stared and wondered how she got so large.

Mrs. Moreno had a strange sense of humor. Once, Yollie and her mother were watching a late-night movie called "They Came to Look." It was about creatures from the underworld who had climbed through molten lava to walk the earth. But Yollie, who had played soccer all day with the kids next door, was too tired to be scared. Her eyes closed but sprang open when her mother screamed, "Look, Yollie! Oh, you missed a scary part. The guy's face was all ugly!"

But Yollie couldn't keep her eyes open. They fell shut again and stayed shut, even when her mother screamed and slammed a heavy palm on the arm of her chair.

"Mom, wake me up when the movie's over so I can go to bed," mumbled Yollie.

"OK, Yollie, I wake you," said her mother through a mouthful of popcorn.

But after the movie ended, instead of waking her daughter, Mrs. Moreno laughed under her breath, turned the TV and lights off, and tiptoed to bed. Yollie woke up in the middle of the night and didn't know where she was. For a moment she thought she was dead. Maybe something from the underworld had lifted her from her house and carried her into the earth's belly. She blinked her sleepy eyes, looked around at the darkness, and called, "Mom? Mom, where are you?" But there was no answer, just the throbbing hum of the refrigerator.

Finally, Yollie's grogginess cleared and she realized her mother had gone to bed, leaving her on the couch. Another of her little jokes.

But Yollie wasn't laughing. She tiptoed into her mother's bedroom with a glass of water and set it on the nightstand next to the alarm clock. The next morning, Yollie woke to screams. When her mother reached to turn off the alarm, she had overturned the glass of water.

Yollie burned her mother's morning toast and gloated. "Ha! Ha! I got you back. Why did you leave me on the couch when I told you to wake me up?"

Despite their jokes, mother and daughter usually got along. They watched bargain matinees together, and played croquet in the summer and checkers in the winter. Mrs. Moreno encouraged Yollie to study hard because she wanted her daughter to be a doctor. She bought Yollie a desk, a typewriter, and a lamp that cut glare so her eyes would not grow tired from hours of studying.

Yollie was slender as a tulip, pretty, and one of the smartest kids at Saint Theresa's. She was captain of crossing guards, an altar girl, and a whiz in the school's monthly spelling bees.

"Tienes que estudiar mucho," Mrs. Moreno said every time she propped her work-weary feet on the hassock. "You have to study a lot, then you can get a good job and take care of me."

"Yes, Mama," Yollie would respond, her face buried in a book. If she gave her mother any sympathy, she would begin her stories about how she had come with her family from Mexico with nothing on her back but a sack with three skirts, all of which were too large by the time she crossed the border because she had lost weight from not having enough to eat.

Everyone thought Yollie's mother was a riot. Even the nuns

laughed at her antics. Her brother Raul, a nightclub owner, thought she was funny enough to go into show business.

But there was nothing funny about Yollie needing a new outfit for the eighth-grade fall dance. They couldn't afford one. It was late October, with Christmas around the corner, and their dented Chevy Nova had gobbled up almost one hundred dollars in repairs.

"We don't have the money," said her mother, genuinely sad because they couldn't buy the outfit, even though there was a little money stashed away for college. Mrs. Moreno remembered her teenage years and her hardworking parents, who picked grapes and oranges, and chopped beets and cotton for meager pay around Kerman. Those were the days when "new clothes" meant limp and out-of-style dresses from Saint Vincent de Paul.

The best Mrs. Moreno could do was buy Yollie a pair of black shoes with velvet bows and fabric dye to color her white summer dress black.

"We can color your dress so it will look brand-new," her mother said brightly, shaking the bottle of dye as she ran hot water into a plastic dish tub. She poured the black liquid into the tub and stirred it with a pencil. Then, slowly and carefully, she lowered the dress into the tub.

Yollie couldn't stand to watch. She *knew* it wouldn't work. It would be like the time her mother stirred up a batch of molasses for candy apples on Yollie's birthday. She'd dipped the apples into the goo and swirled them and seemed to taunt Yollie by singing *"Las Mañanitas"* to her. When she was through, she set the apples on wax paper. They were hard as rocks and hurt the kids' teeth. Finally they had a contest to see who could break the apples open by throwing them against the side of the house. The apples shattered like grenades, sending the kids scurrying for cover, and in an odd way the birthday party turned out to be a success. At least everyone went home happy.

To Yollie's surprise, the dress came out shiny black. It looked brand-new and sophisticated, like what people in New York wear. She beamed at her mother, who hugged Yollie and said, "See, what did I tell you?"

The dance was important to Yollie because she was in love with Ernie Castillo, the third-best speller in the class. She bathed, dressed, did her hair and nails, and primped until her mother yelled, "All right already." Yollie sprayed her neck and wrists with Mrs. Moreno's Avon perfume and bounced into the car.

Mrs. Moreno let Yollie out in front of the school. She waved and told her to have a good time but behave herself, then roared off, blue smoke trailing from the tail pipe of the old Nova.

Yollie ran into her best friend, Janice. They didn't say it, but each thought the other was the most beautiful girl at the dance; the boys would fall over themselves asking them to dance.

The evening was warm but thick with clouds. Gusts of wind picked up the paper lanterns hanging in the trees and swung them, blurring the night with reds and yellows. The lanterns made the evening seem romantic, like a scene from a movie. Everyone danced, sipped punch, and stood in knots of threes and fours, talking. Sister Kelly got up and jitterbugged with some kid's father. When the record ended, students broke into applause.

Janice had her eye on Frankie Ledesma, and Yollie, who kept smoothing her dress down when the wind picked up, had her eye on Ernie. It turned out that Ernie had his mind on Yollie, too. He ate a handful of cookies nervously, then asked her for a dance.

"Sure," she said, nearly throwing herself into his arms.

They danced two fast ones before they got a slow one. As they circled under the lanterns, rain began falling, lightly at first. Yollie loved the sound of the raindrops ticking against the leaves. She leaned her head on Ernie's shoulder, though his sweater was scratchy. He felt warm and tender. Yollie could tell that he was in love, and with her, of course. The dance continued successfully, romantically, until it began to pour.

"Everyone, let's go inside—and, boys, carry in the table and the record player," Sister Kelly commanded.

The girls and boys raced into the cafeteria. Inside, the girls, drenched to the bone, hurried to the restrooms to brush their hair and dry themselves. One girl cried because her velvet dress was ruined. Yollie felt sorry for her and helped her dry the dress off with paper towels, but it was no use. The dress was ruined.

Yollie went to a mirror. She looked a little gray now that her mother's makeup had washed away but not as bad as some of the other girls. She combed her damp hair, careful not to pull too hard. She couldn't wait to get back to Ernie.

Yollie bent over to pick up a bobby pin, and shame spread across her face. A black puddle was forming at her feet. Drip, black drip. Drip, black drip. The dye was falling from her dress like black tears. Yollie stood up. Her dress was now the color of ash. She looked around the room. The other girls, unaware of Yollie's problem, were busy grooming themselves. What could she do? Everyone would laugh. They would know she dyed an old dress because she couldn't afford a new one. She hurried from the restroom with her head down, across the cafeteria floor and out the door. She raced through the storm, crying as the rain mixed with her tears and ran into twig-choked gutters.

When she arrived home, her mother was on the couch eating cookies and watching TV.

"How was the dance, *m'ija?* Come watch the show with me. It's really good."

Yollie stomped, head down, to her bedroom. She undressed and threw the dress on the floor.

Her mother came into the room. "What's going on? What's all the racket, baby?"

"The dress. It's cheap! It's no good!" Yollie kicked the dress at her mother and watched it land in her hands. Mrs. Moreno studied it closely but couldn't see what was wrong. "What's the matter? It's just a bit wet."

"The dye came out, that's what."

Mrs. Moreno looked at her hands and saw the grayish dye puddling in the shallow lines of her palms. Poor baby, she thought, her brow darkening as she made a sad face. She wanted to tell her daughter how sorry she was, but she knew it wouldn't help. She walked back to the living room and cried.

The next morning, mother and daughter stayed away from each other. Yollie sat in her room turning the pages of an old *Seventeen,* while her mother watered her plants with a Pepsi bottle.

"Drink, my children," she said loud enough for Yollie to hear. She let the water slurp into pots of coleus and cacti. "Water is all you need. My daughter needs clothes, but I don't have no money."

Yollie tossed her *Seventeen* on her bed. She was embarrassed at last night's tirade. It wasn't her mother's fault that they were poor.

When they sat down together for lunch, they felt awkward about the night before. But Mrs. Moreno had made a fresh stack of tortillas and cooked up a pan of *chile verde,* and that broke the ice. She licked her thumb and smacked her lips.

"You know, honey, we gotta figure a way to make money," Yollie's mother said. "You and me. We don't have to be poor. Remember the Garcias. They made this stupid little tool that fixes cars. They moved away because they're rich. That's why we don't see them no more."

"What can we make?" asked Yollie. She took another tortilla and tore it in half.

"Maybe a screwdriver that works on both ends? Something like that." The mother looked around the room for ideas, but then shrugged. "Let's forget it. It's better to get an education.

If you get a good job and have spare time then maybe you can invent something." She rolled her tongue over her lips and cleared her throat. "The county fair hires people. We can get a job there. It will be here next week."

Yollie hated the idea. What would Ernie say if he saw her pitching hay at the cows? How could she go to school smelling like an armful of chickens? "No, they wouldn't hire us," she said.

The phone rang. Yollie lurched from her chair to answer it, thinking it would be Janice wanting to know why she had left. But it was Ernie wondering the same thing. When he found out she wasn't mad at him, he asked if she would like to go to a movie.

"I'll ask," Yollie said, smiling. She covered the phone with her hand and counted to ten. She uncovered the receiver and said, "My mom says it's OK. What are we going to see?"

After Yollie hung up, her mother climbed, grunting, onto a chair to reach the top shelf in the hall closet. She wondered why she hadn't done it earlier. She reached behind a stack of towels and pushed her chubby hand into the cigar box where she kept her secret stash of money.

"I've been saving a little money every month," said Mrs. Moreno. "For you, *m'ija*." Her mother held up five twenties, a blossom of green that smelled sweeter than flowers on that Saturday. They drove to Macy's and bought a blouse, shoes, and a skirt that would not bleed in rain or any other kind of weather.

Robert Coles

In the early 1960s, as a child psychiatrist practicing in the South, Robert Coles began interviewing children in the cities of Atlanta and New Orleans, talking with the black children who initiated school desegregation, and their white classmates. He compiled the interviews and in 1967 published his first book, *Children of Crisis: A Study of Courage and Fear* from which this excerpt is taken. The book eventually became a five-volume series, for which Dr. Coles received the Pulitzer Prize in 1973. His writing has been called "definitive work on America's poor and powerless in the twentieth century."

Here Coles tells the story of fifteen-year-old John Washington, a poor student from Atlanta, one of ten African American students chosen in that city during the 1960s "to lead his race out of its special schools, and into those shared by the rest of the community."

From *Children of Crisis:*
A Study of Courage and Fear

"We once were slaves, but now we have to free our country as well as ourselves," said a Negro minister to his flock in the summer of 1961. His church is in Atlanta, Georgia, and in the words of one parishioner, "it is a hard-praying one." . . . It was a sermon meant to bolster the spirit of a community set to accomplish part of its liberation; school desegregation would take effect the coming week. Sitting in the church was John Washington, a youth of fifteen who was to be one of ten students (in a city of a million, a state of several million) to lead his race out of its special schools and into those shared by the rest of the community . . .

John was born in South Carolina in the early summer of 1946, the fourth child of Joseph and Hattie (Turner) Washington. His grandparents grew up in the homes of people once slaves—all of his ancestors worked on cotton for generations. His parents took pride in telling me that theirs was the first generation free enough to raise children who would never see a slave. John's birth was attended by his aunt, one of the younger sisters of his mother. His parents were sharecroppers, and until the Second World War had been having an exceedingly hard time of it. Their yearly income had never been more than two hundred dollars. They lived in a cabin at the edge of a large plantation; the cabin still stands, occupied by Mr. Washington's younger brother. He now averages about a thousand dollars a year for farming cotton and tobacco. The land is rich and seemingly inexhaustible. Several times I visited the farm with John—after I had known him for two years—and we both noticed the curious presence of shabby, makeshift living quarters amid abundant wild flowers, heavily cultivated land, and well-fed animals—hogs, chickens, even a goat.

John's father never left that farm until he was drafted to fight in the war. He had his basic training in New Jersey, then went to Europe where he served as a cook for troops fighting in France. He says that he will never be able to forget the sight of men dying in war, but he counts his time in the army as the best and most influential period of his life: "I never had it so good. I ate food I never dreamed I could, even in battle; and I had a good bed and real fine clothes. I saw the world outside, and I figured I wouldn't stay a 'cropper' after that."

He didn't. He came home for a year and tried resuming his earlier life. He had married a nearby girl when she was fourteen, he sixteen. When he was drafted at twenty they had three children. His wife Hattie very much wanted to remain in South Carolina. Her large family lived only a few miles away from his. They were all part of a community. If they were poor beyond description, essentially illiterate and almost totally isolated from the social, cultural, political and economic life of the nation, at least they knew it in their bones; and so they feared the risks and burdens of leaving one another as well as a life both familiar and communal, whatever else it was not. Some, of course, had left, even before the war. Each family had its son or daughter, cousin or neighbor "abroad," in the Southern or Northern cities.

Hattie finally agreed to leave, to emigrate, but not until John had been born in his grandmother's cabin. Her husband Joseph had agreed to wait for the birth. Hattie had hoped that by the time their new child had arrived, Joseph would change his mind about moving. Instead, he was more determined than ever. Their fourth child was their first son; he was given his paternal grandfather's name. Mr. Washington wanted a job in a city. He wanted schooling for his children, particularly his new son. He wanted to go northward, to Philadelphia or New

York. His wife persuaded him to compromise on Atlanta. "I felt safer going to Georgia since we had to go at all," she now recalls, "and if it was to do again, I'd still rather be here than up there North." She didn't like cold weather, snow, distance from her family, large cities or the way people get along in them—shunning one another, making her feel lonely. In Hattie's town white people spoke to her on sight, asked after her. Hattie knew Negroes had a much tougher life to live, but she wasn't sure that moving from one place in America to another would solve *that* problem. . . .

In Atlanta young John began to grow up. Six months after he was born his mother was again pregnant. John eventually was to have seven brothers and sisters. Two brothers followed him, and two sisters followed them. This steadily increasing family settled at first in the outskirts of the city, where Mr. Washington obtained occasional employment as a dishwasher in a restaurant, then as a handyman in a service station. When John was two his parents moved into the neighborhood they now call their own. They have since lived continually in the same apartment, the five sisters in two bedrooms, the three boys in another, the parents in the living room. In addition there is a kitchen. For the entire Washington family—including the relatives in South Carolina and a few north in Chicago—this apartment represents the highest standard of living yet achieved. It is heated, has electricity, is not rat-infested, has running water, and though poorly furnished and crowded in comparison to the way most Americans live, it is by no means unattractive, because Mrs. Washington is a neat housekeeper. . . .

So far as John's parents, older sisters and past teachers can recall, he was not a particularly outstanding boy, either at home or in school. His appetite as an infant and child was normal. He grew normally, suffered the usual childhood ailments. At school he started out hesitantly and without distinction, but gradually gained ground, so that in the sixth

grade he was one of the three or four leading students in his
class. He always excelled in sports, whether in his neighborhood or at school. His parents proudly attributed his agile
manner, his athletic excellence to the rural, farm boy "soul"
in him. "John was born on a farm," his mother once reminded
me, "and that's where his soul got fixed. He can run and jump
because that's what you do when you live where we did. People say he's so strong, and his muscles are so good, but we're
not surprised. He carries my daddy's body, and he'll hand it
down, too—if the city don't take it out of him, somehow." . . .
John entered junior high school (and adolescence) at twelve.
He took up with a girl in his class, a rather attractive and quiet
girl who then dreamed of being a nurse, and afterward became
one. John continued to see her over the years, though they
became "old friends" rather than courting friends. I noticed
that they drew closer together—at his behest—when he faced
the ordeal of desegregation.

He became involved in that ordeal quite casually. He was a
tenth grader in one of the Negro high schools in Atlanta. He
had been thinking of quitting school, as many of his friends
had been doing with increasing frequency. He fought with his
parents over this, and the considerations at issue tell about his
home life. His father had been drinking for many years, but
until John was about ten had managed to confine his intake
to weekend bouts. John remembers as a child that his father
would simply disappear, sometimes coming home for brief pe-
riods, sometimes lying down to sleep in hallways or alleys and
then being picked up by the police and jailed, dried out and
returned home, or brought to his family directly. However, he
generally kept sober during the week, and kept his job out of
jeopardy. About the time John entered high school his father's
controls weakened; he insidiously began weekday drinking.
Mrs. Washington apparently saw what was coming, and obtained work at a nearby factory where she helped assemble
children's toys. She called upon her religious faith more than

ever at that time, and attributes her job to divine intervention: "I saw him going for the bottle worse than ever, and I prayed to God for guidance. He told me to go and find a job, and let it be between Him and my husband, what will come from the drinking. So I looked, and I found one, and it's a good job, too." . . .

[But] John stayed in high school, and obligingly set to work studying harder than ever before. Listening to him talk about it several years later, I felt he must have been relieved to see his own struggles and decisions act to stabilize his family. . . .

When the city of Atlanta and the state of Georgia yielded to a federal court order requiring a start toward school desegregation, they chose to begin with the last two years of high school. John was a sophomore at this time and like all his classmates was confronted with the choice of applying or not for transfer the next year to a white high school. The school board would then act upon the applications, selecting the children it judged suitable to make the move. . . .

Walking home one day with his friends, he heard some say yes, they would, some say no, they wouldn't think of going through mobs or sitting through insults at a white school. John recalls the atmosphere and conversation as follows: "We were just kidding around, like any other time; only that day it was about integration and what we would do now that it was coming to Atlanta. We kept on daring one another and teasing each other. My friend Kenny said he was going to do it, regardless; and the girls let out a big cheer and hugged and kissed him. Then Larry called him a fool. He said we would be giving up the best two years of our lives for nothing but trouble. He meant the end of high school, and the dances and football games—everything you hope for when you're beginning high school. Well, we most of us said we would do it—I think more to be the hero before the girls. Then they fell to arguing just like we did. My best girl then was Betty, and she told me she would sign up if I would, but we had to promise we both meant it to one another. I can still remember the bargain. She said, 'No joking' and I said, 'No joking,' and that was it. A week later we went down singing to get the forms and apply. I didn't even tell my folks until it came time to get their signatures, and that was where the trouble started. They said no, sir. I tried to tell them we were all going to do it, but it didn't cut any ice with them. Momma started praying out loud, and quoting the Bible to me about getting into heaven by being poor, and if I tried to go to school with whites and rise up, I'll probably lose my soul. And Daddy told me I'd get myself killed, and they'd get him to lose his job, one way or another. For a while I thought I was out of the running before I even started; and a lot of my friends had the same trouble."

In a sense the week of struggle for his parents' signatures became a real time of intimacy and discussion between the three of them. It was also a confrontation of the generations, the past incredulous at what the present seemed to expect as its due. John heard from his parents stories of experiences which they themselves had long since "forgotten": accounts of terror, humiliation and repudiation which had formerly been handed down from parent to child as an inheritance, to be told and later relived. John was particularly moved by his mother's insistence that his generation was the first to be spared the worst of it—the constant possibility of lynching, the near-total lack of hope, the daily scorn that permitted no reply, no leeway. To be free of that, to be safe from night riders, to have steady work, to be left mostly alone, all that seemed enough. "They wanted me to be glad I could walk on the sidewalk," John summarized their conversations, "because they used to have to move into the gutter in their town when a white man approached them. But I told them that once you walk on the sidewalk, you look in the windows of the stores and restaurants, and you want to go there, too. They said, maybe *my* children, and I said *me*, so that my children will be the first really free Negroes. They always told me that they would try to spare me what they went through; so I told them I wanted to spare my children going through any mobs. If there were mobs for us to face, we should do it right now. And besides, I told them they were contradicting themselves. My mother always brags about how wonderful the farm life was, and my daddy says he thought the city would save him, and it drove him to drink, so it's too bad he ever left South Carolina. Suddenly, though, all the truth was coming out." When I asked him how *he* explained their opposing sentiments he replied briefly—and for me his words are unforgettable— "I guess people can believe different things at different times."

As he persisted they relented. Eventually they gave their reluctant, apprehensive endorsements. They apparently were proud as well as filled with foreboding as they signed their names, itself not an easy task for either of them. John must have sensed their pride. He described an unexpected rise of sentiment in himself as he watched his parents sign their permission: "I think I got more emotional over that than anything else that happened; even more than walking in the building the first day."

Before walking into any school building for white children he would have to meet the standards of school officials worried about how to implement an uncongenial court order in the face of an uncertain and fearful population. John expected to be one of hundreds of new Negro students. He may have been dimly aware that no Southern city had yet taken more than a handful of Negro children to start desegregation, but neither he nor his friends ever gave much thought to the likelihood that only a few of them might be chosen. To some extent they believed—and correctly—that their city was determined to secure their safety. That belief, that faith, helped these children forget or "overlook" some of the possible dangers in the future. John put it to me quite concisely one day several weeks before those dangers actually started coming to his attention: "I try not to think about what's going to happen when school starts. I just go from day to day. We never thought it would be a picnic, but we figured we'd just take what comes, and then we could have stories to tell afterward."

John was interviewed, along with many of his friends, by school officials who were trying to make their choices more rationally and thoughtfully than some of their counterparts had done in other Southern cities. John realized during the interviews that a quiet and sincere presence was wanted, that an inflammatory or argumentative one was feared. He was asked by the school system's deputy superintendent how he would manage insults and even attacks upon himself. He replied that he would ignore them. If anyone threatened to injure him or interfere with his activities, he would call for help from others, namely his teachers. He was pointedly asked whether he would strike back if hit. He said he would not. He was asked why. He said he would only be inviting worse injury by doing so; he would, after all, be outnumbered, literally a thousand to one. I asked him, on hearing him tell of this exchange, how he expected to maintain that degree of almost fearless restraint. My question was: "John, in your own mind—apart from what you told them in the interview—do you think you would act that way if one or two boys pushed or shoved you, and called you names?" He replied: "That's where my daddy is right. He told me a long time ago, 'The only way a colored man can win is to fool the white man into thinking he's won.' I don't think that's always right, but it has to be like that until we get strong enough to make it even steven."

John was chosen, one of ten in a city of a million. He was surprised and quite disappointed rather than honored to learn that he and a girl he casually knew would be the only two of their race to enter the large "white" high school near his "old" one. . . .

For three summer months he awaited his role in desegregation. He worked at cutting lawns, emptying trash, helping his father by substituting at the gas station, or selling Cokes at local baseball games. I saw very little evidence of anxiety in him. He did become concerned with his "strength," and accordingly set himself a routine of exercise. His sister asked him whether he was worried about trouble in the fall, and he impatiently denied it. He had noticed he was short-winded on occasion, and that alone was the reason for his exercise. I was on the lookout for "trouble," but his appetite held up; he slept well; he seemed to his family quieter and more relaxed than usual.

The week before school started, the threats on his life, on his family's life, reached their terrible and bizarre peak. The telephone calls came in round the clock, angry voices talking of dynamite, alarmed voices talking of "racial amalgamation," plaintive voices urging John to reconsider his ill-advised decision "before it is too late." His parents—and especially his older sisters—wanted the phone changed. A city detective watching their home advised them to change their number. John would not hear of it: "I'm going to have to get used to that, so we might as well start now." Such a response showed how firmly and stubbornly he was girding himself. As I look back—and only in retrospect can I see it and say it—his willingness to take on the constant irritation and heckling of the telephone calls foreshadowed his future capacity to deal with similar episodes in school. At the time I failed to understand why he wouldn't let his family follow their inclinations and the advice of the police department. . . . I failed to recognize this youth's desire to have his preliminary struggle with the enemy on "home territory," and win it.

On the first day of school he was escorted and driven to school by city detectives. I watched him walk up to the door of the high school, heavily guarded by police, the students and teachers waiting inside for him, and wondered how he felt, what he was thinking, and whether in fact he had any words to describe those seconds. Everybody else seemed to have words: national and local political leaders, reporters, observers, all noted how important it was for a Southern city to initiate school desegregation without violence. There was none.

Certainly the white children and their teachers felt themselves in the presence of history; and so did John. He told his mother later that he said a prayer she long ago taught him as he left the police car; when that was finished, still walking toward the school, he looked quickly at the building and thought of words he had heard from his grandparents as a boy: "It's going to get better for us, don't you ever forget that." Approaching the front door, he thought of the classroom and pictured the students sitting, waiting for him to enter, and then watching him as he did.

They were doing just that, watching closely, and would continue to do so for two years. They stared at him and looked away from him. At the end of the first class some of them heckled him. A few days later he found insulting words scribbled on his books. Some of the students tried very hard to be friendly, though most of them kept an apprehensive distance from him. He, too, watched apprehensively; but he also worked hard in school, studied earnestly at home, and took things as they came each day.

During his two years in a desegregated high school I kept trying to learn how he managed to cope with the constant strains. I kept careful track of his moods, particularly so because I became puzzled at his altogether remarkable composure in the face of various social provocations or intellectual hurdles. In the first place, he was woefully unprepared for the transfer academically. He had prepared himself for unfriendliness, but not for the long hours of homework required to catch up with, not to say keep abreast of, his fellow students. Meeting these problems daily and a host of others he had never expected, he survived and—I came to see—flourished. . . .

John and I went to a basketball game at his high school. The opposing team was from a school not yet desegregated.

John as the only Negro in the audience attracted attention from the visitors by his mere presence. Indeed, a good part of the audience eventually paid more attention to him than the game. After the game, as we started leaving, one heckler after another confronted us. They had also seen the game, and now that it was over they turned their attention to John. Their language was awful, their behavior threatening. Were it not for quick action by hastily summoned police, there might well have been a riot. I was quite alarmed, and afterward sad and very angry. John was astonishingly steadfast during the episode, and rather composed afterward. I had known him for several months by then, and so I felt free enough to say what I did: "I don't know how you can take that sort of treatment; I really don't." He smiled, and looked at me as if he understood my problems and would try to help me as best he could. In a moment he did. He started with gentle criticism of me: "You don't know how I can take it because you haven't ever *had* to take it." He paused. "You see, when I grew up I had to learn to expect that kind of treatment; and I got it, so many times I hate to remember and count them. Well, now I'm getting it again, but it's sweet pain this time, because whatever they may say to me or however they try to hurt me, I know that just by sticking it out I'm going to help end the whole system of segregation; and that can make you go through anything. Yes, when they get to swearing and start calling me 'nigger' I think of the progress we're making, I'm making, every minute; then I know I can take even worse than we had tonight. I saw much worse happen to my momma and me when I was eight or nine, and we were shopping, and a woman decided she belonged ahead of us in a line in a store downtown. She slapped my momma, and momma didn't do a thing. I got so angry I kicked the lady and shoved her; so she called the police and soon the whole store seemed after us. The worst of it was that I got the beating of my life from my parents for doing that. You see, we just grow up to take it. But not you, you don't have to, and that's the difference." . . .

As I have watched John grow from a youth to a young man, and reflected upon his capacity to endure the simple trials not only of growing but of growing in a home such as his, of growing while a student in a white school, while taking a leading part in an important social change, I have found the limits of my own particular professional training rather severely defined.

John, after all, came from a very grim home, psychiatrically speaking. Both parents have serious mental disorders, the father at the very least a heavy drinker, the mother at the very least subject to distracted, suspicious fits of not very coherent religious preoccupations. John's childhood was characterized by poverty and what we now call "cultural disadvantage." He had a mediocre early education. When he decided to apply for an education at a white school he was not deeply or specially involved in the civil rights struggle. He belonged to no organization working for desegregation. He was not "enlisted" or encouraged to seek an application form; it was almost a matter of a moment's whim, a teen-ager's dare, a response to the company he kept, to their collective teasing of one another—fear and desire blended into a challenge.

Yet, this rather "ordinary" youth survived handily two years of an academic schedule far more burdensome and severe than any he had ever been taught to expect or endure. He also survived the daily loneliness and fear of his special position at school. Finally, he survived the ugliness and nastiness of threats, foul language, even some shoves and pokes in the corridors and corners of the school and in the streets nearby.

What accounts for such durability, such a hardy spirit against such odds? Where did John find his strength? . . .

John went on to college, to do quite well there. "That high

school became my life," John told me the day after he graduated from it. It was his answer to my curiosity about "what enabled him to do it." "That school glued me together; it made me stronger than I ever thought I could be, and so now I don't think I'll be able to forget what happened. I'll probably be different for the rest of my life."

Richard Ford

Richard Ford was born in 1944 to parents who settled in Jackson, Mississippi, after leaving Arkansas and wandering through the area. "I was displaced well before I could become placed," Ford has said, and his writing is often about shiftless working people looking to establish themselves.

Today Ford lives part of each year in Montana and part in New Orleans. "Optimists" is a short story from an early collection of stories by Ford called *Rock Springs,* praised by the *Los Angeles Times* as "a sad and quiet set of literary snapshots from one section of America's 'voiceless'—poor, sad, unemployed men and women from Montana."

Great Falls, Montana, in 1959, is a town "going downhill." It's a bad time for the railroads there, and fifteen-year-old Frank Brinson, the narrator of this haunting story, senses the political tensions between his father, Roy, a union switch-engineer fireman for the Great Northern Railway, and an anti-union neighbor who comes to play cards one night. When the neighbor accuses Brinson's father of being a "feather-bedder"—an employee needlessly hired by the union—the result is the precise moment when an entire family's circumstance is forever changed.

Optimists

All of this that I am about to tell happened when I was only fifteen years old, in 1959, the year my parents were divorced, the year when my father killed a man and went to prison for it, the year I left home and school, told a lie about my age to fool the Army, and then did not come back. The year, in other words, when life changed for all of us and forever—ended, really, in a way none of us could ever have imagined in our most brilliant dreams of life.

My father was named Roy Brinson, and he worked on the Great Northern Railway, in Great Falls, Montana. He was a switch-engine fireman, and when he could not hold that job on the seniority list, he worked the extra-board as a hostler, or as a hostler's helper, shunting engines through the yard, onto and off the freight trains that went south and east. He was thirty-seven or thirty-eight years old in 1959, a small, young-appearing man, with dark blue eyes. The railroad was a job he liked, because it paid high wages and the work was not hard, and because you could take off days when you wanted to, or even months, and have no one to ask you questions. It was a union shop, and there were people who looked out for you when your back was turned. "It's a workingman's paradise," my father would say, and then laugh.

My mother did not work then, though she *had* worked—at waitressing and in the bars in town—and she had liked working. My father thought, though, that Great Falls was coming to be a rougher town than it had been when he grew up there, a town going downhill, like its name, and that my mother should be at home more, because I was at an age when trouble came easily. We lived in a rented two-story house on Edith

Street, close to the freight yards and the Missouri River, a house where from my window at night I could hear the engines as they sat throbbing, could see their lights move along the dark rails. My mother was at home most of her time, reading or watching television or cooking meals, though sometimes she would go out to movies in the afternoon, or would go to the YWCA and swim in the indoor pool. Where she was from—in Havre, Montana, much farther north—there was never such a thing as a pool indoors, and she thought that to swim in the winter, with snow on the ground and the wind howling, was the greatest luxury. And she would come home late in the afternoon, with her brown hair wet and her face flushed, and in high spirits, saying she felt freer.

The night that I want to tell about happened in November. It was not then a good time for railroads—not in Montana especially—and for firemen not at all, anywhere. It was the featherbed time, and everyone knew, including my father, that they would—all of them—eventually lose their jobs, though no one knew exactly when, or who would go first, or, clearly, what the future would be. My father had been hired out ten years, and had worked on coal-burners and oil-burners out of Forsythe, Montana, on the Sheridan spur. But he was still young in the job and low on the list, and he felt that when the cut came young heads would go first. "They'll do something for us, but it might not be enough," he said, and I had heard him say that other times—in the kitchen, with my mother, or out in front, working on his motorcycle, or with me, fishing the whitefish up the Missouri. But I do not know if he truly thought that or in fact had any reason to think it. He was an optimist. Both of them were optimists, I think.

I know that by the end of summer in that year he had stopped taking days off to fish, had stopped going out along the coulee rims to spot deer. He worked more then and was gone more, and he talked more about work when he was home: about what the union said on this subject and that, about court cases in Washington, D.C., a place I knew nothing of, and about injuries and illnesses to men he knew, that threatened their livelihoods, and by association with them, threatened his own—threatened, he must've felt, our whole life.

Because my mother swam at the YWCA she had met people there and made friends. One was a large woman named Esther, who came home with her once and drank coffee in the kitchen and talked about her boyfriend and laughed out loud for a long time, but who I never saw again. And another was a woman named Penny Mitchell whose husband, Boyd, worked for the Red Cross in Great Falls and had an office upstairs in the building with the YWCA, and who my mother would sometime play canasta with on the nights my father worked late. They would set up a card table in the living room, the three of them, and drink and eat sandwiches until midnight. And I would lie in bed with my radio tuned low to the Calgary station, listening to a hockey match beamed out over the great empty prairie, and could hear the cards snap and laughter downstairs, and later I would hear footsteps leaving, hear the door shut, the dishes rattle in the sink, cabinets close. And in a while the door to my room would open and the light would fall inside, and my mother would set a chair back in. I could see her silhouette. She would always say, "Go back to sleep, Frank." And then the door would shut again, and I would almost always go to sleep in a minute.

—

It was on a night that Penny and Boyd Mitchell were in our house that trouble came about. My father had been working his regular bid-in job on the switch engine, plus a helper's job off the extra-board—a practice that was illegal by the railroad's rules, but ignored by the union, who could see bad times coming and knew there would be nothing to help it when they came, and so would let men work if they wanted to. I was in the kitchen, eating a sandwich alone at the table, and my mother was in the living room playing cards with Penny and Boyd Mitchell. They were drinking vodka and eating the other sandwiches my mother had made, when I heard my father's motorcycle outside in the dark. It was eight o'clock at night, and I knew he was not expected home until midnight.

"Roy's home," I heard my mother say. "I hear Roy. That's wonderful." I heard chairs scrape and glasses tap.

"Maybe he'll want to play," Penny Mitchell said. "We can play four-hands."

I went to the kitchen door and stood looking through the dining room at the front. I don't think I knew something was wrong, but I think I knew something was unusual, something I would want to know about firsthand.

My mother was standing beside the card table when my father came inside. She was smiling. But I have never seen a look on a man's face that was like the look on my father's face at that moment. He looked wild. His eyes were wild. His whole face was. It was cold outside, and the wind was coming up, and he had ridden home from the train yard in only his flannel shirt. His face was red, and his hair was strewn around his bare head, and I remember his fists were clenched white, as if there was no blood in them at all.

"My God," my mother said. "What is it, Roy? You look crazy." She turned and looked for me, and I knew she was thinking that this was something I might not need to see. But she didn't say anything. She just looked back at my father, stepped toward him and touched his hand, where he must've been coldest. Penny and Boyd Mitchell sat at the card table, looking up. Boyd Mitchell was smiling for some reason.

"Something awful happened," my father said. He reached and took a corduroy jacket off the coat nail and put it on, right in the living room, then sat down on the couch and hugged his arms. His face seemed to get redder then. He was wearing black steel-toe boots, the boots he wore every day, and I stared at them and felt how cold he must be, even in his own house. I did not come any closer.

"Roy, what is it?" my mother said, and she sat down beside him on the couch and held his hand in both of hers.

My father looked at Boyd Mitchell and at his wife, as if he hadn't known they were in the room until then. He did not know them very well, and I thought he might tell them to get out, but he didn't.

"I saw a man be killed tonight," he said to my mother, then shook his head and looked down. He said, "We were pushing into that old hump yard on Ninth Avenue. A cut of coal cars. It wasn't even an hour ago. I was looking out my side, the way you do when you push out a curve. And I could see this one open boxcar in the cut, which isn't unusual. Only this guy was in it and was trying to get off, sitting in the door, scooting. I guess he was a hobo. Those cars had come in from Glasgow tonight. And just the second he started to go off, the whole cut buckled up. It's a thing that'll happen. But he lost his balance just when he hit the gravel, and he fell backwards underneath. I looked right at him. And one set of trucks rolled right over his foot." My father looked at my mother then. "It hit his foot," he said.

"My God," my mother said and looked down at her lap.

My father squinted. "But then he moved, he sort of bucked himself like he was trying to get away. He didn't yell, and I could see his face. I'll never forget that. He didn't look scared, he just looked like a man doing something that was hard for him to do. He looked like he was concentrating on something. But when he bucked he pushed back, and the other trucks caught his hand." My father looked at his own hands then, and made fists out of them and squeezed them.

"What did you do?" my mother said. She looked terrified.

"I yelled out. And Sherman stopped pushing. But it wasn't that fast."

"Did you do anything then," Boyd Mitchell said.

"I got down," my father said, "and I went up there. But here's a man cut in three pieces in front of me. What can you do? You can't do very much. I squatted down and touched his good hand. And it was like ice. His eyes were open and roaming all up in the sky."

"Did he say anything?" my mother said.

"He said, 'Where am I today?' And I said to him, 'It's all right, bud, you're in Montana. You'll be all right.' Though, my God, he wasn't. I took my jacket off and put it over him. I didn't want him to see what had happened."

"You should've put tourniquets on," Boyd Mitchell said gruffly. "That could've helped. That could've saved his life."

My father looked at Boyd Mitchell then as if he had forgotten he was there and was surprised that he spoke. "I don't know about that," my father said. "I don't know anything about those things. He was already dead. A boxcar had run over him. He was breathing, but he was already dead to me."

"That's only for a licensed doctor to decide," Boyd Mitchell said. "You're morally obligated to do all you can." And I could tell from his tone of voice that he did not like my father. He hardly knew him, but he did not like him. I had no idea why. Boyd Mitchell was a big, husky, red-faced man with curly hair—handsome in a way, but with a big belly—and I knew only that he worked for the Red Cross, and that my mother was a friend of his wife's, and maybe of his, and that they played cards when my father was gone.

My father looked at my mother in a way I knew was angry. "Why have you got these people over here now, Dorothy? They don't have any business here."

"Maybe that's right," Penny Mitchell said, and she put down her hand of cards and stood up at the table. My mother looked around the room as though an odd noise had occurred inside of it and she couldn't find the source.

"Somebody definitely should've done something," Boyd Mitchell said, and he leaned forward on the table toward my father. "That's all there is to say." He was shaking his head *no*. "That man didn't have to die." Boyd Mitchell clasped his big hands on top of his playing cards and stared at my father. "The unions'll cover this up, too, I guess, won't they? That's what happens in these things."

My father stood up then, and his face looked wide, though it looked young, still. He looked like a young man who had been scolded and wasn't sure how he should act. "You get out of here," he said in a loud voice. "My God. What a thing to say. I don't even know you."

"I know you, though," Boyd Mitchell said angrily. "You're another featherbedder. You aren't good to do anything. You can't even help a dying man. You're bad for this country, and you won't last."

"Boyd, my goodness," Penny Mitchell said. "Don't say that. Don't say that. Don't say that to him."

Boyd Mitchell glared up at his wife. "I'll say anything I want to," he said. "And he'll listen, because he's helpless. He can't do anything."

"Stand up," my father said. "Just stand up on your feet." His fists were clenched again.

"All right, I will," Boyd Mitchell said. He glanced up at his wife. And I realized that Boyd Mitchell was drunk, and it was possible that he did not even know what he was saying, or what had happened, and that words just got loose from him this way, and anybody who knew him knew it. Only my father didn't. He only knew what had been said.

Boyd Mitchell stood up and put his hands in his pockets. He was much taller than my father. He had on a white Western shirt and whipcords and cowboy boots and was wearing a big silver wristwatch. "All right," he said. "Now I'm standing up. What's supposed to happen?" He weaved a little. I saw that.

And my father hit Boyd Mitchell then, hit him from across the card table—hit him with his right hand, square into the chest, not a lunging blow, just a hard, hitting blow that threw my father off balance and made him make a *chuffing* sound with his mouth. Boyd Mitchell groaned, "Oh," and fell down immediately, his big, thick, heavy body hitting the floor already doubled over. And the sound of him hitting the floor in our house was like no sound I had ever heard before. It was the sound of a man's body hitting a floor, and it was only that. In my life I have heard it other places, in hotel rooms and in bars, and it is one you do not want to hear.

You can hit a man in a lot of ways, I know that, and I knew that then, because my father had told me. You can hit a man to insult him, or you can hit a man to bloody him, or to knock him down, or lay him out. Or you can hit a man to kill him. Hit him that hard. And that is how my father hit Boyd Mitchell—as hard as he could, in the chest and not in the face, the way someone might think who didn't know about it.

"Oh my God," Penny Mitchell said. Boyd Mitchell was lying on his side in front of the TV, and she had gotten down on her knees beside him. "Boyd," she said. "Are you hurt? Oh, look at this. Stay where you are, Boyd. Stay on the floor."

"Now then. All right," my father said. "Now. All right." He was standing against the wall, over to the side of where he had been when he hit Boyd Mitchell from across the card table. Light was bright in the room, and my father's eyes were wide and touring around. He seemed out of breath and both his fists were clenched, and I could feel his heart beating in my own chest. "All right, now, you son of a bitch," my father said, and loudly. I don't think he was even talking to Boyd Mitchell. He was just saying words that came out of him.

"Roy," my mother said calmly. "Boyd's hurt now. He's hurt." She was just looking down at Boyd Mitchell. I don't think she knew what to do.

"Oh, no," Penny Mitchell said in an excited voice. "Look up, Boyd. Look up at Penny. You've been hurt." She had her hands flat on Boyd Mitchell's chest, and her skinny shoulders close to him. She wasn't crying, but I think she was hysterical and couldn't cry.

All this had taken only five minutes, maybe even less time. I had never even left the kitchen door. And for that reason I walked out into the room where my father and mother were, and where Boyd and Penny Mitchell were both of them on the floor. I looked down at Boyd Mitchell, at his face. I wanted to see what had happened to him. His eyes had cast back up into their sockets. His mouth was open, and I could see his big pink tongue inside. He was breathing heavy breaths, and his fingers—the fingers on both his hands—were moving, moving in the way a man would move them if he was nervous or anxious about something. I think he was dead then, and I think even Penny Mitchell knew he was dead, because she was saying, "Oh please, please, please, Boyd."

That is when my mother called the police, and I think it is when my father opened the front door and stepped out into the night.

—

All that happened next is what you would expect to happen. Boyd Mitchell's chest quit breathing in a minute, and he turned pale and cold and began to look dead right on our living-room floor. He made a noise in his throat once, and Penny Mitchell cried out, and my mother got down on her knees and held Penny's shoulders while she cried. Then my mother made Penny get up and go into the bedroom—hers and my father's—and lie on the bed. Then she and I sat in the brightly lit living room, with Boyd Mitchell dead on the floor, and simply looked at each other—maybe for ten minutes, maybe for twenty. I don't know what my mother could've been thinking during that time, because she did not say. She did not ask about my father. She did not tell me to leave the room. Maybe she thought about the rest of her life then and what that might be like after tonight. Or maybe she thought this: that people can do the worst things they are capable of doing and in the end the world comes back to normal. Possibly, she was just waiting for something normal to begin to happen again. That would make sense, given her particular character.

Though what I thought myself, sitting in that room with Boyd Mitchell dead, I remember very well, because I have thought it other times, and to a degree I began to date my real life from that moment and that thought. It is this: that situations have possibilities in them, and we have only to be present to be involved. Tonight was a very bad one. But how were we to know it would turn out this way until it was too late and we had all been changed forever? I realized though, that trouble, real trouble, was something to be avoided, inasmuch as once it has passed by, you have only yourself to answer to, even if, as I was, you are the cause of nothing.

In a little while the police arrived to our house. First one and then two more cars with their red lights turning in the street. Lights were on in the neighbors' houses—people came out and stood in the cold in their front yards watching, people I didn't know and who didn't know us. "It's a circus now," my mother said to me when we looked through the window. "We'll have to move somewhere else. They won't let us alone."

An ambulance came, and Boyd Mitchell was taken away on a stretcher, under a sheet. Penny Mitchell came out of the bedroom and went with them, though she did not say anything to my mother, or to anybody, just got in a police car and left into the dark.

Two policemen came inside, and one asked my mother some questions in the living room, while the other one asked me questions in the kitchen. He wanted to know what I had seen, and I told him. I said Boyd Mitchell had cursed at my father for some reason I didn't know, then had stood up and tried to hit him, and that my father had pushed Boyd, and that was all. He asked me if my father was a violent man, and I said no. He asked if my father had a girlfriend, and I said no. He asked if my mother and father had ever fought, and I said no. He asked me if I loved my mother and father, and I said I did. And then that was all.

I went out into the living room then, and my mother was there, and when the police left we stood at the front door, and there was my father outside, standing by the open door of a police car. He had on handcuffs. And for some reason he wasn't wearing a shirt or his corduroy jacket but was bare-chested in the cold night, holding his shirt behind him. His hair looked wet to me. I heard a policeman say, "Roy, you're going to catch cold," and then my father say, "I wish I was a long way from here right now. China maybe." He smiled at the policeman. I don't think he ever saw us watching, or if he did he didn't want to admit it. And neither of us did anything, because the police had him, and when that is the case, there is nothing you can do to help.

—

All this happened by ten o'clock. At midnight my mother and I drove down to the city jail and got my father out. I stayed in the car while my mother went in—sat and watched the high windows of the jail, which were behind wire mesh and bars. Yellow lights were on there, and I could hear voices and see figures move past the lights, and twice someone called out, "Hello, hello. Marie, are you with me?" And then it was quiet, except for the cars that drove slowly past ours.

On the ride home, my mother drove and my father sat and stared out at the big electrical stacks by the river, and the lights of houses on the other side, in Black Eagle. He had on a checked shirt someone inside had given him, and his hair was neatly combed. No one said anything, but I did not understand why the police would put anyone in jail because he had killed a man and in two hours let him out again. It was a mystery to me, even though I wanted him to be out and for our life to resume, and even though I did not see any way it could and, in fact, knew it never would.

Inside our house, all the lights were burning when we got back. It was one o'clock and there were still lights in some neighbors' houses. I could see a man at the window across the street, both his hands to the glass, watching out, watching us.

My mother went into the kitchen, and I could hear her running water for coffee and taking down cups. My father stood in the middle of the living room and looked around, looking at the chairs, at the card table with cards still on it, at the open doorways to the other rooms. It was as if he had forgotten his own house and now saw it again and didn't like it.

"I don't feel I know what he had against me," my father said. He said this to me, but he said it to anyone, too. "You'd think you'd know what a man had against you, wouldn't you, Frank?"

"Yes," I said. "I would." We were both just standing together, my father and I, in the lighted room there. We were not about to do anything.

"I want us to be happy here now," my father said. "I want us to enjoy life. I don't hold anything against anybody. Do you believe that?"

"I believe that," I said. My father looked at me with his dark blue eyes and frowned. And for the first time I wished my father had not done what he did but had gone about things differently. I saw him as a man who made mistakes, as a man who could hurt people, ruin lives, risk their happiness. A man who did not understand enough. He was like a gambler, though I did not even know what it meant to be a gambler then.

"It's such a quickly changing time now," my father said. My mother, who had come into the kitchen doorway, stood looking at us. She had on a flowered pink apron, and was standing where I had stood earlier that night. She was looking at my father and at me as if we were one person. "Don't you think it is, Dorothy?" he said. "All this turmoil. Everything just flying by. Look what's happened here."

My mother seemed very certain about things then, very precise. "You should've controlled yourself more," she said. "That's all."

"I know that," my father said. "I'm sorry. I lost control over my mind. I didn't expect to ruin things, but now I think I have. It was all wrong." My father picked up the vodka bottle, unscrewed the cap and took a big swallow, then put the bottle back down. He had seen two men killed tonight. Who could've blamed him?

"When I was in jail tonight," he said, staring at a picture on the wall, a picture by the door to the hallway. He was just talking again. "There was a man in the cell with me. And I've never been in jail before, not even when I was a kid. But this man said to me tonight, 'I can tell you've never been in jail before just by the way you stand up straight. Other people don't stand that way. They stoop. You don't belong in jail. You stand up too straight.' " My father looked back at the vodka bottle as if he wanted to drink more out of it, but he only looked at it. "Bad things happen," he said, and he let his open hands tap against his legs like clappers against a bell. "Maybe he was in love with you, Dorothy," he said. "Maybe that's what the trouble was."

And what I did then was stare at the picture on the wall, the picture my father had been staring at, a picture I had seen every day. Probably I had seen it a thousand times. It was two people with a baby on a beach. A man and a woman sitting in the sand with an ocean behind. They were smiling at the camera, wearing bathing suits. In all the times I had seen it I'd thought that it was a picture in which I was the baby, and the two people were my parents. But I realized as I stood there, that it was not me at all; it was my father who was the child in the picture, and the parents there were his parents—two people I'd never known, and who were dead—and the picture was so much older than I had thought it was. I wondered why I hadn't known that before, hadn't understood it for myself, hadn't always known it. Not even that it mattered. What mattered was, I felt, that my father had fallen down now, as much as the man he had watched fall beneath the train just hours before. And I was as helpless to do anything as he had been. I wanted to tell him that I loved him, but for some reason I did not.

—

Later in the night I lay in my bed with the radio playing, listening to news that was far away, in Calgary and in Saskatoon, and even farther, in Regina and Winnipeg—cold, dark cities I knew I would never see in my life. My window was raised above the sill, and for a long time I had sat and looked out, hearing my parents talk softly down below, hearing their footsteps, hearing my father's steel-toed boots strike the floor, and then their bedsprings squeeze and then be quiet. From out across the sliding river I could hear trucks—stock trucks and grain trucks heading toward Idaho, or down toward Helena, or into the train yards where my father hostled engines. The neighborhood houses were dark again. My father's motorcycle sat in the yard, and out in the night air I felt I could hear even the falls themselves, could hear every sound of them, sounds that found me and whirled and filled my room—could even feel them, cold and wintry, so that warmth seemed like a possibility I would never know again.

After a time my mother came in my room. The light fell on my bed, and she set a chair inside. I could see that she was looking at me. She closed the door, came and turned off my radio, then took her chair to the window, closed it, and sat so that I could see her face silhouetted against the streetlight. She lit a cigarette and did not look at me, still cold under the covers of my bed.

"How do you feel, Frank," she said, smoking her cigarette.
"I feel all right," I said.
"Do you think your house is a terrible house now?"
"No," I said.
"I hope not," my mother said. "Don't feel it is. Don't hold anything against anyone. Poor Boyd. He's gone."
"Why do you think that happened?" I said, though I didn't think she would answer, and wondered if I even wanted to know.

My mother blew smoke against the window glass, then sat and breathed. "He must've seen something in your father he just hated. I don't know what it was. Who knows? Maybe your father felt the same way." She shook her head and looked out into the streetlamp light. "I remember once," she said. "I was still in Havre, in the thirties. We were living in a motel my father part-owned out Highway Two, and my mother was around then, but wasn't having any of us. My father had this big woman named Judy Belknap as his girlfriend. She was an Assiniboin. Just some squaw. But we used to go on nature tours when he couldn't put up with me anymore. She'd take me. Way up above the Milk River. All this stuff she knew about, animals and plants and ferns—she'd tell me all that. And once we were sitting watching some gadwall ducks on the ice where a creek had made a little turn-out. It was getting colder, just like now. And Judy just all at once stood up and clapped. Just clapped her hands. And all these ducks got up, all except for one that stayed on the ice, where its feet were frozen, I guess. It didn't even try to fly. It just sat. And Judy said to me, 'It's just a coincidence, Dottie. It's wildlife. Some always get left back.' And that seemed to leave her satisfied for some reason. We walked back to the car after that. So," my mother said. "Maybe that's what this is. Just a coincidence."

She raised the window again, dropped her cigarette out, blew the last smoke from her throat, and said, "Go to sleep,

Frank. You'll be all right. We'll all survive this. Be an optimist."

When I was asleep that night, I dreamed. And what I dreamed was of a plane crashing, a bomber, dropping out of the frozen sky, bouncing as it hit the icy river, sliding and turning on the ice, its wings like knives, and coming into our house where we were sleeping, leveling everything. And when I sat up in bed I could hear a dog in the yard, its collar jingling, and I could hear my father crying, "Boo-hoo-hoo, boo-hoo-hoo,"—like that, quietly—though afterward I could never be sure if I had heard him crying in just that way, or if all of it was a dream, a dream I wished I had never had.

—

The most important things of your life can change so suddenly, so unrecoverably, that you can forget even the most important of them and their connections, you are so taken up by the chanciness of all that's happened and by all that could and will happen next. I now no longer remember the exact year of my father's birth, or how old he was when I last saw him, or even when that last time took place. When you're young, these things seem unforgettable and at the heart of everything. But they slide away and are gone when you are not so young.

My father went to Deer Lodge Prison and stayed five months for killing Boyd Mitchell by accident, for using too much force to hit him. In Montana you cannot simply kill a man in your living room and walk off free from it, and what I remember is that my father pleaded no contest, the same as guilty.

My mother and I lived in our house for the months he was gone. But when he came out and went back on the railroad as a switchman the two of them argued about things, about her wanting us to go someplace else to live—California or Seattle were mentioned. And then they separated, and she moved out. And after that I moved out by joining the Army and adding years to my age, which was sixteen.

I know about my father only that after a time he began to live a life he himself would never have believed. He fell off the railroad, divorced my mother, who would now and then resurface in his life. Drinking was involved in that, and gambling, embezzling money, even carrying a pistol, is what I heard. I was apart from all of it. And when you are the age I was then, and loose on the world and alone, you can get along better than at almost any other time, because it's a novelty, and you can act for what you want, and you can think that being alone will not last forever. All I know of my father, finally, is that he was once in Laramie, Wyoming, and not in good shape, and then he simply disappeared from view.

A month ago I saw my mother. I was buying groceries at a drive-in store by the interstate in Anaconda, Montana, not far from Deer Lodge itself, where my father had been. It had been fifteen years, I think, since I had seen her, though I am forty-three years old now, and possibly it was longer. But when I saw her I walked across the store to where she was and I said, "Hello, Dorothy. It's Frank."

She looked at me and smiled and said, "Oh, Frank. How are you? I haven't seen you in a long time. I'm glad to see you now, though." She was dressed in blue jeans and boots and a Western shirt, and she looked like a woman who could be sixty years old. Her hair was tied back and she looked pretty, though I think she had been drinking. It was ten o'clock in the morning.

There was a man standing near her, holding a basket of groceries, and she turned to him and said, "Dick, come here and meet my son, Frank. We haven't seen each other in a long time. This is Dick Spivey, Frank."

I shook hands with Dick Spivey, who was a man younger than my mother but older than me—a tall, thin-faced man with coarse blue-black hair—and who was wearing Western boots like hers. "Let me say a word to Frank, Dick," my mother said, and she put her hand on Dick's wrist and squeezed it and smiled at him. And he walked up toward the checkout to pay for his groceries.

"So. What are you doing now, Frank," my mother asked, and put her hand on my wrist the way she had on Dick Spivey's, but held it there. "These years," she said.

"I've been down in Rock Springs, on the coal boom," I said. "I'll probably go back down there."

"And I guess you're married, too."

"I was," I said. "But not right now."

"That's fine," she said. "You look fine." She smiled at me. "You'll never get anything fixed just right. That's your mother's word. Your father and I had a marriage made in Havre—that was our joke about us. We used to laugh about it. You didn't know that, of course. You were too young. A lot of it was just wrong."

"It's a long time ago," I said. "I don't know about that."

"I remember those times very well," my mother said. "They were happy enough times. I guess something *was* in the air, wasn't there? Your father was so jumpy. And Boyd got so mad, just all of a sudden. There was some hopelessness to it, I suppose. All that union business. We were the last to understand any of it, of course. We were trying to be decent people."

"That's right," I said. And I believed that was true of them.

"I still like to swim," my mother said. She ran her fingers back through her hair as if it were wet. She smiled at me again. "It still makes me feel freer."

"Good," I said. "I'm happy to hear that."

"Do you ever see your dad?"

"No," I said. "I never do."

"I don't either," my mother said. "You just reminded me of him." She looked at Dick Spivey, who was standing at the front window, holding a sack of groceries, looking out at the parking lot. It was March, and some small bits of snow were falling onto the cars in the lot. He didn't seem in any hurry. "Maybe I didn't appreciate your father enough," she said.

"Who knows? Maybe we weren't even made for each other. Losing your love is the worst thing, and that's what we did." I didn't answer her, but I knew what she meant, and that it was true. "I wish we knew each other better, Frank," my mother said to me. She looked down, and I think she may have blushed. "We have our deep feelings, though, don't we? Both of us."

"Yes," I said. "We do."

"So. I'm going out now," my mother said. "Frank." She squeezed my wrist, and walked away through the checkout and into the parking lot, with Dick Spivey carrying their groceries beside her.

But when I had bought my own groceries and paid, and gone out to my car and started up, I saw Dick Spivey's green Chevrolet drive back into the lot and stop, and watched my mother get out and hurry across the snow to where I was, so that for a moment we faced each other through the open window.

"Did you ever think," my mother said, snow freezing in her hair. "Did you ever think back then that I was in love with Boyd Mitchell? Anything like that? Did you ever?"

"No," I said. "I didn't."

"No, well, I wasn't," she said. "Boyd was in love with Penny. I was in love with Roy. That's how things were. I want you to know it. You have to believe that. Do you?"

"Yes," I said. "I believe you."

And she bent down and kissed my cheek through the open window and touched my face with both her hands, held me for a moment that seemed like a long time before she turned away, finally, and left me there alone.

PART THREE

I Took My Place, Bent My Head and Went to Work

Cathy Song

Born in Honolulu, Hawaii, in 1955, Cathy Song attended Wellesley College and Boston University. Her first book of poetry, *Picture Bride,* was selected as winner of the 1982 Yale Series of Younger Poets Award and was also nominated for the National Book Critics Circle Award.

This poem is from Song's latest collection, *School Figures,* published in 1994. Cathy Song lives in Honolulu.

The Grammar of Silk

On Saturdays in the morning
my mother sent me to Mrs. Umemoto's sewing
    school.
It was cool and airy in her basement,
pleasant—a word I choose
to use years later to describe
the long tables where we sat
and cut, pinned, and stitched,
the Singer's companionable whirr,
the crisp, clever bite of scissors
parting like silver fish a river of calico.

The school was in walking distance
to Kaimuki Dry Goods
where my mother purchased my supplies—
small cards of buttons,
zippers and rickrack packaged like licorice,
lifesaver rolls of thread
in fifty-yard lengths,
spun from spools, tough as tackle.
Seamstresses waited at the counters
like librarians to be consulted.
Pens and scissors dangled like awkward pendants
across flat chests,
a scarf of measuring tape flung across a shoulder,

time as a pincushion bristled at the wrist.
They deciphered a dress's blueprints
with an architect's keen eye.

This evidently was a sanctuary,
a place where women confined with children
conferred, consulted the oracle,
the stone tablets of the latest pattern books.
Here mothers and daughters paused in symmetry,
offered the proper reverence—
hushed murmurings for the shantung silk
which required a certain sigh,
as if it were a piece from the Ming Dynasty.

My mother knew there would be no shortcuts
and headed for the remnants,
the leftover bundles with yardage
enough for a heart-shaped pillow,
a child's dirndl, a blouse without darts.
Along the aisles
my fingertips touched the titles—
satin, tulle, velvet,
peach, lavender, pistachio,
sherbet-colored linings—
and settled for the plain brown-and-white
    composition
of polka dots on kettle cloth
my mother held up in triumph.

She was determined that I should sew
as if she knew what she herself was missing,

a moment when she could have come up for air—
the children asleep,
the dishes drying on the rack—
and turned on the lamp
and pulled back the curtain of sleep.
To inhabit the night,
the night as a black cloth, white paper,
a sheet of music in which she might find herself
    singing.

On Saturdays at Mrs. Umemoto's sewing school,
when I took my place beside the other girls,
bent my head and went to work,
my foot keeping time on the pedal,
it was to learn the charitable oblivion
of hand and mind as one—
a refuge such music affords the maker—
the pleasure of notes in perfectly measured time.

Lorna Dee Cervantes

Lorna Dee Cervantes credits poetry with giving her a ladder out of her "welfare class" neighborhood in a San Jose, California, barrio. Owing to poverty and racism, Cervantes says she never considered college until a group of young Chicanos calling themselves the Brown Berets came to her school one day. "One came up to me and said, 'You look pretty smart, are you thinking of college?' " This was the moment when Cervantes passionately began reading and writing.

"Cannery Town in August" is taken from Cervantes's first book of poetry, *Emplumada*. For her writing, Cervantes won a 1982 American Book Award. Her second book of poetry was published in 1991 and is titled *From the Cables of Genocide: Poems on Love and Hunger*. Today Cervantes lives in Boulder, Colorado, with her husband and son.

Cannery Town in August

All night it humps the air.
Speechless, the steam rises
from the cannery columns. I hear
the night bird rave about work
or lunch, or sing the swing shift
home. I listen, while bodyless
uniforms and spinach specked shoes
drift in monochrome down the dark
moon-possessed streets. Women
who smell of whiskey and tomatoes,
peach fuzz reddening their lips and eyes—
I imagine them not speaking, dumbed
by the can's clamor and drop
to the trucks that wait, grunting
in their headlights below.
They spotlight those who walk
like a dream, with no one
waiting in the shadows
to palm them back to living.

Gary Soto

Poet and short story writer Gary Soto worked as a young man in the fields of the San Joaquin Valley of California. "Field Poem" is from his collection of poems titled *The Elements of San Joaquin*. His short story "Mother and Daughter" also appears in this anthology.

Field Poem

When the foreman whistled
My brother and I
Shouldered our hoes,
Leaving the field.
We returned to the bus
Speaking
In broken English, in broken Spanish
The restaurant food,
The tickets to a dance
We wouldn't buy with our pay.

From the smashed bus window,
I saw the leaves of cotton plants
Like small hands
Waving good-bye.

Luis J. Rodriguez

The author of five books, including *Always Running: La Vida Loca, Gang Days in L.A.,* Luis J. Rodriguez was born on the Mexico–U.S. border and raised in the toughest and poorest sections of Watts and East Los Angeles during the 1960s and 1970s. Rodriguez once led an L.A. gang, had numerous close calls with death, and almost committed suicide.

Rodriguez's father was a janitor at a library and made his son spend a summer on the job with him, where the younger Rodriguez started improving his vocabulary and reading. Rodriguez was also influenced by an ex-convict who was a poet.

"Night Shift at St. Regis" is taken from his collection *Trochemoche*, which means "helter-skelter" in Spanish. It describes what it's like to work late and hard in the St. Regis paper mill.

Night Shift at St. Regis

I worked several months at the St. Regis
Paper Company as a "utility man."
My job was to move immense rolls of paper,
cut their steel wrappings with tools
that resembled car theft equipment (more on this
later) and attach them to the back of paper-bag
making machines, usually run by women,
with hefty guys as bag catchers on the other end.
A 24-hour operation, I started in the graveyard
shift. My fellow operatives were usually
African and Mexican, with a *güero* face here and
    there.
My *compadre* Tony also worked at St. Regis.
A Jewish-Italian who once lived in the
mostly Mexican-and-Black Aliso Village
Housing Projects in East L.A.,
Tony was sometimes more Chicano in manner
than some Chicanos I knew,
but he also had this kind of brash,
take-care-of-business, I-know-what-I'm-
talking-about "white guy" demeanor;
still he was my best friend, my *compa,*
and we tried never to let each other down.
Me and my other partners—including Paul,
the Fremont High School drop-out from South

Central L.A., and Leo, the Hopi-Laguna homeboy
who lived in the Pico Gardens Housing Projects—
were this multi-national crew
of young revolutionaries, taking on schools,
capitalists, sell-outs, boot-lickers,
and neo-nazi-white-supremacists,
(we loved the fight, good or otherwise);
Being employed at St. Regis
was how we handed ourselves over to the world.
To stay awake on those God-awful hours,
I slept during the day in the makeshift bombshelter
that my future mother-in-law had built
in her City Terrace backyard.
She believed the *communistas* were going
to drop the bomb any day—and she was ready.
Truth be told, it probably couldn't survive a minor
fireworks display, but the place was great for sleeping
since it was dark, burrowed deep, and I didn't need
to place aluminum foil on any windows.
I would arrive to work near the midnight hour,
tools in hand, and step into the din
of the gigantic machinery, punching in on
a time clock, and falling into place as the
previous shifts' utility man groggily left the mill floor.

The work required the same gestures, the same
dance every night, hauling rolled paper taller than me
into alignment behind machines that
cranked out thousands of paper bags per shift.
Sometimes, I'd get so damn beat

that my motions became like in a dream
and my eyelids descended against my will.
Once I fell asleep standing up
—and almost toppled into a machine's gearworks!
But I couldn't rest until the designated breaks.
And the dance continued
until dawn broke through the shattered
glass of the overhead windows near the corrugated
   tin roof.
One morning, as I tottered to my car in the parking
   lot,
a police car pulled up behind me.
"Hold it right there, buddy!" an officer exclaimed
while climbing out of the car.
Carajo, it had been a while since police had snuck up
on me. And although I now was a crime-free
   working stiff,
I apparently still had the "criminal" stain.
"What you got in your hands?" another officer
barked, as he merged right from his partner's left.
"These are my work tools," I replied,
too weary to get too agitated.
"Yeah, what kind of work—stealing cars?" he
   blurted out.
"No, I'm over at St. Regis; if you like, we can walk
   over
and talk to the foreman."
Great idea. It should've worked. But not before they
forced my hands over the car's hood,
had me open my car with the keys, and threatened

to take me in when I tried to further explain myself.
But I held my own, maintaining
my innocence while remaining calm, even after
the officers claimed there were many car thefts in the
     area
and that my tools were similar to those belonging
to a thief (actually car theft tools, such as a jimmy
     bar,
looked nothing like my "utility man" chisel and steel
hammer. But I supposed they were close).
Finally, when my request to check my job status sank
     in,
the officers backed off.
I also began to look more like a tired,
overworked, and quite legit young employee
who was planning to get married in a couple of
     months.
"Okay, we'll let you go for now (thanks for the
     favor),
but whoever is stealing these cars will be caught!"
(Adam 12, where are you when we need you?)

St. Regis offered no perks and little advancement
except perhaps to become a utility man on the
afternoon turn. But I gave it my all. Sometimes,
I actually liked being there; something about
the rhythms, the lateness of hour, the way the day
crowds out the night and the sun climbs up
on the sky in slow, calculated steps.
Then, just before my six-months' probation period

ended, I got called into Johnny Brown's office;
he was the plant's graveyard supervisor.
"Sit down, young man," he said, not looking up.
"I've been watching your performance
for some time now. I must say, I see much lacking
in your speed, much lacking in desire."
I had no idea what he was talking about.
"If you want to remain on this job, you'll have to
pick up the pace. You're slowing down the whole
production. You have to catch up. There's
much at stake here. We can't afford any
loss time. You want a future with St. Regis,
you have to sharpen up, get on the stick,
put your best foot forward. Understand?"
Sure, but this didn't seem to correspond
to what I was doing. For a second,
I thought maybe he had me confused, but no—
it was my personnel file in front of his face!
As I left his office, I felt devastated:
I had heaved a lot of energy into the job,
and still I didn't seem to make the grade.
Johnny Brown spoke in a tedious tone,
but it was authoritative and final.
I thought for sure I wouldn't make my probation,
that I'd probably have to call off the wedding,
because without a job, what kind of home
could I provide my bride!
I walked out that day with my stomach
in knots; I couldn't even knock out as usual.

I called Tony to tell him I wasn't going to make it at
    St. Regis.
Tony listened intently, an obese silence
on the other end of the line.
Then, in the same banal voice as Johnny Brown's,
he repeated word for word what the man had told
    me.
Hey? How did you know what he said?
"That's Johnny Brown," Tony assured.
"He says the same thing to everybody
who's near their end of probation. You're all right.
If you were really that bad, he would've fired you."
Well, I don't appreciate this at all.
"I know, it stinks," Tony continued. "But that's his
    way
of keeping the new employees under his thumb.
For people like Johnny Brown, you'll never be
good enough! He's just a hack.
He's never done the work you're doing.
Don't worry about it."
Oh.

I stayed on at St. Regis a few more months
and eventually did get hitched.
I also stopped getting pestered by police
in the parking lot.
And I got used to the graveyard shift,
when the darkness swam easily in my bones,
the vampire came out,

and the bloodlust overwhelmed me (just kidding).
On top of this, I learned to trundle the paper
as fast as anyone at the plant,
which is nothing to sniff at, let me tell you,
when one works at St. Regis.

Raymond Carver

When he died of lung cancer in 1988 at the age of fifty, short story writer, poet and essayist Raymond Carver was eulogized by the *New York Times* as the "Writer and Poet of the Working Poor." During his lifetime he published ten books of poetry and prose. Carver was born in 1938 in Clatskanie, Oregon, to Clevie Raymond Carver, a sawmill worker, and his wife Ella, a waitress. Carver came from "the hardscrabble world of the down-and-out blue-collar character in his stories," and Carver himself once said, "I'm a paid-in-full member of the working poor . . . They're my people."

This poem is a reflection on Carver's father, Clevie, a wanderer from Arkansas who went from job to job in the Pacific Northwest and "couldn't keep money" because it "burned a hole in his pocket." Carver says his father "walked, hitched rides and rode in empty boxcars when he went from Arkansas to Washington State in 1934, looking for work. I don't think he dreamed much. I believe he was simply looking for steady work at decent pay."

Through poetry, a son examines a photograph of his young father for clues to his own character and habits.

Photograph of My Father
in His Twenty-second Year

October. Here in this dank, unfamiliar kitchen
I study my father's embarrassed young man's face.
Sheepish grin, he holds in one hand a string
of spiny yellow perch, in the other
a bottle of Carlsberg beer.

In jeans and flannel shirt, he leans
against the front fender of a 1934 Ford.
He would like to pose brave and hearty for his
    posterity,
wear his old hat cocked over his ear.
All his life my father wanted to be bold.

But the eyes give him away, and the hands
that limply offer the string of dead perch
and the bottle of beer. Father, I love you,
yet how can I say thank you, I who can't hold my
    liquor either
and don't even know the places to fish.

PART FOUR

Take a Stand on High Ground

Zora Neale Hurston

Zora Neale Hurston is best known today as the author
of the novel *Their Eyes Were Watching God*, published
in 1937, and as a participant in the Harlem Renaissance. Hurston's mother died when Hurston was a
child, and her father, a carpenter and Baptist minister,
moved the family to Eatonville, Florida, when she was
three.

As a teenager, Hurston worked a string of menial
jobs and then began coursework at Howard University.
In Washington, Hurston began writing her first stories
and poems about the life she observed, and attending
a literary salon of leading black activists and writers.

Henry Louis Gates, a leading black scholar, calls
Their Eyes Were Watching God "a bold feminist novel,
the first to be so in the African American tradition."

In this excerpt, narrator Janie Crawford tells her best
friend, Pheoby, that life began at sixteen "at her grandmother's gate." Janie's story then blends with her
grandmother's, Old Nanny, as Old Nanny reaches
painfully back into her past to recount life as a slave,
the arrival of Janie's mother into the world, and what
these events mean for Janie as she steps across three
generations of poverty into womanhood.

From *Their Eyes Were Watching God*

Janie saw her life like a great tree in leaf with the things suffered, things enjoyed, things done and undone. Dawn and doom was in the branches.

"Ah know exactly what Ah got to tell yuh, but it's hard to know where to start at.

"Ah ain't never seen mah papa. And Ah didn't know 'im if Ah did. Mah mama neither. She was gone from round dere long before Ah wuz big enough tuh know. Mah grandma raised me. Mah grandma and de white folks she worked wid. She had a house out in de back-yard and dat's where Ah wuz born. They was quality white folks up dere in West Florida. Named Washburn. She had four gran'chillun on de place and all of us played together and dat's how come Ah never called mah Grandma nothin' but Nanny, 'cause dat's what everybody on de place called her. Nanny used to ketch us in our devilment and lick every youngun on de place and Mis' Washburn did de same. Ah reckon dey never hit us ah lick amiss 'cause dem three boys and us two girls wuz pretty aggravatin', Ah speck.

"Ah was wid dem white chillun so much till Ah didn't know Ah wuzn't white till Ah was round six years old. Wouldn't have found it out then, but a man come long takin' pictures and without askin' anybody, Shelby, dat was de oldest boy, he told him to take us. Round a week later de man brought de picture for Mis' Washburn to see and pay him which she did, then give us all a good lickin'.

"So when we looked at de picture and everybody got pointed out there wasn't nobody left except a real dark little girl with long hair standing by Eleanor. Dat's where Ah wuz s'posed to be, but Ah couldn't recognize dat dark chile as me. So Ah ast, 'where is me? Ah don't see me.'

"Everybody laughed, even Mr. Washburn. Miss Nellie, de Mama of de chillun who come back home after her husband dead, she pointed to de dark one and said, 'Dat's you, Alphabet, don't you know yo' ownself?'

"Dey all useter call me Alphabet 'cause so many people had done named me different names. Ah looked at de picture a long time and seen it was mah dress and mah hair so Ah said:

" 'Aw, aw! Ah'm colored!'

"Den dey all laughed real hard. But before Ah seen de picture Ah thought Ah wuz just like de rest.

"Us lived dere havin' fun till de chillun at school got to teasin' me 'bout livin' in de white folks back-yard. Dere wuz uh knotty head gal named Mayrella dat useter git mad every time she look at me. Mis' Washburn useter dress me up in all de clothes her gran'chillun didn't need no mo' which still wuz better'n what de rest uh de colored chillun had. And then she useter put hair ribbon on mah head fuh me tuh wear. Dat useter rile Mayrella uh lot. So she would pick at me all de time and put some others up tuh do de same. They'd push me 'way from de ring plays and make out they couldn't play wid nobody dat lived on premises. Den they'd tell me not to be takin' on over mah looks 'cause they mama told 'em 'bout de hound dawgs huntin' mah papa all night long. 'Bout Mr. Washburn and de sheriff puttin' de bloodhounds on de trail tuh ketch mah papa for whut he done tuh mah mama. Dey didn't tell about how he wuz seen tryin' tuh git in touch wid mah mama later on so he could marry her. Naw, dey didn't talk dat part of it atall. Dey made it sound real bad so as tuh crumple mah feathers. None of 'em didn't even remember whut his name wuz, but dey all knowed de bloodhound part by heart. Nanny didn't love tuh see me wid mah head hung down, so she figgered it would be mo' better fuh me if us had uh house. She got de land and everything and then Mis' Washburn helped out uh whole heap wid things."

Pheoby's hungry listening helped Janie to tell her story. So she went on thinking back to her young years and explaining them to her friend in soft, easy phrases while all around the house, the night time put on flesh and blackness.

She thought awhile and decided that her conscious life had commenced at Nanny's gate. On a late afternoon Nanny had called her to come inside the house because she had spied Janie letting Johnny Taylor kiss her over the gatepost.

It was a spring afternoon in West Florida. Janie had spent most of the day under a blossoming pear tree in the backyard. She had been spending every minute that she could steal from her chores under that tree for the last three days. That was to say, ever since the first tiny bloom had opened. It had called her to come and gaze on a mystery. From barren brown stems to glistening leaf-buds; from the leaf-buds to snowy virginity of bloom. It stirred her tremendously. How? Why? It was like a flute song forgotten in another existence and remembered again. What? How? Why? This singing she heard that had nothing to do with her ears. The rose of the world was breathing out smell. It followed her through all her waking moments and caressed her in her sleep. It connected itself with other vaguely felt matters that had struck her outside observation and buried themselves in her flesh. Now they emerged and quested about her consciousness.

She was stretched on her back beneath the pear tree soaking in the alto chant of the visiting bees, the gold of the sun and the panting breath of the breeze when the inaudible voice of it all came to her. She saw a dust-bearing bee sink into the sanctum of a bloom; the thousand sister-calyxes arch to meet the love embrace and the ecstatic shiver of the tree from root to tiniest branch creaming in every blossom and frothing with delight. So this was a marriage! She had been summoned to behold a revelation. Then Janie felt a pain remorseless sweet that left her limp and languid.

After a while she got up from where she was and went over the little garden field entire. She was seeking confirmation of the voice and vision, and everywhere she found and acknowledged answers. A personal answer for all other creations except herself. She felt an answer seeking her, but where? When? How? She found herself at the kitchen door and stumbled inside. In the air of the room were flies tumbling and singing, marrying and giving in marriage. When she reached the narrow hallway she was reminded that her grandmother was home with a sick headache. She was lying across the bed asleep so Janie tipped on out of the front door. Oh to be a pear tree—*any* tree in bloom! With kissing bees singing of the beginning of the world! She was sixteen. She had glossy leaves and bursting buds and she wanted to struggle with life but it seemed to elude her. Where were the singing bees for her? Nothing on the place nor in her grandma's house answered her. She searched as much of the world as she could from the top of the front steps and then went on down to the front gate and leaned over to gaze up and down the road. Looking, waiting, breathing short with impatience. Waiting for the world to be made.

Through pollinated air she saw a glorious being coming up the road. In her former blindness she had known him as shiftless Johnny Taylor, tall and lean. That was before the golden dust of pollen had beglamored his rags and her eyes.

In the last stages of Nanny's sleep, she dreamed of voices. Voices far-off but persistent, and gradually coming nearer. Janie's voice. Janie talking in whispery snatches with a male voice she couldn't quite place. That brought her wide awake. She bolted upright and peered out of the window and saw Johnny Taylor lacerating her Janie with a kiss.

"Janie!"

The old woman's voice was so lacking in command and reproof, so full of crumbling dissolution,—that Janie half believed that Nanny had not seen her. So she extended herself outside of her dream and went inside of the house. That was the end of her childhood.

Nanny's head and face looked like the standing roots of some old tree that had been torn away by storm. Foundation of ancient power that no longer mattered. The cooling palma christi leaves that Janie had bound about her grandma's head with a white rag had wilted down and become part and parcel of the woman. Her eyes didn't bore and pierce. They diffused and melted Janie, the room and the world into one comprehension.

"Janie, youse uh 'oman, now, so—"

"Naw, Nanny, naw Ah ain't no real 'oman yet."

The thought was too new and heavy for Janie. She fought it away.

Nanny closed her eyes and nodded a slow, weary affirmation many times before she gave it voice.

"Yeah, Janie, youse got yo' womanhood on yuh. So Ah mout ez well tell yuh whut Ah been savin' up for uh spell. Ah wants to see you married right away."

"Me, married? Naw, Nanny, no ma'am! Whut Ah know 'bout uh husband?"

"Whut Ah seen just now is plenty for me, honey, Ah don't want no trashy nigger, no breath-and-britches, lak Johnny Taylor usin' yo' body to wipe his foots on."

Nanny's words made Janie's kiss across the gatepost seem like a manure pile after a rain.

"Look at me, Janie. Don't set dere wid yo' head hung down. Look at yo' ole grandma!" Her voice began snagging on the prongs of her feelings. "Ah don't want to be talkin' to you like dis. Fact is Ah done been on mah knees to mah Maker many's de time askin' *please*—for Him not to make de burden too heavy for me to bear."

"Nanny, Ah just—Ah didn't mean nothin' bad."

"Dat's what makes me skeered. You don't mean no harm. You don't even know where harm is at. Ah'm ole now. Ah can't be always guidin' yo' feet from harm and danger. Ah wants to see you married right away."

"Who Ah'm goin' tuh marry off-hand lak dat? Ah don't know nobody."

"De Lawd will provide. He know Ah done bore de burden in de hear uh de day. Somebody done spoke to me 'bout you long time ago. Ah ain't said nothin' 'cause dat wasn't de way Ah placed you. Ah wanted yuh to school out and pick from a higher bush and a sweeter berry. But dat ain't yo' idea, Ah see."

"Nanny, who—who dat been askin' you for me?"

"Brother Logan Killicks. He's a good man, too."

"Naw, Nanny, no ma'am! Is dat whut he been hangin' round here for? He look like some ole skull-head in de grave yard."

The older woman sat bolt upright and put her feet to the floor, and thrust back the leaves from her face.

"So you don't want to marry off decent like, do yuh? You just wants to hug and kiss and feel around with first one man and then another, huh? You wants to make me suck de same sorrow yo' mama did, eh? Mah ole head ain't gray enough. Mah back ain't bowed enough to suit yuh!"

The vision of Logan Killicks was desecrating the pear tree, but Janie didn't know how to tell Nanny that. She merely hunched over and pouted at the floor.

"Janie."

"Yes, ma'am."

"You answer me when Ah speak. Don't you set dere poutin' wid me after all Ah done went through for you!"

She slapped the girl's face violently, and forced her head back so that their eyes met in struggle. With her hand uplifted for the second blow she saw the huge tear that welled up from

Janie's heart and stood in each eye. She saw the terrible agony and the lips tightened down to hold back the cry and desisted. Instead she brushed back the heavy hair from Janie's face and stood there suffering and loving and weeping internally for both of them.

"Come to yo' Grandma, honey. Set in her lap lak yo' use tuh. Yo' Nanny wouldn't harm a hair uh yo' head. She don't want nobody else to do it neither if she kin help it. Honey, de white man is de ruler of everything as fur as Ah been able tuh find out. Maybe it's some place way off in de ocean where de black man is in power, but we don't know nothin' but what we see. So de white man throw down de load and tell de nigger man tuh pick it up. He pick it up because he have to, but he don't tote it. He hand it to his womenfolks. De nigger woman is de mule uh de world so fur as Ah can see. Ah been prayin' fuh it tuh be different wid you. Lawd, Lawd, Lawd!"

For a long time she sat rocking with the girl held tightly to her sunken breast. Janie's long legs dangled over one arm of the chair and the long braids of her hair swung low on the other side. Nanny half sung, half sobbed a running chant-prayer over the head of the weeping girl.

"Lawd have mercy! It was a long time on de way but Ah reckon it had to come. Oh Jesus! Do Jesus! Ah done de best Ah could."

Finally, they both grew calm.

"Janie, how long you been 'lowin' Johnny Taylor to kiss you?"

"Only dis one time, Nanny. Ah don't love him at all. Whut made me do it is—oh, Ah don't know."

"Thank yuh, Massa Jesus."

"Ah ain't gointuh do it no mo', Nanny. Please don't make me marry Mr. Killicks."

" 'Tain't Logan Killicks Ah wants you to have, baby, it's protection. Ah ain't gittin' ole, honey. Ah'm *done* ole. One mornin' soon, now, de angel wid de sword is gointuh stop by here. De day and de hour is hid from me, but it won't be long. Ah ast de Lawd when you was uh infant in mah arms to let me stay here till you got grown. He done spared me to see de day. Mah daily prayer now is tuh let dese golden moments rolls on a few days longer till Ah see you safe in life."

"Lemme wait, Nanny, please, jus' a lil bit mo'."

"Don't think Ah don't feel wid you, Janie, 'cause Ah do. Ah couldn't love yuh no more if Ah had uh felt yo' birth pains mahself. Fact uh de matter, Ah loves yuh a whole heap more'n Ah do yo' mama, de one Ah did birth. But you got to take in consideration you ain't no everyday chile like most of 'em. You ain't got no papa, you might jus' as well say no mama, for de good she do yuh. You ain't got nobody but me. And mah head is ole and tilted towards de grave. Neither can you stand alone by yo'self. De thought uh you bein' kicked around from pillar tuh post is uh hurtin' thing. Every tear you drop squeezes a cup uh blood outa mah heart. Ah got tuh try and do for you befo' mah head is cold."

A sobbing sigh burst out of Janie. The old woman answered her with little soothing pats of the hand.

"You know, honey, us colored folks is branches without roots and that makes things come round in queer ways. You in particular. Ah was born back due in slavery so it wasn't for me to fulfill my dreams of whut a woman oughta be and to do. Dat's one of de hold-backs of slavery. But nothing can't stop you from wishin'. You can't beat nobody down so low till you can rob 'em of they will. Ah didn't want to be used for a work-ox and a brood-sow and Ah didn't want mah daughter used dat way neither. It sho wasn't mah will for things to happen lak they did. Ah even hated de way you was born. But, all de same Ah said thank God, Ah got another chance. Ah wanted to preach a great sermon about colored women sittin' on high, but they wasn't no pulpit for me. Freedom found me wid a baby daughter in mah arms, so Ah said Ah'd take a broom and a cook-pot and throw up a highway through de wilderness for her. She would expound what Ah feft. But somehow she got lost offa de highway and next thing Ah knowed here you was in de world. So whilst Ah was tendin' you of nights Ah said Ah'd save de text for you. Ah been waitin' a long time, Janie, but nothin' Ah been through ain't too much if you just take a stand on high ground lak Ah dreamed."

Old Nanny sat there rocking Janie like an infant and thinking back and back. Mind-pictures brought feelings, and feelings dragged out dramas from the hollows of her heart.

"Dat mornin' on de big plantation close to Savannah, a rider come in a gallop tellin' 'bout Sherman takin' Atlanta. Marse Robert's son had done been kilt at Chickamauga. So he grabbed his gun and straddled his best horse and went off wid de rest of de gray-headed men and young boys to drive de Yankees back into Tennessee.

"They was all cheerin' and cryin' and shoutin' for de men dat was ridin' off. Ah couldn't see nothin' cause yo' mama wasn't but a week old, and Ah was flat uh mah back. But pretty soon he let on he forgot somethin' and run into mah cabin and made me let down mah hair for de last time. He sorta wropped his hand in it, pulled mah big toe, lak he always done, and was gone after de rest lak lightnin'. Ah heard 'em give one last whoop for him. Then de big house and de quarters got sober and silent.

"It was de cool of de evenin' when Mistis come walkin' in mah door. She throwed de door wide open and stood dere lookin' at me outa her eyes and her face. Look lak she been livin' through uh hundred years in January without one day of spring. She come stood over me in de bed.

" 'Nanny, Ah come to see that baby uh yourn.'

"Ah tried not to feel de breeze off her face, but it got so cold in dere dat Ah was freezin' to death under the kivvers. So Ah couldn't move right away lak Ah aimed to. But Ah knowed Ah had to make haste and do it.

" 'You better git dat kivver offa dat youngun and dat quick!'
she clashed at me. "Look lak you don't know who is Mistis
on dis plantation, Madam. But Ah aims to show you.'

"By dat time I had done managed tuh unkivver mah baby
enough for her to see de head and face.

" 'Nigger, whut's yo' baby doin' wid gray eyes and yaller
hair?' She begin tuh slap mah jaws ever which a'way. Ah never
felt the fust ones 'cause Ah wuz too busy gittin' de kivver back
over mah chile. But dem last lick burnt me lak fire. Ah had
too many feelin's tuh tell which one tuh follow so Ah didn't
cry and Ah didn't do nothin' else. But then she kept on astin
me how come mah baby look white. She asted me dat maybe
twenty-five or thirty times, lak she got tuh sayin' dat and
couldn't help herself. So Ah told her, 'Ah don't know nothin'
but what Ah'm told tuh do, 'cause Ah ain't nothin' but uh
nigger and uh slave.'

"Instead of pacifyin' her lak Ah thought, look lak she got
madder. But Ah reckon she was tired and wore out 'cause she
didn't hit me no more. She went to de foot of de bed and wiped
her hands on her handksher. 'Ah wouldn't dirty mah hands
on yuh. But first thing in de mornin' de overseer will take you
to de whippin' post and tie you down on yo' knees and cut de
hide offa yo' yaller back. One hundred lashes wid a raw-hide
on yo' bare back. Ah'll have you whipped till de blood run
down to yo' heels!' Ah mean to count de licks mahself. And
if it kills you Ah'll stand de loss. Anyhow, as soon as dat brat
is a month old Ah'm going to sell it offa dis place.'

"She flounced on off and left her wintertime wid me. Ah
knowed mah body wasn't healed, but Ah couldn't consider
dat. In de black dark Ah wrapped mah baby de best Ah
knowed how and made it to de swamp by de river. Ah knowed
de place was full uh moccasins and other bitin' snakes, but Ah
was more skeered uh whut was behind me. Ah hide in dere
day and night and suckled de baby every time she start to cry,
for fear somebody might hear her and Ah'd git found. Ah ain't

sayin' uh friend or two didn't feel mah care. And den de Good
Lawd seen to it dat Ah wasn't taken. Ah don't see how come
mah milk didn't kill mah chile, wid me so skeered and worried
all de time. De noise uh de owls, skeered me; de limbs of dem
cypress trees took to crawlin' and movin' round after dark,
and two three times Ah heered panthers prowlin' round. But
nothin' never hurt me 'cause de Lawd knowed how it was.

"Den, one night Ah heard de big guns boomin' lak thunder.
It kept up all night long. And de next mornin' Ah could see
uh big ship at a distance and a great stirrin' round. So Ah
wrapped Leafy up in moss and fixed her good in a tree and
picked mah way on down to de landin'. The men was all in
blue, and Ah heard people say Sherman was comin' to meet
de boats in Savannah, and all of us slaves was free. So Ah run
got mah baby and got in quotation wid people and found a
place Ah could stay.

"But it was a long time after dat befo' de Big Surrender at
Richmond. Den de big bell ring in Atlanta and all de men in
gray uniforms had to go to Moultrie, and bury their swords
in de ground to show they was never to fight about slavery no
mo'. So den we knowed we was free.

"Ah wouldn't marry nobody, though Ah could have uh heap
uh times, 'cause Ah didn't want nobody mistreating mah baby.
So Ah got with some good white people and come down here
in West Florida to work and make de sun shine on both sides
of de street for Leafy.

"Mah Madam help me wid her just lak she been doin' wid
you. Ah put her in school when it got so it was a school to
put her in. Ah was 'spectin' to make a school teacher outa her.

"But one day she didn't come home at de usual time and
Ah waited and waited, but she never come all dat night. Ah
took a lantern and went round askin' everybody but nobody
ain't seen her. De next Mornin' she come crawlin' in on her
hands and knees. A sight to see. Dat school teacher had done

hid her in de woods all night long, and he had done raped mah baby and run on off just before day.

"She was only seventeen, and somethin' lak dat to happen! Lawd a'mussy! Look lak Ah kin see it all over gain. It was a long time before she was well, and by dat time we knowed you was on de way. And after you was born she took to drinkin' likker and stayin' out nights. Couldn't git her to stay here and nowhere else. Lawd knows where she is right now. She ain't dead, 'cause Ah'd know it by mah feelings, but sometimes Ah wish she was at rest.

"And, Janie, maybe it wasn't much, but Ah done de best Ah kin by you. Ah raked and scraped and bought dis lil piece uh land so you wouldn't have to stay in de white folks' yard and tuck yo' head befo' other chillun at school. Dat was all right when you was little. But when you got big enough to understand things, Ah wanted you to look upon yo'self. Ah don't want yo' feathers always crumpled by folks throwin' up things in yo' face. And Ah can't die easy thinkin' maybe de menfolks white or black is makin' a spit cup outa you. Have some sympathy fuh me. Put me down easy, Janie, Ah'm a cracked plate."

Dean Torres

High school student Dean Torres lives on the Lower East Side of New York, a poor community in which "most of the teens have this low self-esteem attitude." In this essay he struggles to comprehend what he has seen happen to some of his friends, and argues for better living and working conditions for the poor.

Doing What It Takes to Survive

What does it take to put food on the table, put clothes on your back, and keep a roof over your head? What would you do if you couldn't get a good job: sell drugs, go on welfare, or try to find a minimum wage job like McDonald's that pays $5 an hour?

I think a lot about how I'm going to support myself. When I finish high school, I plan to join the military.

Many of my friends don't know what they want to do in life, but we're all hoping to have a good career. We want to be somebody.

A lot of people have all these goals in life that they want to capture, but things around them intimidate them, like people they know dying or ending up dealing drugs or taking drugs and ruining their chances for success. That's what they see in their neighborhood.

—

In my community, on the Lower East Side, most of the teens have this low self-esteem attitude that they'll never get a job in the real world, because they don't want to work hard, they don't have any job experience and they don't have the college education to get a job in big business.

The majority of these kids either got kicked out or dropped out of high school.

I'm guessing they didn't want to do the hard work because they didn't know how to deal with the pressure, or they were simply too lazy to do it.

—

For some of my friends, the easiest way to earn decent money is by hustling, so that's what they do. If they don't hustle, it seems like the only option is a dead-end job.

It doesn't help that places like Burger King or McDonald's pay $5.15 an hour. The minimum wage should be at least $6 or $7 an hour.

Some of them feel they're better off on welfare, so at least they can get a little money without having to work for it.

I know a few people who are or used to be on welfare, like a woman I know named Tricia.

And a lot of my friends are selling drugs because they are too lazy to go out and find a job, like a good friend of mine, who we call Venom.

Tricia and Venom, and other people I know like them, feel like they have no other choice but to deal drugs or take them or end up on welfare.

Both of them thought they could get through by dealing drugs temporarily until they found a real job, but unfortunately, things ended up a lot worse than they expected.

—

Tricia, who used to live in the Bronx, decided to go on welfare because she thought she had no other options.

She had no job to support her kids or herself, and she was hanging out with the wrong crowd of people.

They encouraged her to take drugs, and to support her kids and her habit, she started dealing, too.

Tricia thought it would do her and her kids some good to get the little welfare money she received every month.

Tricia also was purposely getting pregnant while she was on welfare so that she could get more money from the welfare department. Now she has seven kids.

But going on welfare and having more kids only made matters worse.

Things got so bad that her kids were taken away from her

196 • Doing What It Takes to Survive

and put in foster homes. (Tricia's mother took in two of them, but she couldn't care for all seven.)

—

I'm not sure exactly how ACS found out, but I think someone informed them that her home was no place for any child to live in.

It was a rat-infested, one-bedroom apartment with no heat and broken windows. It looked like an abandoned apartment with people still living in it.

Even after Tricia's kids were taken, she was still heavy into the drugs and about to get kicked out of her apartment.

But when she realized her kids were really gone, Tricia woke up and decided that she had to get her life together. It was like someone just came and took away her pride. Tricia knew that she had to sacrifice for her children.

She found herself some help through a friend, who got her into a rehab program, and she went out looking for a job. After searching for months, she finally found a decent job, starting at $8 an hour.

—

Eventually, Tricia got custody of her kids back and moved away from the Bronx.

Now she is living in Hamilton, North Carolina, and working at an even better job.

I'm pretty proud of Tricia, but it's too bad that she had to get so low before she realized what drugs were doing to her and her kids.

Unfortunately, I see other people following in her footsteps, not realizing which path they are walking down.

My friend we call Venom (because he's supposed to be deadly) started dealing drugs about three years ago, and has already been in and out of jail. But he has no plans to stop.

—

Venom was always acting tough, although I think he just plays the street role so people will know that he doesn't take no mess.

Now he does his street pharmacy to take care of himself, his girlfriend and his one-year-old daughter.

Venom dropped out of high school when he was seventeen and went for his GED, because he said it was too much stress on his shoulders and he couldn't deal with it.

On top of that, his girlfriend, Keeshia, was pregnant, so he needed a job. V got into selling drugs because it was money in his pocket.

He still refuses to do the right thing and make money legally.

"It's hard finding a job," he claims, but I don't think he's ever tried looking for one. The problem with Venom is that he tries to find the easy way out of things all the time.

—

I don't know how he got hooked up into selling drugs, though. When he started, I wasn't feeling him and I didn't approve of it.

Dealing is too risky and he's my friend, so it's my job to tell him that it's not such a good idea.

But Venom is his own person, and he can't see another way to take care of his responsibilities. And I guess it's good that he makes sure his daughter is taken care of, and that he tries to be a father.

The mother of his daughter, Keeshia, is working to support herself and the baby, and she's not happy with what Venom is doing.

She doesn't want him buying their daughter things with drug money.

They had a big argument about that, but to Venom, dealing

is his career and his life. For him, this is the only way to survive.

He always says, "I'm doing this for my daughter." But Keeshia says, "No, you're doing this for yourself," and before you know it they're throwing words back and forth at each other.

—

From the looks of it, Venom's probably never going to change and he won't learn his lesson.

It is so easy for the kids in my neighborhood to get into selling drugs because they grow up knowing a lot of people who deal.

So when they realize that it's hard to find a job these days, especially for minorities, they feel like selling drugs is their best option, since looking for a job didn't work for a lot of people they know.

I think my friends need to take responsibility for their lives by staying in school and away from drugs. But I also think the government can do more to help poor people.

It seems like this country just doesn't care about the poor, only the rich.

The government should do a better job providing child care so mothers can go back to work, and should work harder to help the unemployed find jobs that pay enough to actually support a family.

—

Poverty is a big problem in America.

In my neighborhood, some people turn to selling drugs because they think they can't make decent money any other way.

If they take a minimum wage job, they'll have to work extremely hard at a boring job, and all they'll be making is chump change.

But whether you're selling drugs or taking them, somehow, some way, I think you're setting yourself up to be trapped, and you'll regret your choice later on, when it finally catches up to you and you land in jail or wake up one morning and realize that your life is gone.

—

The best way to prevent all of that from happening is to not get involved with drugs at all.

Stay out of trouble by finding yourself something to do— get involved with some kind of activity or stay in your house and find something to do, even if it's only talking on the phone with your boyfriend or girlfriend. At least you'll be doing something positive.

I stay out of trouble by not hanging around negative people and by not hanging in my neighborhood.

I either stay in the house, go to school, or find things to do with my girlfriend or my family, and just live my life as calmly as possible.

I realize that taking or selling drugs isn't worth it, because I've seen family and friends go through it. I take it as a lesson to me not to do it.

When I look at some of the people I know, like Tricia and Venom, it makes me sad and angry at the same time.

Sad for them and mad at the world, because people know what's going on in these poor communities and it seems like nobody helps. But when poor people do something wrong— like selling drugs or abusing welfare—everyone gets upset, even though they know our situation and make no effort to give us the help that we need the most.

—

I think our country could do a lot more to help the poor, if people tried harder. Sometimes I see the government working to improve things, though, and that makes me feel hopeful.

The Housing Authority has been trying to fix things up in my neighborhood—and it has. Before, my project used to look like a dead and deserted place with dead trees and run-down benches outside. It didn't feel like a place you'd want to come home to.

Now that it has been reconstructed, it looks like a new place, with brand-new benches and strong, healthy trees.

It didn't cost the government too much to make the people in my neighborhood feel a little better about their lives.

When I see how much nicer they've made my home, it makes me feel like, with a little effort, there can be a change for people who live in poverty—all over the ghetto.

Mildred Taylor

Mildred Taylor was born in 1943 in Jackson, Mississippi. When she was ten, Taylor's father moved her family to Toledo, Ohio, into a middle-class neighborhood. Taylor was the only black child in her class, an experience she never forgot. Then a story she wrote for a contest sponsored by the Council on Interracial Books for Children won in the African American catagory. Titled *Song of the Trees,* it was the basis for the first in a series of books Taylor would write about the Logan family and their struggle to hang on to their land in the racially divided state of Mississippi during the Depression. The second book in the series, *Roll of Thunder, Hear My Cry,* won the 1977 Newberry Award for "the most distinguished contribution to American literature for children." Two more books about the Logan family followed: *Let the Circle Be Unbroken* and *The Road to Memphis.* Taylor credits her father's stories of growing up in the South as the inspiration for her series.

In this excerpt the four Logan children: Stacey, Christopher-John, "Little Man," and the narrator, Cassie, must walk to school each day, because, as their mother tells them, "the county did not provide buses for its black students." Tired of being intentionally splattered with mud by the white bus driver hauling white children to school, the four Logan children hatch a plot to bring this humiliating ritual to an end.

From *Roll of Thunder, Hear My Cry*

By the end of October the rain had come, falling heavily upon the six-inch layer of dust which had had its own way for more than two months. At first the rain had merely splotched the dust, which seemed to be rejoicing in its own resiliency and laughing at the heavy drops thudding against it; but eventually the dust was forced to surrender to the mastery of the rain and it churned into a fine red mud that oozed between our toes and slopped against our ankles as we marched miserably to and from school.

To shield us from the rain, Mama issued us dried calfskins which we flung over our heads and shoulders like stiff cloaks. We were not very fond of the skins, for once they were wet they emitted a musty odor which seeped into our clothing and clung to our skins. We preferred to do without them; unfortunately, Mama cared very little about what we preferred.

Since we usually left for school after Mama, we solved this problem by dutifully cloaking ourselves with the skins before leaving home. As soon as we were beyond Big Ma's eagle eyes, we threw off the cloaks and depended upon the overhanging limbs of the forest trees to keep us dry. Once at school, we donned the cloaks again and marched into our respective classrooms properly attired.

If we had been faced only with the prospect of the rain soaking through our clothing each morning and evening, we could have more easily endured the journey between home and school. But as it was, we also had to worry about the Jefferson Davis school bus zooming from behind and splashing us with the murky waters of the road. Knowing that the bus driver liked to entertain his passengers by sending us slipping along the road to the almost inaccessible forest banks washed to a smooth baldness by the constant rains, we continuously looked over our shoulders when we were between the two crossroads so that we could reach the bank before the bus was upon us. But sometimes the rain pounded so heavily that it was all we could do to stay upright, and we did not look back as often nor listen as carefully as we should; we consequently found ourselves comical objects to cruel eyes that gave no thought to our misery.

No one was more angered by this humiliation than Little Man. Although he had asked Mama after the first day of school why Jefferson Davis had two buses and Great Faith had none, he had never been totally satisfied by her answer. She had explained to him, as she had explained to Christopher-John the year before and to me two years before that, that the county did not provide buses for its black students. In fact, she said, the county provided very little and much of the money which supported the black schools came from the black churches. Great Faith Church just could not afford a bus, so therefore we had to walk.

This information cut deeply into Little Man's brain, and each day when he found his clean clothes splashed red by the school bus, he became more and more embittered until finally one day he stomped angrily into the kitchen and exploded, "They done it again, Big Ma! Just look at my clothes!"

Big Ma clucked her tongue as she surveyed us. "Well, go on and get out of 'em, honey, and wash 'em out. All of y'all, get out of them clothes and dry yo'selves," she said, turning back to the huge iron-bellied stove to stir her stew.

"But, Big Ma, it ain't fair!" wailed Little Man. "It just ain't fair."

Stacey and Christopher-John left to change into their work clothes, but Little Man sat on the side bench looking totally dejected as he gazed at his pale-blue pants crusted with mud from the knees down. Although each night Big Ma prepared a pot of hot soapy water for him to wash out his clothing, each day he arrived home looking as if his pants had not been washed in more than a month.

Big Ma was not one for coddling any of us, but now she turned from the stove and, wiping her hands on her long white apron, sat down on the bench and put her arm around Little Man. "Now, look here, baby, it ain't the end of the world. Lord, child, don't you know one day the sun'll shine again and you won't get muddy no more?"

"But, Big Ma," Little Man protested, "ifn that ole bus driver would slow down, I wouldn't get muddy!" Then he frowned deeply and added, "Or ifn we had a bus like theirs."

"Well, he don't and you don't," Big Ma said, getting up. "So ain't no use frettin' 'bout it. One day you'll have a plenty of clothes and maybe even a car of yo' own to ride 'round in, so don't you pay no mind to them ignorant white folks. You jus' keep on studyin' and get yo'self a good education and you'll be all right. Now, go on and wash out yo' clothes and hang 'em by the fire so's I can iron 'em 'fore I go to bed."

Turning, she spied me. "Cassie, what you want, girl? Go change into yo' pants and hurry on back here so's you can help me get this supper on the table time yo' mama get home."

That night when I was snug in the deep feathery bed beside Big Ma, the tat-tat of the rain against the tin roof changed to a deafening roar that sounded as if thousands of giant rocks were being hurled against the earth. By morning the heavy rain had become a drizzle, but the earth was badly sodden from the night's downpour. High rivers of muddy water flowed in the deep gullies, and wide lakes shimmered on the roads.

As we set out for school the whiteness of the sun attempted to penetrate the storm clouds, but by the time we had turned north toward the second crossing it had given up, slinking meekly behind the blackening clouds. Soon the thunder rolled across the sky, and the rain fell like hail upon our bent heads.

"Ah, shoot! I sure am gettin' tired of this mess," complained T. J.

But no one else said a word. We were listening for the bus. Although we had left home earlier than usual to cover the northern road before the bus came, we were not overly confident that we would miss it, for we had tried this strategy before. Sometimes it worked; most times it didn't. It was as if the bus were a living thing, plaguing and defeating us at every turn. We could not outwit it.

We plodded along feeling the cold mud against our feet, walking faster and faster to reach the crossroads. Then Christopher-John stopped. "Hey, y'all, I think I hear it," he warned.

We looked around, but saw nothing.

"Ain't nothin' yet," I said.

We walked on.

"Wait a minute," said Christopher-John, stopping a second time. "There it is again."

We turned but still there was nothing.

"Why don't you clean out your ears?" T. J. exclaimed.

"Wait," said Stacey, "I think I hear it too."

We hastened up the road to where the gully was narrower and we could easily swing up the bank into the forest.

Soon the purr of a motor came closer and Mr. Granger's sleek silver Packard eased into view. It was a grand car with chrome shining even in the rain, and the only one like it in the county, so it was said.

We groaned. "Jus' ole Harlan," said T. J. flippantly as the expensive car rounded a curve and disappeared, then he and Claude started down the bank.

Stacey stopped them. "Long as we're already up here, why don't we wait awhile," he suggested. "The bus oughta be here soon and it'll be harder to get up on the bank further down the road."

"Ah, man, that bus ain't comin' for a while yet," said T. J. "We left early this mornin', remember?"

Stacey looked to the south, thinking. Little Man, Christopher-John and I waited for his decision.

"Come on, man," T. J. persuaded. "Why stay up here waitin' for that devilish bus when we could be at school outa this mess?"

"Well . . ."

T. J. and Claude jumped from the bank. Then Stacey, frowning as if he were doing this against his better judgment, jumped down too. Little Man, Christopher-John, and I followed.

Five minutes later we were skidding like frightened puppies toward the bank again as the bus accelerated and barreled down the narrow rain-soaked road; but there was no place to which we could run, for Stacey had been right. Here the gullies were too wide, filled almost to overflowing, and there were no briars or bushes by which we could swing up onto the bank.

Finally, when the bus was less than fifty feet behind us, it veered dangerously close to the right edge of the road where we were running, forcing us to attempt the jump to the bank; but all of us fell short and landed in the slime of the gully.

Little Man, chest-deep in water, scooped up a handful of mud and in an uncontrollable rage scrambled up to the road and ran after the retreating bus. As moronic rolls of laughter and cries of "Nigger! Nigger! Mud eater!" wafted from the open windows, Little Man threw his mudball, missing the wheels by several feet. Then, totally dismayed by what had happened, he buried his face in his hands and cried.

T. J climbed from the gully grinning at Little Man, but Stacey, his face burning red beneath his dark skin, glared so fiercely at T. J. that he fell back. "Just one word outa you, T. J.," he said tightly. "Just one word."

Christopher-John and I looked at each other. We had never seen Stacey look like this, and neither had T. J.

"Hey, man, I ain't said nothin'! I'm jus' as burnt as you are."

Stacey glowered at T. J. a moment longer, then walked swiftly to Little Man and put his long arm around his shoulders, saying softly, "Come on, Man. It ain't gonna happen no more, least not for a long while. I promise you that."

Again, Christopher-John and I looked questioningly at each other, wondering how Stacey could make such a rash promise. Then, shrugging, we hurried after him.

When Jeremy Simms spied us from his high perch on the forest path, he ran hastily down and joined us.

"Hey," he said, his face lighting into a friendly grin. But no one spoke to him.

The smile faded and, noticing our mud-covered clothing, he asked, "Hey, St-Stacey, wh-what happened?"

Stacey turned, stared into his blue eyes and said coldly, "Why don't you leave us alone? How come you always hanging 'round us anyway?"

Jeremy grew even more pale. "C-cause I just likes y'all," he stammered. Then he whispered, "W-was it the bus again?"

No one answered him and he said no more. When we reached the crossroads, he looked hopefully at us as if we might relent and say good-bye. But we did not relent and as I glanced back at him standing alone in the middle of the crossing, he looked as if the world itself was slung around his neck. It was only then that I realized that Jeremy never rode the bus, no matter how bad the weather.

As we crossed the school lawn, Stacey beckoned Christopher-John, Little Man, and me aside. "Look," he whispered, "meet me at the toolshed right at noon."

"Why?" we asked.

He eyed us conspiratorily. "I'll show y'all how we're gonna stop that bus from splashing us."

"How?" asked Little Man, eager for revenge.

"Don't have time to explain now. Just meet me. And be on time. It's gonna take us all lunch hour."

"Y-you mean we ain't gonna eat no lunch!" Christopher-John cried in dismay.

"You can miss lunch for one day," said Stacey, moving away. But Christopher-John looked sourly after him as if he greatly questioned the wisdom of a plan so drastic that it could exclude lunch.

"You gonna tell T. J. and Claude?" I asked.

Stacey shook his head. "T. J.'s my best friend, but he's got no stomach for this kinda thing. He talks too much, and we couldn't include Claude without T. J."

"Good," said Little Man.

At noon, we met as planned and ducked into the unlocked toolshed where all the church and school garden tools were kept. Stacey studied the tools available while the rest of us watched. Then, grabbing the only shovels, he handed one to me, holding on to the other himself, and directed Little Man and Christopher-John to each take two buckets.

Stealthily emerging from the toolshed into the drizzle, we eased along the forest edge behind the class buildings to avoid being seen. Once on the road, Stacey began to run. "Come on, hurry," he ordered. "We ain't got much time."

"Where we going?" asked Christopher-John, still not quite adjusted to the prospect of missing lunch.

"Up to where that bus forced us off the road. Be careful now," he said to Christopher-John, already puffing to keep up.

When we reached the place where we had fallen into the gully, Stacey halted. "All right," he said, "start digging." Without another word, he put his bare foot upon the top edge of the shovel and sank it deep into the soft road. "Come on, come on," he ordered, glancing up at Christopher-John, Little Man and me, who were wondering whether he had finally gone mad.

"Cassie, you start digging over there on that side of the road right across from me. That's right, don't get too near the edge. It's gotta look like it's been washed out. Christopher-John, you and Little Man start scooping out mud from the middle of the road. Quick now," he said, still digging as we began to carry out his commands. "We only got 'bout thirty minutes so's we can get back to school on time."

We asked no more questions. While Stacey and I shoveled ragged holes almost a yard wide and a foot deep toward each other, dumping the excess mud into the water-filled gullies, Little Man and Christopher-John scooped bucketfuls of the red earth from the road's center. And for once in his life, Little Man was happily oblivious to the mud spattering upon him.

When Stacey's and my holes merged into one big hole with Little Man's and Christopher-John's, Stacey and I threw down our shovels and grabbed the extra buckets. Then the four of us ran back and forth to the gullies, hastily filling the buckets with the murky water and dumping it into the hole.

Now understanding Stacey's plan, we worked wordlessly until the water lay at the same level as the road. Then Stacey waded into the gully water and pulled himself up onto the forest bank. Finding three rocks, he stacked them to identify the spot.

"It might look different this afternoon," he explained, jumping down again.

Christopher-John looked up at the sky. "Looks like it's gonna rain real hard some more."

"Let's hope so," said Stacey. "The more rain, the better. That'll make it seem more likely that the road could've been washed away like that. It'll also keep cars and wagons away." He looked around, surveying the road. "And let's hope don't nothin' come along 'fore that bus. Let's go."

Quickly we gathered our buckets and shovels and hurried back to school. After returning the tools to the toolshed, we stopped at the well to wash the mud from our arms and feet, then rushed into our classes, hoping that the mud caked on our clothes would go unnoticed. As I slipped into my seat Miss Crocker looked at me oddly and shook her head, but when she did the same thing as Mary Lou and Alma sat down, I decided that my mud was no more noticeable than anyone else's.

Soon after I had settled down to the boredom of Miss Crocker, the rain began to pound down again, hammering with great intensity upon the tin roof. After school it was still raining as the boys and I, avoiding T. J. and Claude, rushed along the slippery road recklessly bypassing more cautious students.

"You think we'll get there in time to see, Stacey?" I asked.

"We should. They stay in school fifteen minutes longer than we do and it always takes them a few minutes to load up."

When we reached the crossing, we glanced toward Jefferson Davis. The buses were there but the students had not been dismissed. We hastened on.

Expecting to see the yard-wide ditch we had dug at noon, we were not prepared for the twelve-foot lake which glimmered up at us.

"Holy smokes! What happened?" I exclaimed.

"The rain," said Stacey. "Quick, up on the bank." Eagerly, we settled onto the muddy forest floor and waited.

"Hey, Stacey," I said, "won't that big a puddle make that ole driver cautious?"

Stacey frowned, then said uncertainly, "I don't know. Hope not. There's big puddles down the road that ain't deep, just water heavy."

"If I was to be walking out there when the bus comes, that ole bus driver would be sure to speed up so's he could splash me," I suggested.

"Or maybe me," Little Man volunteered, ready to do anything for his revenge.

Stacey thought a moment, but decided against it. "Naw. It's

better none of us be on the road when it happens. It might give 'em ideas."

"Stacey, what if they find out we done it?" asked Christopher-John nervously.

"Don't worry, they won't," assured Stacey.

"Hey, I think it's coming," whispered Little Man.

We flattened ourselves completely and peered through the low bushes.

The bus rattled up the road, though not as quickly as we had hoped. It rolled cautiously through a wide puddle some twenty feet ahead; then, seeming to grow bolder as it approached our man-made lake, it speeded up, spraying the water in high sheets of backward waterfalls into the forest. We could hear the students squealing with delight. But instead of the graceful glide through the puddle that its occupants were expecting, the bus emitted a tremendous crack and careened drunkenly into our trap. For a moment it swayed and we held our breath, afraid that it would topple over. Then it sputtered a last murmuring protest and died, its left wheel in our ditch, its right wheel in the gully, like a lopsided billy goat on its knees.

We covered our mouths and shook with silent laughter.

As the dismayed driver opened the rear emergency exit, the rain poured down upon him in sharp-needled darts. He stood in the doorway looking down with disbelief at his sunken charge; then, holding on to the bus, he poked one foot into the water until it was on solid ground before gingerly stepping down. He looked under the bus. He looked at the steaming hood. He looked at the water. Then he scratched his head and cursed.

"How bad is it, Mr. Grimes?" a large, freckle-faced boy asked, pushing up one of the cracked windows and sticking out his head. "Can we push it out and fix it?"

"Push it out? Fix it?" the bus driver echoed angrily. "I got me a broken axle here an' a water-logged engine no doubt and no tellin' what-all else and you talkin' 'bout fixin' it! Y'all come on, get outa there! Y'all gonna have to walk home."

"Mister Grimes," a girl ventured, stepping hesitantly from the rear of the bus, "you gonna be able to pick us up in the mornin'?"

The bus driver stared at her in total disbelief. "Girl, all y'all gonna be walkin' for at least two weeks by the time we get this thing hauled outa here and up to Strawberry to get fixed. Now y'all get on home." He kicked a back tire, and added, "And get y'all's daddies to come on up here and give me a hand with this thing."

The students turned dismally from the bus. They didn't know how wide the hole actually was. Some of them took a wild guess and tried to jump it; but most of them miscalculated and fell in, to our everlasting delight. Others attempted to hop over the gullies to the forest to bypass the hole; however, we knew from much experience that they would not make it.

By the time most of the students managed to get to the other side of the ditch, their clothes were dripping with the weight of the muddy water. No longer laughing, they moved spirit-lessly toward their homes while a disgruntled Mr. Grimes leaned moodily against the raised rear end of the bus.

Oh, how sweet was well-maneuvered revenge!

With that thought in mind, we quietly eased away and picked our way through the dense forest toward home.

—

At supper Mama told Big Ma of the Jefferson Davis bus being stuck in the ditch. "It's funny, you know, such a wide ditch in one day. I didn't even notice the beginning of it this morn-ing—did you, children?"

"No'm," we chorused.

"You didn't fall in, did you?"

"We jumped onto the bank when we thought the bus would be coming," said Stacey truthfully.

"Well, good for you," approved Mama. "If that bus hadn't been there when I came along, I'd probably have fallen in myself."

The boys and I looked at each other. We hadn't thought about that.

"How'd you get across, Mama?" Stacey asked.

"Somebody decided to put a board across the washout."

"They gonna haul that bus outa there tonight?" Big Ma inquired.

"No, ma'am," said Mama. "I heard Mr. Granger telling Ted Grimes—the bus driver—that they won't be able to get it out until after the rain stops and it dries up a bit. It's just too muddy now."

We put our hands to our mouths to hide happy grins. I even made a secret wish that it would rain until Christmas.

Mama smiled. "You know I'm glad no one was hurt—could've been too with such a deep ditch—but I'm also rather glad it happened."

"Mary!" Big Ma exclaimed.

"Well, I am," Mama said defiantly, smiling smugly to herself and looking very much like a young girl. "I really am."

Big Ma began to grin. "You know somethin'? I am too."

Then all of us began to laugh and were deliciously happy.

Sylvia Watanabe

Sylvia Watanabe was born in Hawaii on the island of Maui. She writes about post–World War II life for Japanese Americans on Maui as its sugar plantations are dying and splashy resorts begin moving into its modest villages. "Talking to the Dead," the title story of the anthology from which "The Ghost of Fred Astaire" is taken, won the O. Henry Award for best American short story. Watanabe now makes her home in Michigan. "I first began writing," she has said, "because I wanted to record a way of life which I loved and which seemed in danger of dying away . . . I wanted to save my parents' and grandparents' stories . . ."

In "The Ghost of Fred Astaire," a female Japanese American Fred Astaire impersonator returns to her village and relatives, trying to create Hollywood glamour in a seedy village dance studio.

The Ghost of Fred Astaire

After Great Uncle Kazuhiro Sato died, his daughter Minerva returned to the village to claim her inheritance—a run-down two-story rooming house called the Bachelor Palms. Grandmother says that the place started going to seed when the Paradise Mortuary opened next door and it became rumored that the spirits of the newly departed were taking up residence in Great Uncle's establishment. Up until then, he and his wife, Grandmother's younger sister Miho, had run a prosperous business providing for the single, mostly Filipino men who worked on the nearby sugar plantation. For thirty-five years, until she expired in the midst of preparing a Thanksgiving dinner, Aunt Miho cooked over a hundred meals a day. "Someday all this will be yours," Great Uncle promised Cousin Minerva. But the summer she turned eighteen, Minerva ran away from all that cooking to pursue a tap dancing career in Hollywood.

"It was like stabbing the old man through the heart," Grandmother says with her usual knack for understatement. And that wasn't the worst of it. The whole time Great Uncle was threatening to disown their daughter, Aunt Miho was supplying her with funds enclosed in notes that said, "Be a success. If you come back, I'll never forgive you." When Minerva finally realized that Hollywood didn't offer much of a market for female Japanese American impersonators of Fred Astaire, Aunt Miho wrote her, "Don't give up. This is a free country. You can be anything you want."

Cousin Minerva was inspired by her mother's advice. She moved to San Francisco and changed her name to Mi Ho Min. She learned Chinese. She auditioned for Sinbad Ah Soon's All-Girl Revue at the Seven Happiness Nightclub in Chinatown.

After she was hired on, she sent home photos of herself with the other girls in the show. "Here I am with Ginger Rogers Wong," the captions on back of the pictures said. "This is me with the Mae West of the East." She mailed her mother an airplane ticket to come see her perform, but Great Uncle wouldn't hear of it. Then, a few years later when Aunt Miho died, Min did not return for the funeral. For a long time, the rest of the family lost track of her—though for a while following Pearl Harbor, a rumor circulated through the village that she had escaped being interned and was enjoying a prosperous nightclub career under her newly acquired identity.

"It was just a rumor," Mother reminds us whenever Grandmother tells this story.

But Grandmother says that no form of underhandedness is beyond someone without a sense of Filial Obligation.

"Aunt Miho didn't see it that way," Mother objects.

"Your Aunt Miho was a foolish woman," Grandmother replies.

Personally, I don't much care about the family politics. I am more interested in getting the facts straight. For instance, where did Cousin Min learn to tap dance? And just how good was her Chinese?

Whenever I bring up these questions, Mother says, "The only fact you need to remember is that Minerva is a member of this family."

—

After Great Uncle died without a will, it was Mother who hired the detective agency which traced Cousin Min to the retirement home in Santa Monica. She spoke to Min on the phone a couple of times but couldn't persuade her to return, and Grandmother began talking about selling the Palms to one of the Canadian or Japanese real estate companies which were scouting out property around the village. "Let *them* worry about the ghosts," she said. Then, one evening, as we were sitting down to dinner, an airport taxi stopped in front of the house.

Our father pushed through the screen door and stepped out onto the porch—the rest of us not far behind. "You looking for someone?" he asked.

The cab door opened, and a slim figure in a white linen suit and straw Panama got out.

"Wow," my sister Ruby whispered.

"Don't stare," I whispered back, staring. I felt uneasy, as if I were looking at something I couldn't name.

"Well," Grandmother said. "Minerva Sato."

I noticed that Pearlie Woo had also come out across the road and was gesturing at her husband inside their house. Pearlie's neighbor Haru Hanabusa looked up from watering her ginger bushes and did not look away. From all over the neighborhood, I could feel people's eyes on us.

"Cousin Min, so good to see you," Mother called. She pushed our father forward. "Need help with your luggage?"

Min said, "I wouldn't mind a hand, though that one case is all I brought." Father went around to the back of the cab where the driver was struggling to unload an enormous steamer trunk. Between the two of them, they managed to get it out of the car and grunt it up the walk onto the porch. "I can take it from here," Father said, staggering into the house.

Cousin Min paid the driver. Then she turned toward us and took off her hat. Her hair was white and cut as short as a man's. Her skin was the color of parchment. She went to Mother and they put their arms around each other like old friends—the one so tall and pale, the other short and dark. For an instant, I didn't know why, I wanted to run down there and pull them apart.

If I believed in intuition, I might say I had it then, though Ruby blames my aversion to Cousin Min on a disinclination to anything new. Of course, that's not the way she puts it; she calls me a stick-in-the-mud. Maybe that's true, if it means that

I want things to be orderly, that I like them to add up. But as I've said before, there are too many things about Cousin Min that do not.

Then, there were the small inconveniences. Father threw his back out trying to haul her trunk up the stairs and ended up missing work for nearly a week, which he spent yelling orders at me from the living room couch. Mother began serving breakfast for dinner because Cousin Min claimed that years of working nights in show business had permanently altered her gastronomical clock. And for her entire stay with us, Ruby and I had to camp out on Grandmother's floor—a situation which Grandmother did not take to graciously. She complained that we snored, passed wind, exuded heat. In the middle of the night, she'd prod me awake to open the window. "How can anyone sleep with you two breathing up all the air?" she'd say. Only Ruby, who was just eight and didn't know enough not to, seemed to be having a good time.

Meanwhile, Cousin Min's trunk remained where Father had abandoned it at the bottom of the staircase in the hall. For days it sat there, a repository of mysteries, blocking the way to the second floor. Whenever I passed, I could not help touching the gold locks or running a hand along its gleaming black surface, and several times, I caught Ruby sitting on the stairs, gazing down at it.

Then, one afternoon, Min accompanied Mother and Grandmother to a Ladies Auxiliary meeting in town. Father was still at work, and Ruby and I had the house to ourselves.

"Come on, Myra," she called from the living room, where she was waiting to help me fold newspapers. In those days, I still had a delivery route, and a lot of the girls at my high school teased me for that. They also poked fun at the errand and odd job business I was trying to get started and began calling me Odd Job after the character in the James Bond movie. I just told them he was even scarier in the book.

Back in elementary school, I skipped a few grades, so all

those girls are older than me; some even have boyfriends with driver's licenses. But I want to go places where a boyfriend with a driver's license can't take me. I'm aiming for the Ivy League. I want to major in business and, someday, own my own company. When I leave here, no one's going to tell stories about me like I've heard all my life about Cousin Min.

"So, how do we know that this person who claims to be Min is really who she says she is?" I asked Ruby as we sat folding newspapers. I was trying to spook her.

"Because Grandmother said," Ruby answered. "And so did Mother. You heard them."

I said, "Then, how do we know that they were right? It's not as if anyone asked for an I.D. check."

"Well, because," Ruby said.

I went to the bookshelf and pulled out the family photo album. After flipping through the pages, I took the album over to her and pointed out a snapshot of the young Minerva in front of the Bachelor Palms. "Doesn't look a bit like you-know-who," I said.

"But it *is* her." Ruby sounded confident. "I've seen proof."

She was not making any sense, and it was beginning to irritate me. I asked, "What proof?"

She said, "Other pictures. Things. Things in her trunk." Her eyes widened, and she covered her mouth with her hand.

I put down the album and moved slowly toward her. "And how did you get your hands on those? What do you suppose *she* would do if she knew you were snooping?"

"I didn't snoop," Ruby protested. "Cousin Min showed me."

I grabbed for her, but she sidestepped and yelled, "Fold your own dumb newspapers." Then she dashed for the door, but this time I got her.

She began to squeal. I clapped my hand over her mouth, and we scuffled out into the hall. "I want you to show me," I said. "Show me those *things*."

Now we are kneeling before Cousin Min's trunk, and I order her to open it.

She reaches for the heavy brass locks. Snap! Snap! The sound echoes through the quiet house, and the smell of cedar wafts toward us.

"Look," Ruby says, showing me a narrow black cylinder that fits into the palm of her hand. She pulls at one end and the cylinder telescopes into a gold-tipped walking stick. Next, she holds up a black fabric disk, about the size of a dinner plate, and waves it to one side; it opens into an elegant silk top hat. She flourishes the hat and raps the walking stick smartly against the wooden floor. We both laugh.

There is the sound of clapping behind us, and Cousin Min comes down the stairs. "Just the thought of going to one of those hen parties gives me a headache," she says taking the hat and walking stick. "I used these in a production of 'Puttin' on the Ritz.' " Then she is on her knees beside me, unzipping a garment bag, and a cloud of feathers drifts out into the hall. As she drapes me with a white silk dress covered with ostrich plumes, she says, "Ginger wore this when we danced 'Cheek to Cheek.' "

I think, Who is she kidding?, but I feel giddy. I glance over at Ruby, who is already lost.

"You still aren't sure about me, are you, Myra?" Cousin Min says, then unrolls a poster with a huge, color photograph on the front. It is unmistakably her, and she is dressed in black tie and tails. The words MI HO MIN NIGHTLY are printed in large red letters above her head.

She says, "In those days, I could do all of Fred's moves and, some said, better. He was a class act, but so was I. Everyone knew he shied away from flash, so I made sure I never did." She takes photo after photo from the trunk and lays them down in front of us. "Somersaults, backflips, handstands, the buck and wing. I did 'em all. Drove audiences crazy. Then in '52—or was it '54?—he came out with the ceiling dance in

Royal Wedding. After that, all people wanted was camera tricks." Her voice has turned bitter.

"Tell us about the magic shoes," Ruby says.

Min looks up.

My sister reaches into the trunk and lifts out a pair of black and gold wingtips.

Min takes them, then says, "Sinbad had these custom-made at his uncle's factory in Hong Kong. He told me that as long as I wore them, I could give Astaire a run for his money." She turns the pair over and points to a row of Chinese characters inscribed on each instep. "They say, 'Good Fortune Dance.' Those words were branded on every shoe." She sits quietly, staring off for a while, then removes one of her house slippers and takes off her sock. "But here is something even Sinbad never knew about." Her voice is a whisper, drawing us close. On the sole of her foot, the words "Good Fortune Dance" have been tattooed in blue.

—

The next day was Saturday, and I'd spent the morning organizing my new errand service, which I'd decided to call Odd Jobs by Odd Job. I'd lined up customers and arranged to take on a partner, a friend I'd started out with at elementary school, named Winston Lee. From the beginning, our partnership has worked like this: I bring in the business, and he gets it done. Since the whole thing was my idea in the first place, I take 60 percent of the profits, and he keeps the rest, plus tips. I was considering whether I could afford to quit my newspaper route when I walked into the kitchen and found Ruby eating tuna sandwiches with Cousin Min. It was the first time I'd ever seen Min up and about before afternoon.

"We made one for you," Ruby said. "But hurry up and finish it because we've got to catch the bus."

"I'm taking you to the movies," Min added. "They're showing *That's Entertainment* over at the Pagoda Theater."

She had caught me off guard. Since that business with the tattoos, I was not exactly eager to spend another afternoon with her.

"It's the middle of the day," Grandmother said, coming into the kitchen. She and Mother had just returned from doing the food shopping. "Whoever heard of going to the movies in the middle of the day?"

"Besides, I'm kind of busy," I said.

"But you've got to see this movie," Min said. "It includes all of Fred Astaire's most famous numbers. I'll treat."

Mother looked up from putting food away in the refrigerator. "Go on, Myra. You can't be too busy to turn down an offer like that." She went to her purse and handed me a dollar. "Here, the popcorn's on me."

Grandmother frowned. She was counting on me to resist, but the crisp new bill in my hand had weakened my resolve. "Really, Myra." She sounded disgusted. I hesitated, but Ruby was already running off to fetch her pocketbook and put on her shoes.

It takes an hour and a half by bus to get to the Pagoda Theater, which is in the resort across the bay. During the ride over, Cousin Min didn't say much—not that she was a great conversationalist, but you could almost feel the gloom thickening around her. Ruby, on the other hand, would not shut up. Between choruses of "A Hundred Bottles of Beer in the Wall," she gave me a minute-by-minute account of every "Leave It to Beaver" rerun she'd ever seen.

There was a line at the box office when we arrived. It was hot, and red dust blew off the road and stuck to our sweaty skins. The starch in Min's suit had wilted. There were stares and whispered remarks as we purchased our tickets, then pushed our way through the crowd in the lobby. I was ready to sit in the first row we came to, but Min insisted on getting closer to the screen, and I could feel people staring again as we made our way down to the front. After we'd settled into our seats, the worst part was over, and by the time the lights had dimmed, I was almost feeling my old self again. During the previews, Min bought the popcorn.

But once the movie got started, it was all I could do to keep my eyes open. First, there was some guy playing a ukulele to a bunch of chorus girls doing the Charleston Hula. Then, Jimmy Durante singing that song he always sings. Then, a lady tap dancing on a row of giant birthday cakes.

I must have dozed off because the next thing I knew, Ruby is nudging me awake, and Astaire is dancing up the walls and across the ceiling of some hotel room, singing, "You're all the world to me."

"Leave me alone," I snap, but she persists.

"Hey, Myra, *wake up*." I look where she is pointing, at the stage in front of the movie screen, and there is Cousin Min leaping, and whirling, and tapping up a storm, with the gold tips of her shoes glittering and the picture flickering all around her. I close my eyes, and when I open them again, she is still up there. "We've got to make her stop," I say. But Ruby looks as if she is under some kind of spell, just like when we were going through Min's trunk the afternoon before.

The teenage boys behind us begin whistling and yelling. Others join them. Some people throw things. Finally, the manager comes down and escorts us from the auditorium. He hands Ruby and me a couple of Three Musketeers bars from the concession stand on our way out. I almost throw mine into a trash can in front of the theater, but then I slip it into my pocket instead. Ruby opens hers right away. "Piggy," I say, reaching toward her, but she skips right past and falls into step beside Cousin Min. Then I notice that Min is humming. Her shoes make a clicking sound against the concrete sidewalk and the gold on them flashes as we head for the bus.

—

After that day, Ruby went tap dancing crazy. You could hear her upstairs in our bedroom, stomping away for hours while Cousin Min yelled instructions over the phonograph and the dishes rattled in the kitchen cupboards. Grandmother began spending most of her time visiting around the neighborhood. Then, one afternoon when I came home from school, the house was quiet. For a minute I thought Ruby had finally come to her senses and things had returned to normal, till I went into the kitchen where she and Min were talking to Mother.

"Guess what!" Ruby cried. Her face had the flushed look it always has when she is getting ready to spill the beans.

"Now, Ruby," Mother said. "This is Minerva's news; don't you think you should let her tell it?"

I didn't like the sound of that.

Mother opened a cardboard bakery box on the table and offered me a slice of chocolate cake.

"What news?" I asked, accepting a large corner piece.

Min smiled. "These last few weeks working with Ruby have made me realize how much I miss my old dancing days."

I began feeling hopeful and said, "You're not leaving, are you?"

"No, silly." Ruby could no longer contain herself. "She's going to open up her very own tap dancing school and stay here forever and ever."

"A what?" I said. "Where?"

"A tap dancing school," Min said. "At my daddy's old rooming house. Ruby and I checked it out this afternoon, and with a bit of renovation, the downstairs parlor would be perfect. There are even a couple of tenants still living there—Domingo Somebody and his wife Rafaela. Domingo is willing to lend a hand."

"But that's not the best part," Ruby said.

"Here, darling." Mother handed her a glass. "Go and get your sister some water."

Min continued. "In a couple of weeks, when we get the studio going, I'll move over to the rooming house, and Ruby can do all her practicing over there."

"Isn't that great, Myra?" Ruby said.

Grandmother pushed through the screen door and came into the kitchen; she was home early. "What's great?" she asked.

"Cousin Min is starting her own dancing school," I said, relishing the prospect of getting my own room back, not to mention the peace and quiet.

"That's great all right," Grandmother said, pulling up a chair. "Just what the world needs. What's for dinner?"

"Come on, Grams," I said. "Why do you always have to be so negative?"

"I'm glad you feel that way," Mother said. "Because I've signed you up for lessons."

"Did you hear that, Myra?" Ruby cried.

I glared at her, then turned to our mother. "Well, I'm not going."

"What do you mean?" Ruby said.

I said, "I am not going to any *stupid* tap dancing lessons, that's what I mean."

"That sounds pretty negative to me," Grandmother said.

Cousin Min got up and left the room. Ruby began to whimper.

"See what you've done?" Mother snatched away my plate and stacked it with the rest of the dirty dishes. "I'm just asking for a little cooperation. Is that too much? All your life, I've done my best—"

My sister's crying grew louder.

"—cooking, cleaning . . ." Mother went on, clattering silverware.

"All right, I'll do it," I said. "Now, Ruby, shut up and don't go blabbing this to anyone."

She wiped her nose with the back of her hand, and nodded. Then she ran out to play in the yard. "Guess what!" I could hear her calling to one of the neighbors. "Myra and I are going to take *tap* dancing lessons!"

—

Cousin Min and Domingo gave the Palms a fresh coat of paint and installed a new floor, stage lights, and wall mirrors in the downstairs parlor. They acquired a termite-eaten piano and had it fumigated. Min framed her old publicity photos and hung them on the walls, and in a place of honor above the reception desk, she put up the color poster of herself.

But weeks passed when Ruby and I were the only students. I can't say I was surprised since that's what you get for not studying your market. Though I tried to point this out to Min, she had her own ideas; she'd already decided that business was suffering from a lack of publicity.

I thought of Grandmother drumming up the old ghost stories on her visits around town, then said, "You'd be surprised how word spreads in a small place like Luhi."

However, Min had had an inspiration, and it was this: she wanted to give Ruby and me free extra lessons in exchange for using us as advertising.

When I suggested that advertising is supposed to make people *want* to buy what you're selling, Min just said, "You've got to think positive. Remember, it's the positive thinkers who inherit the earth."

I was about to protest that wasn't how it went when I saw she was smiling. I told myself I felt sorry for her and couldn't quit then, but there was something in me that wanted to believe what she'd said.

The next thing I knew, Ruby and I were over at the studio three or four times a week, with supervised practice sessions in between. The extra lessons were supposed to help us improve more quickly, but neither of us was going anywhere fast. With her usual optimism, Min decided to sign us up for the annual Lions Club talent show at the county seat. "Remember, girls, think positive," she kept saying. This began to sound desperate as the date drew near.

There were twelve acts ahead of us; we were second to the last. By the time we came up, the auditorium was filled with the buzz of conversation, punctuated by outbreaks of coughing. Backstage, just before we were to go on, I peeked through the curtain at our mother and father in the front row. Grandmother had refused to come. Mother was trying not to look apprehensive, but she kept fidgeting with her hair. In the seat beside her, Father was asleep with his mouth open. "Come on, let's show 'em some real dancing," Min said, then walked out and took her place at the piano.

At the opening of "Tea for Two," Ruby and I enter—diggity, diggity, diggity. My legs are trembling so much it sounds as if I'm sneaking in extra taps. D-diggity d-diggity. "The beat," Ruby hisses at my back. For once there is a smart, self-confident sound to each step she takes. DIGgity. DIGgity. We launch into our shuffle. Doo wop shush. I think I hear Father snoring, but I can't be sure. Min is warbling, "Me for you and you for meeee."

Down in the front row, Mother is jabbing Father with her elbow, but his snoring gains volume, Khhhhhhhhhh. All over the auditorium, people are craning to see where the noise is coming from. I try to tap louder. DIGGITY. DIGGITY. DIGGITY. KKKKKHHHHHHHHHH, Father snores. Suddenly, the audience's attention shifts to something behind me. I listen for Ruby, but it is ominously quiet back there. "Three for two and we're for you," Cousin Min belts out. As casually as possible, I sneak a look. Ruby is untangling herself from the long extension cord attached to the microphone. I whip back around and try to focus on maintaining the pace, which seems to be accelerating with every bar. On the other side of the stage, Ruby has launched herself into fast forward and comes careening over to catch up with me. Diggitydiggitydiggitydiggity. "Ouch!" She kicks herself in the ankle and goes down. There is nothing circumspect about the laughter now. The next time I near stage left, I shuffle off into the wings. Everyone roars. I look for Ruby to follow me, but she has gotten back on her feet and continues dancing. She has a great big grin on her face.

—

After the Lions Club fiasco, I decided to cut my losses and hang up my tap shoes for good. Though Mother voiced some halfhearted protests, it was Ruby who saw my quitting as a major defection.

Meanwhile, Min had gotten permission from the head priest to move her operations to the abandoned Martial Arts Hall at the Buddhist temple. When I asked Ruby what was going on, she hinted that they were planning to out-Astaire Astaire, but refused to say more. I began passing the Hall on my way to and from school, just to keep an eye on things. Once I noticed Domingo unloading lengths of thick brown rope from a pickup. Often I'd hear the sound of hammering.

Then Ruby started having nightmares. One morning when she was dressing for school, I noticed a red streak, like a rash, around her middle.

"How'd you get that?" I asked.

She quickly slipped her dress over her head, and said, "It's nothing. You didn't see anything."

I began pulling her dress up. "You get this over at Min's?"

She shook her head.

"If you don't answer me this minute, I'm going to tell Ma," I said.

"I'll tell her you did it," she cried, and ran out the door.

That afternoon, I went over to the Hall right after school. The doors at the front of the building were locked, so I walked around back and let myself in through an unlatched window.

It was dark inside—except for a spotlight shining down on what looked like a raised wooden platform. In the middle of the spot, a good fifteen feet above the ground, swung my sister.

"You've got to do better than that," a voice said. A second spot came on and there was Min, suspended from another rope right next to her. Min pantomimed a tap step. "How's the lighting from down there, Domingo?"

"Ruby, you come down from there this minute," I hollered. "You're scaring me to death."

Suddenly all the lights went on, and I could see that they were hanging from a weird system of ropes and pulleys held together by a metal scaffolding.

Ruby had stopped struggling and begun to wail. I ran over to Domingo and said, "You bring my sister down, or I'll call the cops!" But he was already lowering her.

"Myra, there's no need to excite yourself," Min called.

Domingo was undoing Ruby's harness. "You okay?" he asked. She had stopped crying.

"Come on, Rube, let's get out of here," I said. She wouldn't come with me at first, so I grabbed her by the wrist and pulled her away.

Behind us, I could hear Min saying, "I don't think the ropes are going to do at all. We'll have to use cables."

—

Min decided to go ahead and launch her new act herself. She put up posters all over town advertising her opening night. "Air Tap, A New Concept in Motion," the posters said. For a whole week, she was the talk of the village. Every conversation began, "Did you hear what Kazuhiro's crazy girl is up to now?"

The show was scheduled to begin at eight o'clock. Min had borrowed extra chairs to accommodate the enormous opening night crowd, but at seven-thirty, Mother, Ruby, and I are the only ones there. At seven forty-five, the head priest shows up. It is so quiet, you can hear the mice squeaking in the walls.

Promptly at eight, the lights dim. A spotlight focuses on stage left. Dressed in black tails, Cousin Min enters to the recorded tune of "I Want to Be a Dancing Man." She soft-shoes up stage and down; right, then left. Each step is clean and precise. The tempo quickens. In spite of myself, I join in on the applause. She runs up one wall and backflips to a standing position. We applaud again. Next, she runs up the opposite wall and somersaults, but instead of landing, she sails right up into the air. We aah in unison. She performs a complicated sequence of tap steps and aerobatic maneuvers, accompanied by our nonstop clapping. Then, as she is coming out of a somersault, there is a sudden, terrible groan, the sound of twisting metal, and—*crash!*—Min flies through a wall of the set and disappears.

For an instant, we are too stunned to move. Domingo comes reeling out from backstage. He is covered with plaster dust and there is a deep gash down the side of his face. "Call a doctor," he moans.

The priest is on his feet.

Someone is yelling, "Is she dead? Is she dead?"

"Shut up, Myra," Mother says. "Take care of your sister."

Ruby is white-faced and too shocked to cry, or even speak. We huddle next to each other as the priest goes to call an ambulance and Mother tends to Cousin Min.

———

Min was in surgery for nine hours. She had three broken ribs, a broken leg, a broken arm, a dislocated elbow, whiplash, a cracked hip, two slipped disks, a bruised spleen, a punctured lung, and a concussion. The doctor said she would probably never dance again.

Three times a week for as long as she was in the hospital,

Ruby and Mother took her reading material and thermoses of seaweed soup. Mother occasionally bullied me into going too. Once, during the ride over, I read an article about Astaire in one of Ruby's movie magazines. The article told about all his most famous dancing stunts and how he'd pulled them off. It had pictures of "Puttin' on the Ritz," "Shoes with Wings On," and the ceiling dance from *Royal Wedding*. It even had a picture of the scene in *The Belle of New York* where he tap-danced in midair. I showed the photos to Ruby and mouthed the words, "Air Tap." When we arrived at the hospital, she left the magazine behind in the car.

—

After Min got out, Mother invited her to stay at our house until she was able to get around on her own. Ruby and I were given the job of helping with her physical therapy—a task I usually tried to avoid by pleading homework or a heavy lineup of Odd Job customers which Winston couldn't handle by himself. But one afternoon, Ruby was sick in bed with the flu and Mother wasn't around, so I had no choice but to pitch in.

"We almost showed up that Astaire, didn't we?" Min said, as I worked on her right leg, bending it at the knee, then straightening it.

"We came this close," she said. "Just wait till next time." I tried to shut out the sound of her voice by concentrating on what I was doing. Bending then straightening.

"Hey, Myra, what's it take to get two words out of you?" she persisted.

I stopped working on her leg, then looked her right in the face and said, "What do you mean next time? You were lucky there was someone around this time to scrape you off the floor."

She flinched just the slightest, then said, "I've had some bad luck. But that's never stopped me."

I said, "Well, it should. Anyway, what's the point? Even if

Astaire knew you were alive, which he does not, there's nothing new about air dancing. He did it twenty years ago, in *The Belle of New York*. Without wires too." I got to my feet.

She was sitting on the floor with her legs sticking out in front of her. The tattoos on her soles looked blurred and faded. I realized they were not words at all but veins showing through her skin.

"Camera tricks!" she called after me, as I headed out of the room. "He did it with camera tricks." I knew she would never be able to get up by herself, but I kept right on going.

—

No one has seen Cousin Min since she's moved back into the Palms. Our mother continues to drop by, but Min refuses her visits.

Ruby has quit tap dancing and has decided to take over my paper route. One evening, as I am showing her where to make deliveries, we pass through Cousin Min's neighborhood. The windows of the rooming house are unlighted, except for the upstairs apartment where Domingo and Rafaela live.

"Hurry up," Ruby says. "It'll be dark soon. This place gives me the creeps at night."

"What's the matter, you worried about ghosts?" I tease.

She laughs nervously. "Maybe."

"Boy, you've sure changed your tune," I say.

Suddenly, she points over at the Palms. "Hey, Myra, look." The words are familiar. When I look where she is pointing, I see something white flitting against the sky. My heart gives a slight start, then I recognize Cousin Min lightly moving across the flat, concrete roof. She is dancing. I think I see the flash of gold on her feet.

"What's she doing up there?" I don't know what else to say. Min dances to the edge of the roof, and my amazement turns to dread. I step forward—to do what?—a shout caught in my throat.

But Ruby does not move.

Then, right before our very eyes, Min lifts her arms—a gesture from dreams of flight—and steps out onto the air. I wait for the plummet, the terrible thud, but it doesn't happen. The air holds her. She dances out above a huge plumeria tree, its white flowers glowing like stars in the gathering dusk. Then, she turns and lights upon the roof again.

"Did you catch *that?*" Ruby says. Her voice is breathless.

My eyes are still on the patch of white up on the roof. "Seeing's not always believing," I say.

Lori Arviso Alvord, M.D.

Dr. Lori Alvord is the country's first female Navajo surgeon. Raised in Crownpoint, New Mexico, "a poor community of working-class families," Alvord says she grew up in "a fragile world" and remembers childhood as "a succession of never-ending worries: would my dad lose his job? Freeze from exposure during one of his [drinking] binges?" Alvord attended Dartmouth College at the age of sixteen on a scholarship. No one from her high school had ever before attended an Ivy League college.

Today she is Associate Dean of Student and Minority Affairs and Assistant Professor of Surgery at Dartmouth Medical School. She has written a book titled *The Scalpel and the Silver Bear: The First Navajo Woman Surgeon Combines Western Medicine and Traditional Healing*.

Here Dr. Alvord narrates the long, long journey from her "childhood home on the eastern border of the Navajo reservation" to state-of-the-art operating rooms in medicine.

Full Circle

"Dr. Alvord, Dr. Alvord, please call the hospital," my beeper goes off with a voice message. I am sitting at the kitchen table in my home in Gallup, New Mexico, just fifty miles from my childhood home of Crownpoint, a tiny town on the eastern border of the Navajo reservation. I am a surgeon, in my fifth year of practice at the Gallup Indian Medical Center. Three decades ago, I played on the mesas surrounding Crownpoint, never dreaming that my life path would turn down the most unexpected of "canyons," leading me back full circle to my home and my people.

As a child, I never dreamed of becoming a doctor, much less a surgeon. We didn't have Navajo doctors, lawyers, or other professionals. I grew up in a poor community of working-class families. Even poorer families, who lacked running water and electricity, lived nearby on the reservation. When I reach back in my mind to my childhood, my past would not have been a predictor of future success. My own family had a precarious existence; my father was Navajo—charming, intelligent, and handsome—but subject to alcoholic binges. My mother was blonde, blue-eyed, and very attractive, but she married my father before she finished high school. He brought her to the reservation to work with him at a trading post when she was two weeks shy of her sixteenth birthday. She had been raised in Belen, a little town along the Rio Grande. They began married life in a remote part of the reservation, a little settlement called Whitehorse Lake. My two younger sisters and I grew up in a fragile world. I remember childhood as a succession of never-ending worries: Would my dad lose his job? Freeze from exposure during one of his binges? Get involved in a car accident that hurt him or someone else? Fear and uncertainty were a part of my everyday life, but our family seemed to respond with an abundance of love for one another, as though that would shelter us if everything else collapsed. During the times when Dad was drinking, though, all bets were off. As a young child, I listened many nights to my parents fighting— the shouting, slurred words, doors slamming, and cars roaring off into the darkness. I remember the craziness of those nights, the despair, the rides in the backseat of an erratic, fast-moving car. When I grew older, Dad woke me up at night to discuss things far too philosophical for a child. I would listen quietly, and talk with him, hoping he would fall asleep, hoping he wouldn't get up and walk out the door into the night . . .

I sought refuge deep in the pages of books, escaping to Russia with Dr. Zhivago, or to Alaska with Jack London's characters. My mother and grandfather had taught me to read before I entered school, and I preferred reading to almost any other pastime. In grade school, I did so well academically that I was accelerated from third to fifth grade, a move which pleased me, but which almost led to my social downfall. Younger and smaller than the other children in my class, I found it hard to fit in, and I began to retreat into solitude. When I emerged from my books, however, the real world was still waiting for me.

Crownpoint was a very small town on the western side of New Mexico. Though there was a significant Native population, all the merchants, teachers, doctors, and engineers were white. I found myself between two worlds: living inside the Navajo world, but sometimes feeling very distant from it; being half-white, but never referring to myself as white.

My father and grandmother had been punished for speaking Navajo in school. Navajos were told that, in order to be successful, they would need to forget their language and culture and adopt American ways. They were warned that if they taught their children Navajo, the children would have a harder time learning in school, and would therefore be at a disadvantage. This pressure to assimilate—along with the complete subjugation of the tribes following the Indian wars of the 1800s, the poverty due to poor grazing lands, forced stock reduction, and lack of jobs—all combined to bring the Navajo people to their knees, and a sense of deep shame prevailed.

My father suffered terribly from this; he had been a straight-A student, sent away to one of the best prep schools in the state. My father wanted to be like the rich, white children who surrounded him, but the differences were too apparent. At home on the reservation, he enjoyed his Navajo lifestyle—hunting deer, fishing, and cherishing the outdoor world. Later, he would bring these loves to our family life; we spent many happy times camping and fishing on mountain lakes in the summer, and hunting deer in the winter. We learned how to track animals, and how to appreciate and respect wildlife. Though hunting is usually a "male" activity, he seemed not to notice that his three children lacked a Y chromosome.

Outside the reservation, however, the world was not so friendly. In his mind, my father rebelled against the limitations of being Navajo in the 1940s and '50s. He went to the University of New Mexico, majoring in pre-med and Latin, until he married my mother and took a job to support her. He began to hate himself for not being able to fit into the white world and for not fulfilling his dreams. He flooded his grief with alcohol. Later in his life, his drinking episodes became much less frequent as he sought to control the disease, but he didn't escape its ultimate outcome. My father's life ended in 1993 in an alcohol-related automobile accident.

As a child, I saw the darkness of this subjugation over our lives, but I did not understand the roots of his anguish until I was a teenager, when I began to read Native American history and absorbed the reality that the all-American hero, Kit Carson, was in fact an arsonist who waged his campaign against the Navajo by burning settlements of men, women, and children to the ground. I read the history of tribe after tribe: the broken treaties, the massacres, the battles that were won not by wits and skill, but by superior weapons technology. I was heartbroken and very angry. With like-minded friends, I watched the takeover of Wounded Knee, South Dakota, and the rise of the American Indian movement. Although I didn't agree with all the principles of the movement, I too wanted to strike out against the America that had done this to my people. It took me years before I understood that this kind of anger was more destructive than beneficial.

Meanwhile, I added courses in Navajo language to my studies. The struggle to become fluent in Navajo began as a teenager and continues to this day, for Navajo is a very complex language, described by linguists as one of the hardest in the world to master. Though I cherished both sides of my heritage, I often felt that I didn't completely belong in either world. I would find, in the non-Indian world, that respect for elders was not present: people talked too much, laughed too loud, asked too many questions, had no respect for privacy, were overly competitive, and put a higher value on material wealth. Navajos, on the other hand, place much more emphasis on a person's relations to family, clan, tribe, and the other inhabitants of the earth, human and nonhuman. In the Navajo world, there are also codes of behavior that were sometimes hard for me to follow as a child. We were taught to be humble and not to draw attention to ourselves, to favor cooperation over competition (so as not to make ourselves "look better" at another's expense, or hurt the feelings of someone else), to avoid prolonged eye contact, to be quiet and reserved, to respect those who were older than us, and to reserve opinions until they were asked for.

This was hardest for me in the classroom, where peer pressure against attracting attention to oneself prevents Navajo children from raising their hands to answer a question in class even though they might know the answer. I enjoyed school and loved learning, so I felt like a racehorse locked in a barn. While I often felt more competitive than my classmates, when it came to college, I found that I wasn't nearly competitive enough.

I made good grades in high school, but I was receiving a marginal education; good teachers were very difficult to recruit, and funding for our little school was often inadequate. I spent many hours in classrooms where nothing was being taught. Nevertheless, my parents always assumed that all their children would go to college. I don't remember any lectures from them on the importance of higher education, just the quiet assurance that they believed in us. My college plans were modest; I assumed I would attend a nearby state school, until I happened to meet another Navajo student who was attending Princeton. I had heard of Princeton, but had no idea where it was. I asked how many Indians were there, and he replied, "Five." I couldn't even imagine a place with only five Indians, since our town was ninety-eight percent Indian! Then he mentioned Dartmouth, which had about fifty Indians on campus at that time, and I felt a little better. "Ivy League" was a term I had heard before, but I had no concept of its meaning. No one from my high school had ever attended an Ivy League college. I learned you had to be "smart" to go to schools like these, and I didn't feel all that smart. I was fourth in my class, not even valedictorian or salutatorian. I decided to apply to Dartmouth anyway—it was so far away and different, like a place out of one of the books I had read. I was flown to visit the college, and it seemed like another reality: the beautiful buildings, the trees, the lush grass. Back at home, I waited anxiously, and one day the letter came: I was accepted, early decision! The year following my acceptance, a student at Crownpoint was given an appointment to West Point, and following that, my younger sister was accepted at Stanford. The trend continues today, and I'm very proud of the role I was able to play, but I must admit that my applying to Dartmouth was more due to chance and destiny than to any well-designed plan.

Dartmouth College was founded in 1769 by a charter from the king of England to provide an "education for Indians." By 1970, that commitment had gone largely unfulfilled and only a handful of Native Americans had actually graduated from the school. In 1970, the college renewed its commitment and developed, in my opinion, the strongest college program for Native Americans as well as a Native American studies program which has also been called the finest in the country.

I came to Dartmouth at the age of sixteen and entered a world so different from my home that I could hardly believe both places existed on the same continent! What a contrast to Crownpoint, my tiny, dusty, reservation bordertown. I felt very lucky to be there, but I was in culture shock. Having come 2,500 miles from home, I was soon very lonely. I had always considered myself to be very independent (and I've been told I'm pretty strongwilled), so I was determined not to give up, even though the obstacles were often enormous.

Academically, I held my own in classes like literature and social sciences due to my strong reading background, but I was totally unprepared for the sciences. I had worked in the hospital pharmacy in high school and loved learning about different medications. I was planning to become a pharmacist, but found myself in a liberal arts college that didn't offer a degree in pharmacy. I decided to prepare for a health career by taking pre-med courses, and tried several science courses my first year. After receiving the first D of my entire life, I retreated. At the time, I assumed that I just wasn't smart enough to handle the sciences. It took me years to realize that my problems with science courses in college stemmed from my previous high school training. I was inadequately prepared to compete with the Ivy Leaguers. After sampling a number of other courses, I finally decided on a double major: a full major in psychology, and a sociology major modified with Native

242 • Full Circle

American studies. I received honors in my freshman seminar as well as in two Native American studies courses that stressed writing. As a result, I found myself thinking of teaching Native American studies as a career, and perhaps also becoming a writer.

Academics and loneliness were not my only struggles; I had trouble connecting with the non-Indian students. At Crownpoint, I was often "gabby" compared to the other students. At Dartmouth, I talked far too little. I blamed my own natural shyness, fear of people, and preference for solitude. It never occurred to me that this was related to my background, that my upbringing was so radically different from my non-Indian classmates' that we shared little common ground. I think I realized this problem years later when I returned home as a surgeon. Though I began encouraging other Navajo students to go to college, I knew that many Navajos would have a much harder time than I did. In fact, many of the other Indian students at Dartmouth, especially those from reservations, were experiencing similar problems, and many ended up leaving school. Navajos, and many other Indians, retreat and withdraw when alone in the midst of predominantly white populations. Very few of the students from traditional communities were able to make the transition; most never wanted to, and many never tried.

Understanding the culture of Dartmouth was like a course in itself. I didn't comprehend the meaning of places like fraternities, or the value systems of students from upper-class families. Had their parents taught them survival skills through camping, tracking, and hunting? Did I have any interest in making four-story-high sculptures out of ice for Winter Carnival? Did they respect their elders, their parents? Did I know which fork to use at a formal dinner? What sort of ceremonies did their "tribes" practice? We had so little in common. While they pondered such burning questions as when the opening day of ski season would be, I was struggling just to stay warm in the frozen New Hampshire winters and not slip on the ice! I was very homesick, wishing I didn't have to miss so many familiar events: the Navajo Tribal Fair, the Zuni Shalako, Laguna feast days, Santa Fe Indian Market, Gallup Ceremonials, and on and on. Everyone at home was having a great time (or so I imagined), eating wonderful food—roasted corn from the Shiprock market, posole, red chile stew, and venison jerky, and I was stuck in the library! I missed the beauty of watching the Apache Devil Dancers or the Pueblo Buffalo Dancers. I missed the splendor of Navajo traditional clothing, showered with silver and turquoise. I missed the pink and purple sunsets of New Mexico. Despite these differences, and my sadness, I took heart in the quality of the education I was receiving. This benefit, along with my own stubbornness and inability to accept failure in myself, was probably what kept me at Dartmouth.

But there was another significant influence in my decision to remain at Dartmouth: the Native American Program. The Native American Program had a tough job: recruiting students like us, who were very high risk—we frequently had only marginal high school preparation, many were reluctant to come to school so far from home, and, like skittish wild horses, some would turn tail and run back home at the least provocation. We were a group of students who found great comfort in one another, for though we came from many different tribes, our experiences at Dartmouth were similar: we came from very different worlds, and we all felt disconnected from the mainstream student body. For minority women, it was even worse. At the time I arrived on the scene, Dartmouth had only recently changed from an all-male to a co-ed student body, and the presence of women was resented by many of the men on campus. Referred to as "co-hogs" instead of co-eds, we were shunned for dates as girls were bused in from nearby women's colleges on weekends. Social activities were dominated by the fraternities, and if we went to their parties at all, we were often ignored. At home I had never had a problem attracting men, so I began questioning myself. Maybe I really wasn't very pretty after all, since these men barely noted my existence. For all these reasons, the small group of Native American students at Dartmouth coalesced into a solid community of students that did almost everything together. We went on many trips: to Native American basketball tournaments in Maine, on Long Island, or at Harvard; to pow wows all over the Northeast; to New York to visit the Indians at the New York City Community House; to Washington, D.C.; even across Canada to attend a wedding in Michigan. Our group was made up of Paiutes, Sioux, Cherokees, Chippewas, Navajos, Pueblos, and many other tribes. We were friends, lovers, rivals, enemies; we felt many things about each other, but in general, whatever we felt, we felt it deeply because we were so close. I have been many places since then and have been a part of other student groups at other colleges—nothing compared to the intensity of the experience of being a member of the Native American student group at Dartmouth.

Through this group, I met another Navajo, Lloyd Brown, who came from a little town about eighty miles north of Crownpoint, and I was instantly attracted to him. Lloyd had shoulder-length thick brown hair and large, expressive brown eyes. I admired Lloyd because he was everything I was not. He was full-blooded Navajo and spoke Navajo fluently, but at the same time, Lloyd was more sophisticated and (I thought) smarter than I was. He had attended high school in Hartford, Vermont, through a program called "A Better Chance," which was administered by a volunteer organization at Dartmouth. This program provided Indian students with the kind of high quality academic preparation at the high school level they would need in order to excel in college. Lloyd had spent three years in high school in Vermont. He had been a starter on their basketball team, and he was much better adjusted to white people than I was. He did better in classes with less effort than I did. We spent several years at Dartmouth together as a couple, before going our separate ways. Lloyd remains a good friend. He is now married and is working to develop businesses on the Navajo reservation.

There was, however, a dark side to Dartmouth: the Indian symbol. For many years, the unofficial mascot of the college had been the "Dartmouth Indian." Native Americans objected strenuously to this symbol, and the college officially discouraged students and alumni from using it, but it was everywhere on campus when I was a student. Imagine, if you can, a young Navajo girl coming to live in a non-Navajo community for the first time, seeing her people portrayed by members of the community as caricatures with paint on their faces, watching them jump around with toy tomahawks, and cheer, "Wah-hoo-wah," supposedly the "sounds that Indians make," at athletic contests. Imagine that she is told that this is meant to convey honor, pride, and respect to "Indians." It didn't make sense, and I was shocked and hurt. If my classmates wanted to respect and honor Indians, I would have brought Navajo code-talkers to Dartmouth, men who fought in World War II and used a special code in the Navajo language to communicate by radio secret military information in the Pacific; it was a "code" the Japanese were never able to break.

The Indian symbol was represented by silly images of Indians with feathers and loincloths. This symbol was widely adopted by many fraternities on campus, and any objection to such use was certain to cause hostility. As Native students, we held protests, we got into fights with fraternity members (yes, some fistfights), and sometimes we cried at night. The college that was chartered to provide education to Indians was doing just that, but it wasn't the education I expected. Dartmouth was built for us, but the welcome mat was often pulled out from under us. This contributed to the sense of isolation I felt while at Dartmouth. I didn't really absorb this until years later,

246 · Full Circle

and I began to ask myself, "Do they really want us here?" Despite all I experienced, I think the answer is yes. Dartmouth has made many favorable changes since then.

I was invited by Dartmouth's president at this time, James Freedman, to serve on the college's Native American Visiting Committee. This committee advises the president on matters relating to the Native American Program, a student support program, and Native American studies, an academic program. One of my first recommendations was to develop programs to build bridges between Native Americans and the rest of the Dartmouth community, possibly by creating "host families" among the faculty, or by developing liaisons between the Native American students and the other organizations on campus. We have much to learn in breaking down the barriers of misunderstanding that separate us.

After graduating from Dartmouth with a double major in psychology and sociology and certification in Native American studies, I decided to take a break before going on to grad school. Once home in New Mexico, I began looking for work in Albuquerque, and my life took a decidedly different turn, much like a car on the freeway veering onto an exit ramp at the very last minute! I had always thought of myself as a "right brain" person. As a child in Crownpoint, I had received an unlikely education in classical piano. In an effort to keep my mind occupied, my mother found a series of piano teachers: the English high school teacher, the Mormon preacher's wife, then finally, a true piano teacher. I took classes all through junior high and high school. I also wrote poetry occasionally, and later embarked on a self-taught education in Impressionist art. I had no plans for a "left brain" career, but a psychology course in neuroanatomy had opened a small door to the world of medicine, and I was fascinated with what I learned about how the brain was "hard wired." While job hunting, I found a job as a research assistant in a neurobiology research lab. I didn't expect to be hired, because of my limited science background, so I was a little surprised when I got the job. My supervisor, Dr. Gary Rosenberg, later told me he thought he could train me to do what I needed to do; since I had a Dartmouth education, I probably had enough innate intelligence to be trainable. I did prove to be trainable—I learned how to run experiments and process and analyze data with statistical packages on computers. Soon Dr. Rosenberg was asking me if I had ever thought about going to medical school. I remember blushing and shaking my head no. "Well, maybe you should think about it," he told me. I smiled. My mind swept back to my years at Dartmouth. With a touch of shame, I remembered my initial failures in chemistry and calculus. What was I thinking? My mind reminded me that I really wasn't smart enough to be considering this. But the thought wouldn't go away. Medicine! Wow! There are some things that seem so far out of reach that you don't dare even dream about them. This was one of them. In high school, I had worked part time at the hospital, in the pharmacy. I loved the rows of medicine bottles, the pretty little pills, each uniquely different, and I would count them very carefully when assigned to help fill a prescription. I thought it would be a very admirable goal to be a pharmacist, but I was so naive as a teenager that I didn't even check to see if Dartmouth had a pharmacy program when I applied. Of course, they didn't! It had been many years since I had thought about studying anything in medicine, even pharmacy. Now, I couldn't let go of the thought. How wonderful it would be to be a doctor, to be able to heal people. It would be a very special gift, a wonderful treasure, and the more I thought about it, the more I thought it might be perfect for me, but was I perfect for it? I had never even met a Navajo physician. I knew of one, Dr. Taylor McKenzie, but no others. What made me think I could do this? I thought about the commitment: four years of medical school, and then a residency which would be three to six years more. This didn't include getting ready for medical school—a year of pre-med science courses I would have to take and pass.

Nevertheless, I decided to consider it, and tested the waters by taking a biology course at night. I did well, but this was a "softer" science. I tried to think of which course intimidated me most, and decided it was physics. I took a physics course on my lunch break, and finished with a B. I was ecstatic! It was the end of the summer of 1980. I went back to Dr. Rosenberg and told him I was quitting. I wanted to go back to college full time to finish my pre-med requirements. Next, I went looking for funding. The scholarships from the college and my tribe had always been there before; now they were nowhere in sight. In order to qualify for these funds, I had to be in a degree-granting college program, yet I was taking a bunch of courses that didn't qualify for loans! I took a deep breath and thought about it. I was so excited about the chance to go to medical school, I decided to keep trying. Luckily, tuition at UNM was fairly reasonable, so I decided to use my savings. I quit my job and went back to school full time. I took a minimum-wage work-study job for twenty hours a week and hoped I would have enough money. I applied for food stamps, ate a lot of beans and rice that year, and somehow made it. I needed eight more science courses, and took four per semester. Rather than wait out another year, I applied to medical schools that same fall and took the Medical College Admissions Test in October. It was a gamble, because I had taken less than half of the science courses I needed for the test. I told myself that this year's application was really just a "dry run," and I didn't really expect to get in that year.

My scores came back in the 7-9 range, on a 1-15 scale, with an 11 in reading. I knew most students needed 10 or better to qualify, but I pointed out in my application that I had yet to take most of my science courses. I applied to four medical schools: University of New Mexico, Stanford, U.C.

San Francisco, and U.C. San Diego. At the time, San Francisco was the highest-ranked medical school in the country. Stanford was not far behind.

My first interview was at UNM. I remember it distinctly as a turning point in my life. My interviewer and I sat down. He looked at my application and said, "I see you've applied to Stanford." I expected to hear him say, "What makes you think you can get into Stanford?" Instead, he said, "I think Stanford will probably accept you. What can we do to get you to come to UNM?" I was completely speechless for a few moments, taking it all in. I thought to myself, "I have a spot in a medical school! I'm going to medical school! The only question now is where?" I thanked him and said I would definitely consider UNM. I was accepted at all four medical schools, and while common sense told me to go to UCSF, I chose Stanford instead for a number of reasons—primarily because my sister Karen was there as an undergraduate and was incredibly lonely. Also, however, I was intimidated by San Francisco—I was afraid of the city. I had never lived in an urban environment. Stanford was much more rural and it had a beautiful campus. In addition, the curriculum was more flexible.

I realized that medicine seemed to be a perfect choice; I had always wanted to help people, and this was a direct and powerful way to do it. But I was fueled by another strong drive: I wanted to be able to provide for my family if anything happened to my father. I had a strong need to protect the people I loved and to eliminate some of the insecurity our family continually experienced.

Medical school was extremely challenging. I studied like I had never studied before—long hours every night, often into the morning. I knew I wasn't as naturally brilliant as everyone else, so I would have to work overtime to make up for it. The biggest stress of medical school was convincing myself I could do it. I had a very real fear of failure that persisted all the way through my training, well past medical school, into residency, and beyond. There was just no way of knowing whether I was capable of all this. Competition was keen; there were over five thousand applications for eighty-six class slots per year. I feared the other students and felt like a poor relation invited to the ball, because I had no connection to places like these. No family or community members had been here before and I came from a very poor part of the world—a world so vastly different from what I was experiencing that I often could hardly believe I was really there. Though I did have a Dartmouth degree behind me, this was a whole new echelon. Until very recently, I battled with this inferiority complex, which finally left me only after I became board certified in general surgery.

While classroom demands were tough, clinical medicine was even tougher. I spent long hours in the hospital, up all night every third night, trying to absorb everything I was experiencing without falling asleep from exhaustion. In addition to my sleep deprivation, a more subtle problem occurred. I didn't fully comprehend it, though, until much later, when I began caring for Indian patients. As a medical student, we were learning to interview patients and perform physical examinations, and I was having a real problem with it. I disliked asking the questions and I hated doing the examinations. I was very uncomfortable with the whole process and I began to question whether I was really meant to be a physician. I finally realized that I was facing a cultural barrier, an impasse; in the Navajo world, it is considered improper to ask a personal question unless the subject is first brought up by the other person. It is improper to even hold hands or touch in public, and traditional clothing covers a person from head to toe. I found I was breaking rule after rule by asking intimate, probing questions, and touching total strangers in every place imaginable. Yet I knew these were not Navajos, these were Californians, and they expected this treatment as part of their visit. Once my mind was able to capture the reasons for my extreme discomfort, I was able to do what was expected of me with much greater ease. I tried to make sure that everything was done in a respectful manner, and I told myself that I learned what I needed from the interview and exam in order to give the patients good medical care. Later, for my Indian patients, I developed techniques of asking questions without being overly probing or invading their privacy, sometimes gathering the information I needed over several interviews, rather than in one lengthy interview on my first visit with a patient. I kept all of their bodies covered except for the small part I was examining and tried to make them feel as comfortable as possible in an uncomfortable situation.

In my third year of medical school, I did a summer assignment at a hospital very close to my home: Acoma-Canyoncito-Laguna Hospital. I met a Native American physician working there named Ron Lujan. I had met other Native physicians before, but Dr. Lujan was different—he was a surgeon. Full-blooded Taos, he had a style of interacting with Indian patients that was deeply caring and respectful, accented with a touch of humor. His patients were crazy about him, and I was astonished. Here, thirty miles from my parents' doorstep, was the man I would learn the most from, for not only did he know how to relate to his patients, he was a surgeon! At first, I could not get over it; I didn't know Native surgeons existed. I took my first steps into the world of the operating room with him. It was a strange and beautiful experience: it was like walking into a place I had known all my life, and into a place I knew I was supposed to be. As he taught me the initial steps to an operation, how to hold and use the tools, and how to gently enter the world inside the human body, I watched, listened, and sometimes held my breath, for the experiences had a spiritual component that I had not expected. Entrusted with the lives of these patients, Dr. Lujan made it clear that this was nothing that could be undertaken lightly. He did his best to try to dissuade me from considering surgery as a career. "The hours are longer and harder than for any other medical profession, the years of training are the longest, and once you're done, your lifestyle will still be very hard," he warned me.

But I was not to be deterred. "I can't help it, there is nothing else I would rather do, there is nothing else I want to do. I love this and I feel this is what I am supposed to do."

"Okay," he replied, "but don't say I didn't warn you." Once he was sure of my decision, the training began in earnest. "You will be questioned because you are Indian. They will think you don't know what you're doing." He was referring to affirmative action and the backlash that led to an assumption that minorities hadn't rightfully attained their place in professional society. He continued, "Therefore you must be better than everyone else: you will have to study longer, work harder, to rise above this. You will have to prove yourself." He was right, of course. And I could sometimes feel it—when a nurse questioned an order I wrote or when doctors sent patients to me for surgical evaluations, and then questioned my decisions. I made sure I made the right decisions, that my arguments were correct, and yet part of me became very angry. I am rarely questioned these days, for I have worked with the same people in my hospital for many years, and I don't have to prove myself on a daily basis, but I remember the past—this type of discrimination is so subtle one can barely point a finger at it. Yet it exists.

I returned many times to work with Dr. Lujan, learning more with each visit. I began to understand the naturalness of Native physicians working with Native patients, a harmony that is most certainly the way things are meant to be. These patients deserve doctors who understand their culture, lifestyle, and ways of thinking: doctors who have respect for them. At times in this hospital, we realized a dream—an O.R. team completely composed of Indians. Our nurse anaesthetist is Laguna and the O.R. nurses are also Indian, so when Lujan and

I face one another across the operating table, a dream comes to life. I see a visual example of a primary goal of our people: that of creating our own professionals, who will lead our communities, in order to control our own destiny as a people.

When I returned to Stanford to do my regular hospital rotations, I had a clear advantage in general surgery, for I had seen much of it already. My professors thought that I had been planning to train in surgery for many years. My evaluations were rated as excellent. This helped my decision to apply for a residency in general surgery. While most students had ten to twenty programs they applied to, I chose only three: University of New Mexico, Stanford, and a program in Phoenix. UNM was at the top of the list this time; after four years in California, I wanted very badly to come home. Phoenix didn't receive all my letters of recommendation in time, and this application was forfeited. I interviewed with a woman pediatric surgeon at UNM who wrote me a letter saying she was very impressed with my interview, and could I please come back and interview with the chairman of the department. I went back immediately. Then I relaxed—UNM liked me. I was a Stanford graduate and a resident of New Mexico, what more could they want? The applications are processed by computer match; the applicant ranks the surgery programs from the most desired to least desired, the surgery programs do the same with the list of applicants. Each list goes into a computer and the computer matches the applicant with a surgery program. Finally, on an anxious day called Match Day, the results are announced, and your fate is determined. Some students don't match at all, which is very frightening; you are faced with a choice of trying to get a spot in a program that didn't completely fill, choosing another specialty, or waiting a year.

The night before Match Day, I had a dream. In the dream, I opened my letter and found that I had matched in general surgery at Stanford Hospital. I cried and cried because it meant I wouldn't be going home. I woke up, realized it was just a dream, sighed with relief, and went back to sleep. The next day, I went to Match Day, opened the letter and found I had indeed matched at Stanford. I laughed at myself, my dream, and the fact that I had already cried, so there was no need to do that again. I knew also that I was one of a privileged few; there were hundreds of applications for only four positions in the surgery program at Stanford. I realized that my mind had not dared to hope for this, and instead had focused on UNM. In fact, I soon found that destiny, always the best navigator, had made the right choice. I learned that UNM was spoken of as a "good ole boys" program; they had not matched a woman there in many years, and the residents weren't very happy there. Stanford, on the other hand, was training more women and more minorities than any comparable program. The hours, while rigorous, were more humane than those of most programs, and the training was excellent. I trained for six years, spending my last year there as a chief resident. I owed three years of service to the Indian Health Service for scholarships while in medical school, and so returned home to work in Gallup, deciding to stay on after my obligation was finished.

My life as a surgeon is hard, as Dr. Lujan said it would be, but extremely rewarding. It is like anything of great value—difficult to achieve, and once obtained, treasured beyond measure. It is a beautiful discipline, in that part of it is an art form, because performing surgery well requires a precise choreography of the hands, eyes, and mind. Beyond that, however, is the part which is hardest for me—the fact that patients place their lives in our hands, and an error during an operation, or in the management of a patient afterward, can cause serious damage or death. This level of responsibility, this weight, can be very hard to shoulder. It comes with the trauma patient who is wheeled through the doors after a gunshot wound or a car accident, losing blood rapidly, and facing certain death without intervention; it lies in the patient who is crashing in the Intensive Care Unit from a severe infection, and is so ill that an operation is risky. These cases and others come to you in dreams, keep you up all night, and never really leave your side. It is like riding a spirited stallion—it can be the ride of your life, but it is so fast and dangerous that you never want to ride again.

Because medicine is so competitive and because the surgical profession requires so much effort and discipline, it commands its own respect. For me, a young Indian girl who came from the reservation, from a family without money or power and with little education, it sometimes feels like I'm basking in the sun—though the clouds might roll in at any minute. I fear I may wake up one day to find it has all been a dream. This immense difference between my childhood, my culture, and my profession, has often been hard to reconcile. It is as though I am living in two parallel worlds that exist side by side but only rarely intersect. Native American friends who see me in action at the hospital or hear me speaking "medicalese" on the phone often have a hard time integrating that doctor with the woman they know. Surgeons and others I work with rarely see the woman who goes to a medicine man for advice during her pregnancy. My roles are complicated and even I get lost in them sometimes. Yet I have found a unique place in my culture as a role model for young people and as a human cultural "bridge" for Navajo people. I have given countless commencement addresses and speeches to groups at the request of Navajo communities. What I tell them often involves my passion for their success as individuals and as communities. I encourage them to learn who they are, respect themselves, and believe in themselves and in each other. These attributes are linked to and enriched by appreciating and preserving their culture—and will help them to be successful. My hopes and dreams are wrapped up in theirs: it is a dream for healthy, strong Navajo families and communities.

I entered medicine as a way to help my people, and, at the time, I thought that meant help in the most literal form, to fight disease. Now I find that my career is helping my people in ways I never imagined, for as they see my success, they are better able to realize their own potential.

Robert Coles

Child psychiatrist Robert Coles wrote a five-volume, Pulitzer Prize-winning series about children in America called *Children of Crisis*. The second volume of *Children of Crisis* was published at a time of great national worry over the fate of the poor in what President Lyndon Johnson called "the Great Society." In the foreword to the book Dr. Coles pointed out that such children "number millions, I regret to say," and need "what millions of my kind of words cannot provide: bread, clean water, decent housing, and in general, a world more welcoming, a kinder and more decent world than they now know."

In this excerpt, Dr. Coles listens as a little white girl named Sally, who lives with her family of ten up in the hollows of Appalachia, explains what she does when she "loses her spirits." An excerpt from the first volume of *Children of Crisis* also appears in this anthology.

From *Children of Crisis:*
Migrants, Sharecroppers, Mountaineers

What of the Sallys who by the thousands live up those hollows and creeks, the poorest of the poor, those whose minds and hearts and souls have significantly given way, having suffered beyond any reasonable limit, even where people know how to take hardship in their stride? They are the families and the children whose extreme condition—of life and limb and spirit—has been described by Appalachian people themselves, specifically, the people of the hollows and creeks of Kentucky or West Virginia or western North Carolina. For all their misery they see quite clearly what is happening to them and others like them. Sally herself, for example, can spell out unselfconsciously and even casually some of the distinguishing characteristics that set her apart, say, from Herbie, a boy of eight who lives not far away in the same hollow. "Herbie is nice," she has told me many, many times, and she means it in every sense of the word. That is, she likes Herbie for his goodness, his largeness and generosity of character, as it were, his kindness, his pleasing and agreeable nature, his modest and well-mannered way of getting along with people: "He's honest; he never will cheat in school or when we play. They're kin of ours, Herbie's family, but not too close from what I hear. Herbie's daddy had a job in the mines, but then he got fired because they were closing down the mines, some of them, and laying off people on account of the machines. They had some money during the time he was working, and my daddy says once you've had money you never can forget it. Herbie says his daddy can't recall the last time he saw a paycheck, but you can see his folks went and got things with the money—the television and the stove and the refrigerator. In our place there's no electricity, none—so we couldn't have television or a refrigerator, even if we had the money to buy them. We don't need electricity. We have the stove. All we need is wood for it, and my daddy goes and finds coal up the hollow and digs out the pieces. The trouble is a lot of the time he's under, real bad under, and then we have to do his chores, and my mother will be crying and then we all start and it's then I wish I was staying down the hollow a bit, maybe with Herbie and his folks—they're the best people you could ever meet."

When her father goes "real bad under" he has been drinking too much. Her mother tries hard to stop "the old man's habit," as she refers to him and his drinking. After a while, though, she also starts drinking, first slowly but then with a certain desperate acceleration that strikes terror into the minds of her seven children, who run for cover—to the woods and to kinfolk down the hollow. Sally's parents live as far up the hollow as one can go. From their cabin one can see a truly splendid view of the Appalachians: the hills close by and far; the low-hanging white clouds and the higher gray clouds; the mist or the drizzle or the fog; and, near at hand, everywhere the green of the trees. The cabin is black, tar-paper black, and stands on four cement blocks. The cabin lacks curtains but does indeed possess that old stove, the place where life-giving food is prepared and life-preserving heat is given off. Near the stove there are three beds with mattresses but nothing else. Ten human beings use the mattresses: Sally's grandmother, her parents, and the seven children in the family. The cabin possesses a table but only one chair to go with it, and two other old "sitting chairs," both of which are battered and tattered, with springs in each quite visible.

The children sit and eat outside under the trees, or inside on the floor, or near the house on the ground; or else they walk out in front of the house, in which case they often remain standing and hunch over their food. The children commonly use their hands to eat, or share a limited number of forks (four), spoons (five), and knives (seven) with their parents and grandmother. The children also share clothes: two pairs of shoes, both in serious need of repair, two ragged winter jackets, and three very old pairs of winter gloves. The children, let it be said, also share something else—the hollow: its hills and land, its vast, imposing view, its bushes and shrubs and plants and animals and water and silence and noise, its seclusion and isolation, and also its people, a few families, a few dozen people, but for Sally a whole crowded, complicated sustaining world. . . . She lets me know that she wishes her father didn't lose control and drink so much and take to shooting wildly at animals that no one but he can see. She lets me know that she wishes her mother didn't then begin to weaken and eventually also fall apart. She lets me know that she can imagine a better state of affairs, can for a second or two here and there wish and dream for that, but mostly, for most seconds of most days, she makes do with things as they are. She lets me know that her mother and father, her brothers and sisters, her grandmother, who is weak and pain-ridden and at fifty-two a very, very old woman, all wonder whether the strain and turmoil, the cumulatively devastating episodes of meanness and terror and sorrow and disorder will ever stop and leave a time of peace and plenty.

Sally's eyes and ears notice a good deal more than her school performance would indicate, and her observations about her family and their troubles show once again a mixture of intelligence and hurt that are really inseparable—except in the minds of those who want for their own reasons to dwell exclusively on one thing or another; that is, see in Sally only the grace which goes with suffering that somehow becomes transcended, or see in Sally only evidence of a ravaged and "depressed" and "disadvantaged" and "border-line" mind. . . . "I like to go up to the field there, on top of the hill, and look over. You can see far, far away. You're closer to the sun. You're near the sky. Once when I was real little my grandma took me up there. My daddy had gone real bad, and he was shooting. My mother was crying so hard I thought she'd turn into water and there'd be nothing left of her. My grandma took me on her shoulder and ran. My brother wouldn't go with her. He said if he was going to be hit, it might as well be a bullet. I don't know what happened to the others. They might have gone by themselves, my older sister and my other brother. Up there we stood, in the field. My grandma put me down and told me what to do—stand there and don't move. She kept telling me things: that there was this mountain and that one, and she'd been told who lived near each one, and if the mountain had a name, what it was. She was listening while she was talking, I guess, because after a while she said we could go back, because it sounded quiet again back there— and we did. I can see her leaning toward me and picking me up. She said she liked carrying me on her back. She told me never to forget that we had this field to go to, and you're able to see as far as anyone on God's earth can, and if you lose your spirits and feel real down, then go up there and talk to God and He'll hear you from that field, if He's ever going to, because you're so near to Him and there's no one else to be bothering Him and asking something of Him at the same time as you are. And I do, I talk with Him. I do."

She does. She goes up there and finds a certain rest, a sense of nearness to Someone or Something that is said to help, that can be called upon and begged and urged to help, that is "up there, where Heaven is," that is waiting and may well take notice. "He'll hear, I know He will," Sally once insisted. Perhaps I did wonder whether she wasn't just a little worried He might *not* hear; but I also have to remind myself that Sally does believe—predominantly and consistently and to her great relief and joy—that He *is* there, and He *will* help, and in *His* way. Why, I came to ask myself when I was with her, do people like me make so very much of the "primitive" and superstitious and "neurotic" quality in the faith of a child like Sally? Why did I look with such suspicion for so long at her flight upward, her flight to the field on top of the hill, her flight to God, her flight, really, for a vision of the widest possible world available. Once when she and I and her little sister and a cousin of hers stood on the top of that hill, for an hour or so the children told me about the mountain "over yonder," and pointed out to me several likely (and utterly lovely) spots God's Spirit might single out for a visit. I shared my doubts and misgivings and suspicions. I asked the children if they thought God's Spirit "really" came to those places they had shown me. Sally in particular smiled and said she didn't know how to answer me. But in fact she did. She quietly and gracefully remarked that "God comes for those who wait for Him," and then she changed the subject.

Andrew Lam

Andrew Lam was born in Saigon, Vietnam and, at the age of eleven, fled his homeland with his mother, aunt, sister, and grandmother, "when the Communist tanks came rolling into Saigon." They ended up in a refugee camp in Guam while his father was left behind, then emigrated to the United States. "One day I was reading my favorite book in my mother's rose garden," Lam writes, "and the next day I am running for my life with a small backpack in which I only managed to save my stamp collection . . . Everything else was burnt." Today Andrew Lam is an associate editor with the Pacific News Service, a short story writer, and a regular commentator on National Public Radio. He is currently working on his first short story collection.

In Lam's short story, Cao Long Nguyen, a poor refugee from Vietnam, enters an eighth grade public school classroom for the first time.

Show and Tell

Mr. K. brought in the new kid near the end of the semester during what he called oral presentations and everybody else called eighth grade Show and Tell. This is Cao Long Nguyen, he said, and he's from Vietnam and mean old Billy said cool. What's so cool? Kevin asked. That's where my dad came back from with this big old scar on his chest and a bunch of grossed-out stories, Billy said, and that's where they have helicopters and guns and VCs and Mr. K said, Be quiet, Billy.

Cao Long Nguyen is a Vietnamese refugee, Mr. K said, and he wrote "Cao Long Nguyen—Refugee" in blue on the blackboard. Cao doesn't speak any English yet, but he'll learn soon enough so let's give him a welcome hand, shall we, and we applauded but some of us booed him just for the hell of it and the new kid blushed like a little girl. He looked at his shoes that said Bata and I never heard of that brand before. Then Mr. K gave him a seat in front of me and he sat down and he smelled a little like eucalyptus and he started drawing in his Hello Kitty notebook even when Show and Tell already started and it was my turn.

I didn't want it to be my turn. I hated being in front of the class as much as I hated anything. But I had to do it like everybody else. So I brought my family tree chart and taped it on the blackboard under "Cao Long Nguyen—Refugee" and Billy said Bobby's so poor he only got half a tree and everybody laughed. Well, not everybody. Mr. K didn't laugh. He said, Shh Billy, how many times do I have to tell you to be quiet in my class? And the new kid he didn't laugh neither. He just stared at my tree like he knew what it was but I doubt it, 'cause it didn't even look like a tree. Then when he saw me looking at him, he blushed and pretended like he was busy drawing but I knew he wasn't.

It's only half a tree 'cause my mama wouldn't tell me about the other half. Your daddy was a jackass, she said when I asked, and that's all she ever said about him. But mama, it's for my Show and Tell, I said, and she said so what.

So nothing, that's what. So my daddy hangs alone on this little branch on the left side. He left when I was four or something like that so I don't remember him very well. Only my sister Charlene remembers him, Charlene's three years older than me. Charlene remembers us having a nice house when my daddy was still around and then she remembers a lot of fights and flying dishes and broken vases. One night when the battle between mama and daddy was the worse, Charlene said she found me hiding in the closet under a bunch of Mama's clothes with my eyes closed and my hands over my ears saying, Stop, please, Stop, please, Stop like I was singing or something. She remembers us moving to California not long after that. I don't. All I remember is this crummy apartment that we lived in my whole life and mama working at Max's diner and smoking and drinking and cussing too goddamn much and always saying we should move somewhere else soon, go back to the South maybe, and then we never ever did.

So I started out with a big lie. I had rehearsed the whole night for it. I said my daddy's dead from a car accident a long, long time ago. I told the class he was an orphan so that's why there's only half a tree. Then I started on the other half. I told about my great-great-granddaddy Charles Boyle the third who was this rich man in New Orleans and who had ten children and a big old plantation during the Civil War but he was on the losing side and lost everything and so he killed himself. And I told about my grand-daddy Jonathan Quentin who became a millionaire from owning a gold mine in Mexico and then he lost it all on alcohol and gambling and then he killed himself. I told about my grandma Mary who was a sweetheart and who had three children and died from cancer and I told about a bunch of cousins who went north and east and west and became pilots and doctors and lawyers and maybe some of them killed themselves too and I wouldn't be a bit surprised 'cause my mama said it's kinda like a family curse or something. Then I saved the best part for last: here's my great-aunt Jenny Ann Quentin, I said, all alone on this little branch 'cause she's an old maid. She's still alive too, I said, ninety-seven years old and with only half a mind and she lives in this broken-down mansion outside of New Orleans and she wears old tattered clothes and talks to ghosts and curses them Yankees for winning the war. I saw her once when I was young, I said. Great-aunt Jenny scared the shit out of me 'cause she had a rifle and everything and she didn't pay her electric bills so her big old house was always dark and scary and there are ghosts living in there in that house and so now I'm done, thank you.

Tommy went after me. He told about stamp collecting and he brought three albums full of pretty stamps, stamps a hundred years old and stamps as far as the Vatican and Sri Lanka and how hard it was for him to have a complete collection of Pope John Paul the Second, and Cindy talked about embroidery and she brought with her two favorite pillowcases with pictures of playing pandas and dolphins that she embroidered herself and she showed us how and everything, and Kevin talked about building a tree house with his dad and how fun it was. He showed us his floor plan and photos of himself hanging out on the tree house, waving and swinging from a rope like a monkey and it looked like a great place to hide too, and then the bell rang.

Robert, Mr. K said, I wonder if you'd be so kind as to take care of our new student and show him the cafeteria. Why me, I said, and made the face like when I had to take the garbage out at home when it wasn't even my turn but Mr. K said, why not you, Robert, you're a nice one.

Oh no, I'm not, I said.

Oh yes, you are, he said, and wiggled his bushy eyebrows up and down like Groucho.

OK, I said, but just today, OK, though I kinda wanted to talk to the new kid anyway about them shoes, and Mr. K said, thank you, Robert Quentin Mitchell. He called the new kid over and put his arm on his shoulders and said Robert, this is Cao, Cao, this is Robert. Robert will take care of you. You both can bring your lunch back here and eat if you want. We're having a speed tournament today, and there's a new X-Men comic book for the winner.

Alright! I said. You're privileged if you get to eat lunch in Mr. K's room. Mr. K has all these games he keeps in the cabinet and at lunch time it's sort of a club and everything. You can eat there if (a) you're a straight A's student, (b) if Mr. K likes and invites you which is not often, or (c) if you know for sure you're gonna get jumped that day if you play outside and you beg Mr. K really, really hard to let you stay. I'm somewhere in between the (b) and (c) category. If you're a bad egg like Billy, who is single-handedly responsible for my (c) situation, you ain't never ever gonna get to eat there and play games, that's for sure.

So, Kal Nguyen Refugee, I said, let's go grab lunch, then we'll come back here for the speed tournament, what'd you say? But the new kid said nothing. He just stared at me and blinked like I'm some kinda strange animal that he ain't never seen before or something. Com'n, I said, and waved him toward me, com'n, follow me, the line's getting longer by the sec', and so finally he did.

We stood in line with nothing to do so I asked him, hey, Kal, where'd you get them shoes?

No undostand, he said, and smiled, *no sspeak engliss.*

Shoes, I said, Bata, Bata and I pointed and he looked down. Oh, Ssues, he said, his eyes shiny and black and wide opened like he just found out for the first time that he was wearing shoes. *Sssues, ssues . . . Saigon.* Yeah? I said, I guess I can't

buy me some here in the good old U.S. of A. then? Mine's
Adidas. They're as old as Mrs. Hamilton, prehistoric if you
ask me but they're still Adidas. A-di-das, go head, Kal, say it.
Adeedoos Suues, he said, *Adeedoos.*
That's right, I said, very good, Kal. Adidas shoes. And
yours, they're Bata shoes and Kal said *theirs Bata ssuees* and
we both looked at each other and grinned like idiots and
that's when Billy showed up. Why you want them gook
shoes anyway, he said, and cut in between us but nobody behind in line said nothing 'cause it's Billy. Why not, I said,
trying to sound tough. Bata sounds kind of nice, Billy. They're
from Saigon.
Bata ssues, the new kid said again, trying to impress Billy.
But Billy wasn't impressed. My daddy said them VCs don't
wear shoes, he said. They wear sandals made from jeep tires
and they live in fuck'n tunnels like moles and they eat bugs
and snakes for lunch. Then afterwards they go up and take
sniper shots at you with their AK-47s.
He don't look like he lived in no tunnel, I said.
Maybe not him, said Billy, but his daddy I'm sure. Isn't that
right, refugee boy? Your daddy a VC? Your daddy the one
who gave my daddy that goddamn scar?
The new kid didn't say nothing. You could tell he pretty
much figured it out that Billy's an asshole 'cause you don't
need no English for that. But all he could say was *no undohsten* and *ssues adeedoos* and those ain't no comeback lines and
he knew it. So he just bit his lip and blushed and kept looking
at me with them eyes.
So, I don't know why, maybe 'cause I didn't want him to
know that I belonged to the (c) category, or maybe 'cause he
kept looking at me, but I said leave him alone, Billy. I was
kinda surprised that I said it. And Billy turned and looked at
me like he was shocked too, like he just saw me for the first
time or something. Then in this loud singsong voice, he said

Bobby's protecting his new boyfriend. Everybody look, Bobby's got a boyfriend and he's gonna suck his VC's dick after lunch.

Everybody started to look.

The new kid kept looking at me too like he was waiting to see what I was gonna do next. What I'd usually do next is shut my trap and pretend that I was invisible or try not to cry like last time when Billy got me in a headlock in the locker room and called me a sissy over and over again 'cause I missed the soft ball at PE even when it was an easy catch. But not now. Now I couldn't pretend to be invisible 'cause too many people were looking. It was like I didn't have a choice. So I said, you know what, Billy, don't mind if I do. I'm sure anything is bigger than yours and everybody in line said Ooohh.

Fuck you, you little faggot, Billy said.

No thanks, Billy, I said, I already got me a new boyfriend, remember?

Everybody said Oohh again and Billy looked real mad. Then I go more scared than mad, my blood pumping. I thought oh my God, what have I done? I'm gonna get my lights punched out for sure. But then, God delivered stupid Becky. She suddenly stuck her beak in. And he's cute, too, she said, almost as cute as you, Bobby. You two'll make a nice faggot couple, I'm sure. So, like, promise me you'll name your firstborn after me, OK?

So, like, I tore at her. That girl could never jump me, not in a zillion years. And I'm sure you're a slut, I said, I'm sure you'd couple with anything that moves. I'm sure there are litters of strayed mutts already named after you. You know, Bitch Becky One, Bitch Becky Two, and, let's not forget, Bow Wow Becky junior and Becky called me asshole and looked away and everyone cracked up, even Billy.

Man, he said, shaking his head, you got some mean mouth on you today. It was like suddenly I was too funny or famous for him to beat up. But after he bought his burger and chocolate milk, he said it real loud so everybody can hear, he said, I'll see you two bitches later. Outside.

Sure, Billy, I said, and waved to him, see yah later, and then after we grabbed our lunch the new kid and me, we made a beeline for Mr. K's.

It was good to be in Mr. K's, I tell you. You don't have to watch over your shoulders every other second. You can play whatever game you want. Or you can read or just talk. So we ate and afterward I showed the new kid how to play speed. He was a quick learner too, if you asked me, but he lost pretty early on in the tournament. Then I lost pretty damn quickly after him. So we sat around and I flipped through the X-Men comic book and tried to explain to the new kid why Wolverine is so cool 'cause he can heal himself with his mutant factor and he has claws that cut through metal, and Phoenix, she's my favorite, Phoenix's so very cool 'cause she can talk to you psychically and she knows how everybody feels without even having to ask them, and best of all, she can lift an eight-wheeler truck with her psycho kinetic energy. That's way cool. The new kid, he listened and nodded to everything I said like he understood. Anyway, after a while, there were more losers than winners and the losers surrounded us and interrogated the new kid like he was a POW or something.

You ever shoot anybody, Cao Long?

Did you see anybody get killed?

How long you been here, Long, long? (haha)?

I hear they eat dogs over there, is that true? Have you ever eaten a dog?

Have you ever seen a helicopter blown up like in the movies?

No undohsten, the new kid answered to each question and smiled or shook his head or waved his hands like shooing flies but the loser flies wouldn't shoo. I mean where else could they go? Mr. K's was it. So the new kid looked at me again when them eyes and I said, OK, OK, Kal, I'll teach you something else. Why don't you say: Hey, fuck heads, leave me alone! Go head, Kal, say it.

Hey-fuck-heads, I said, looking at him.

Hee, Foock headss, he said, looking at me.

Leave. Me. Alone! I said.

Leevenme olone! he said. *Hee, Foock headss. Leevenme olone!*

And everybody laughed. I guess that was the first time they got called fuck heads and actually felt good about it, but Mr. K said, Robert Quentin Mitchell, you watch your mouth or you'll never come back in here again but you could tell he was trying not to laugh himself. So I said, OK, Mr. K but I leaned over and whispered *hey fuck heads, leave me alone* again in the new kid's ear so he'd remember and he looked at me like I'm the coolest guy in the world. *Sthankew Rowbuurt,* he said.

Then after school when I was waiting for my bus, the new kid found me. He gave me a folded piece of paper and before I could say anything he ran away. You'd never guess what it was, really, really good. I was smiling in it. I looked real happy, and older, like a sophomore or something, not like in the seventh grade year book picture where I looked so goofy with my eyes closed and everything and I had to sign my name over it so people wouldn't look. When I got home I taped it on my family tree chart and pinned the chart on my bedroom door and I swear, it smelled like eucalyptus.

Next day at Show and Tell Billy made the new kid cry. He went after Jimmy. Jimmy was this total nerd with thick glasses who told us how "very challenging" it was doing the *New York Times* crossword puzzles 'cause you got to know words like "ubiquitous" and "undulate" and "capricious," totally lame and bogus stuff like that. When he took so long just to do 5 across and 7 horizontal we shot spit balls at him and Mr. K said, stop that. But we got rid of that capricious undulating bozo ubiquitously fast and that was when Billy came up and made the new kid cry.

He brought in his daddy's army uniform and a stack of old magazines. He unfolded the uniform with the name Baxter sewn under US ARMY and put it on a chair. Then he opened one magazine and showed a picture of this naked and bleeding little girl running and crying on this road while these houses behind her were on fire. That's napalm, he said, and it eats into your skin and burns for a long, long time. This girl, Billy said, she got burned real bad, see there, yeah. Then he showed another picture of this monk sitting cross-legged and he was on fire and everything and there were people standing behind him crying out but nobody tried to put the poor man out. That's what you call self-immolation, Billy said. They do that all the time in Nam. This man, he poured gasoline on himself and lit a match 'cause he didn't like the government. Then Billy showed another picture of dead people in black pajamas along this road and he said these are VCs and my dad got at least a dozen of them before he was wounded himself. My dad told me if it weren't for them beatniks and hippies we could have won, Billy said, and that's when the new kid buried his face in his arms and cried and I could see his skinny shoulders go up and down like waves.

That's enough, Billy Baxter, Mr. K said, you can sit down now, thank you.

Oh, man! Billy said, I didn't even get to the part about how my dad got his scar, that's the best part.

Never mind, Mr. K said, sit down, please. I'm not sure whether you understood the assignment but you were supposed to do an oral presentation on what you've done, something that has to do with you, a hobby or a personal project, not the atrocities your father committed in Indochina. Save those stories when you cruise the bars when you're old enough.

Then Mr. K looked at the new kid like he didn't know what to do. That war, he said, I swear. After that it got real quiet in the room and all you could hear was the new kid sobbing.

Cao, Mr. K said finally, real quiet like, like he didn't really want to bother him, Cao, are you all right? Cao Long Nguyen? The new kid didn't answer Mr. K so I put my hand on his shoulder and shook it a little. Hey, Kal, I said, you OK? Then, it was like I pressed an ON button or something, 'cause all of a sudden Kal raised his head and stood up. He looked at me and then he looked at the blackboard. He looked at me again, then the blackboard. Then he marched right up there even though it was Roger's turn next and Roger, he already brought his two pet snakes and everything. But Kal didn't care. Maybe he thought it was his turn 'cause Mr. K called his name and so he just grabbed a bunch of colored chalks on Mr. K's desk and started to draw like a wild man and Mr. K he let him.

We all stared.

He was really, really good, but I guess I already knew that.

First he drew a picture of a boy sitting on this water buffalo and then he drew this rice field in green. Then he drew another boy on a water buffalo and they seemed to be racing. He drew other kids running along the bank with their kites in the sky and you could tell they were laughing and yelling, having a good time. Then he started to draw little houses on both sides of this river and the river ran toward the ocean and the ocean had big old waves. Kal drew a couple standing outside this very nice house and underneath them Kal wrote *Ba* and *Ma*. Then he turned and looked straight at me, his eyes still wet with tears. *Rowbuurt*, he said, tapping the pictures with his chalk, his voice sad but expecting, *Rowbuurt*.

Me? I said. I felt kinda dizzy. Everybody was looking back and forth between him and me now like we were tossing a soft ball between us or something.

Rowbuurt, Kal said my name again and kept looking at me until I said what, what'd you want, Kal?

Kal tapped the blackboard with his chalk again and I saw

in my head the picture of myself taped on the family tree and then, I don't know how but I just kinda knew. So I just took a deep breath and then I said, OK, OK—Kal, uhmm, said he used to live in this village with his mama and papa near where the river runs into the sea, and Kal nodded and smiled and waved his chalk in a circle like he was saying *Go on Robert Quentin Mitchell, you're doing fine, go on.*

So I went on.

And he went on.

I talked. He drew.

We fell into a rhythm.

He had a good time racing them water buffaloes with his friends and flying kites, I said. His village is, hmm, very nice, and . . . and . . . at night he goes to sleep swinging on this hammock and hearing the sound of the ocean behind the dunes and everything.

Then one day, I said, the soldiers named VCs came with guns and they took his daddy away. They put him behind barbed wires with other men, all very skinny, skinny and hungry and they got chains on their ankles and they looked really, really sad. Kal and his mother went to visit his daddy and they stood on the other side of the fence and cried a lot. Yes, it was very, very sad. Then, hmmm, one day his daddy disappeared. No, he didn't disappear, he died, he died.

And Kal and his mother buried him in this cemetery with lots of graves and they lit candles and cried and cried. After that, there was this boat, this really crowded boat, I guess, and Kal and his Mama climbed on it and they went down the river out to sea. Then they got on this island and then they got on an airplane after that and they came here to live in America.

Kal was running out of space. He drew the map of America way too big but he didn't want to erase it. So he climbed on a chair and drew these high-rises right above the rice fields and I recognized the Trans-American building right away, a pyramid underneath a rising moon. Then he drew a big old heart around it. Then he went back to the scene with the man named Ba who stood in the doorway with his wife and he drew a heart around him. Then he went back to the first scene of the two boys racing on the water buffaloes in the rice field and paused a little before he drew tiny tennis shoes on the boys' feet and I heard Billy said that's Bobby and his refugee boyfriend, but I ignored him.

Kal loves America very much, especially San Francisco, I said, he'd never seen so many tall buildings before in his whole life and they're so pretty. Maybe he'll live with his mother someday up in the penthouse when they have lots of money. But he misses home too, and he misses his friends, and he especially misses his daddy who died. A lot. And that's all, I said. I think he's done, thank you.

And he was done. Kal turned around and climbed down from the chair. Then he looked at everybody and checked out their faces to see if they understood, then in this real loud voice he said, *Hee, Foock headss, leevenme olone!* and then he bowed and everybody cracked up and applauded.

Kal started walking back. He was smiling and looking straight at me like he was saying, *Robert Quentin Mitchell, ain't we a team, or what?* and I wanted to say yes, Kal Long Nguyen—Refugee, yes we are, but I just didn't say anything.

"The Love Test," edited by Deborah Stern, from *City Kids, City Teachers: Reports from the Front Row*, edited by William Ayers and Patricia Ford. © 1996 by William Ayers and Patricia Ford. All rights reserved. Reprinted by permission of The New Press.

"The Daily Routine of a Dope Fiend" by Love Shiloh, "Public Housin' Is Straight Hatin' on Us Minorities" by Young Tay B2, and "Jesus Wasn't Listening" by Anonymous, from *The Beat Within*, a weekly publication of writing and art from inside the Bay Area's juvenile halls. Copyright © 1997 Youth Outlook / Pacific News Service. All rights reserved. Reprinted by permission of Pacific News Service, San Francisco.

"Indian Education" from *The Lone Ranger and Tonto Fistfight in Heaven* by Sherman Alexie, The Atlantic Monthly Press. Copyright © 1993 by Sherman Alexie. Reprinted by permission of Grove/Atlantic, Inc.

"Mother and Daughter," from *Baseball in April and Other Stories*, by Gary Soto. Copyright © 1990 by Gary Soto. Reprinted by permission of Harcourt, Inc.

Excerpts from *Children of Crisis: Volume I* by Robert Coles. Copyright © 1964, 1965, 1966, 1967 by Robert Coles. Reprinted by permission of Little, Brown and Company (Inc.).

"Optimists," from *Rock Springs* by Richard Ford. Copyright © 1987 by Richard Ford. Reprinted by permission of Grove/Atlantic, Inc.

"The Grammar of Silk" from *School Figures* by Cathy Song. © 1994. Reprinted by permission of the University of Pittsburgh Press.

"Cannery Town in August" from *Emplumada* by Lorna Dee Cervantes. © 1981. Reprinted by permission of the University of Pittsburgh Press.

"Field Poem" from *The Elements of San Joaquin* by Gary Soto. Copyright © 1977, Gary Soto. All rights reserved. Reprinted by permission of Chronicle Books.

"Nightshift at the St. Regis" from *Troche Moche* (1988) by Luis J. Rodriguez. Reprinted by permission of Curbstone Press. Distributed by Consortium.

"Photograph of My Father in his Twenty-Second Year" from *Fires: Essays, Poems, Stories* by Raymond Carver. Copyright © 1989 by Tess Gallagher. Reprinted by permission of International Creative Management, Inc.

Chapter Two from *Their Eyes Were Watching God* by Zora Neal Hurston. Copyright 1937 by Harper & Row, Publishers, Inc. Renewed 1965 by John